The SAGE Dictionary of Statistics

The SAGE Dictionary of Statistics

a practical resource for students
in the social sciences

Duncan Cramer and Dennis Howitt

SAGE Publications
London ● Thousand Oaks ● New Delhi

First published 2004

SAGE Publications Ltd
1 Oliver's Yard
55 City Road
London EC1Y 1SP

SAGE Publications Inc.
2455 Teller Road
Thousand Oaks, California 91320

SAGE Publications India Pvt Ltd
B-42, Panchsheel Enclave
Post Box 4109
New Delhi 110 017

British Library Cataloguing in Publication data

A catalogue record for this book is available
from the British Library

ISBN 0 7619 4137 1
ISBN 0 7619 4138 X (pbk)

Library of Congress Control Number: 2003115348

Typeset by C&M Digitals (P) Ltd.
Printed in Great Britain by The Cromwell Press Ltd,
Trowbridge, Wiltshire

Contents

To our mothers – it is not their fault that lexicography took its toll.

Preface

Writing a dictionary of statistics is not many people's idea of fun. And it wasn't ours. Can we say that we have changed our minds about this at all? No. Nevertheless, now the reading and writing is over and those heavy books have gone back to the library, we are glad that we wrote it. Otherwise we would have had to buy it. The dictionary provides a valuable resource for students – and anyone else with too little time on their hands to stack their shelves with scores of specialist statistics textbooks.

Writing a dictionary of statistics is one thing – writing a practical dictionary of statistics is another. The entries had to be useful, not merely accurate. Accuracy is not that useful on its own. One aspect of the practicality of this dictionary is in facilitating the learning of statistical techniques and concepts. The dictionary is not intended to stand alone as a textbook – there are plenty of those. We hope that it will be more important than that. Perhaps only the computer is more useful. Learning statistics is a complex business. Inevitably, students at some stage need to supplement their textbook. A trip to the library or the statistics lecturer's office is daunting. Getting a statistics dictionary from the shelf is the lesser evil. And just look at the statistics textbook next to it – you probably outgrew its usefulness when you finished the first year at university.

Few readers, not even ourselves, will ever use all of the entries in this dictionary. That would be a bit like stamp collecting. Nevertheless, all of the important things are here in a compact and accessible form for when they are needed. No doubt there are omissions but even *The Collected Works of Shakespeare* leaves out *Pygmalion*! Let us know of any. And we are not so clever that we will not have made mistakes. Let us know if you spot any of these too – modern publishing methods sometimes allow corrections without a major reprint.

Many of the key terms used to describe statistical concepts are included as entries elsewhere. Where we thought it useful we have suggested other entries that are related to the entry that might be of interest by listing them at the end of the entry under 'See' or 'See also'. In the main body of the entry itself we have not drawn attention to the terms that are covered elsewhere because we thought this could be too distracting to many readers. If you are unfamiliar with a term we suggest you look it up.

Many of the terms described will be found in introductory textbooks on statistics. We suggest that if you want further information on a particular concept you look it up in a textbook that is ready to hand. There are a large number of introductory statistics texts that adequately discuss these terms and we would not want you to seek out a particular text that we have selected that is not readily available to you. For the less common terms we have recommended one or more sources for additional reading. The authors and year of publication for these sources are given at the end of the entry and full details of the sources are provided at the end of the book. As we have discussed some of these terms in texts that we have written, we have sometimes recommended our own texts!

The key features of the dictionary are:

- Compact and detailed descriptions of key concepts.
- Basic mathematical concepts explained.
- Details of procedures for hand calculations if possible.
- Difficulty level matched to the nature of the entry: very fundamental concepts are the most simply explained; more advanced statistics are given a slightly more sophisticated treatment.
- Practical advice to help guide users through some of the difficulties of the application of statistics.
- Exceptionally wide coverage and varied range of concepts, issues and procedures – wider than any single textbook by far.
- Coverage of relevant research methods.
- Compatible with standard statistical packages.
- Extensive cross-referencing.
- Useful additional reading.

One good thing, we guess, is that since this statistics dictionary would be hard to distinguish from a two-author encyclopaedia of statistics, we will not need to write one ourselves.

Duncan Cramer
Dennis Howitt

Some Common
Statistical Notation

Roman letter symbols or abbreviations:

a	constant
df	degrees of freedom
F	F test
$\log n$	natural or Napierian logarithm
M	arithmetic mean
MS	mean square
n or N	number of cases in a sample
p	probability
r	Pearson's correlation coefficient
R	multiple correlation
SD	standard deviation
SS	sum of squares
t	t test

Greek letter symbols:

α (lower case alpha) Cronbach's alpha reliability, significance level or alpha error
β (lower case beta) regression coefficient, beta error
γ (lower case gamma)
σ (lower case delta)
η (lower case eta)
κ (lower case kappa)
λ (lower case lambda)
ρ (lower case rho)
τ (lower case tau)
φ (lower case phi)
χ (lower case chi)

Some common mathematical symbols:

Σ	sum of
∞	infinity
$=$	equal to
$<$	less than
$\leq$	less than or equal to
$>$	greater than
$\geq$	greater than or equal to
$\sqrt{}$	square root

A

a posteriori tests: see *post hoc tests*

a priori comparisons or **tests:** where there are three or more means that may be compared (e.g. analysis of variance with three groups), one strategy is to plan the analysis in advance of collecting the data (or examining them). So, in this context, a priori means before the data analysis. (Obviously this would only apply if the researcher was not the data collector, otherwise it is in advance of collecting the data.) This is important because the process of deciding what groups are to be compared should be on the basis of the hypotheses underlying the planning of the research. By definition, this implies that the researcher is generally disinterested in general or trivial aspects of the data which are not the researcher's primary focus. As a consequence, just a few of the possible comparisons are needed to be made as these contain the crucial information relative to the researcher's interests. Table A.1 involves a simple ANOVA design in which there are four conditions – two are drug treatments and there are two control conditions. There are two control conditions because in one case the placebo tablet is for drug A and in the other case the placebo tablet is for drug B.

An appropriate a priori comparison strategy in this case would be:

- $Mean_a$ against $Mean_b$
- $Mean_a$ against $Mean_c$
- $Mean_b$ against $Mean_d$

Table A.1   *A simple ANOVA design*

Drug A	Drug B	Placebo control A	Placebo control B
$Mean_a =$	$Mean_b =$	$Mean_c =$	$Mean_d =$

Notice that this is fewer than the maximum number of comparisons that could be made (a total of six). This is because the researcher has ignored issues which perhaps are of little practical concern in terms of evaluating the effectiveness of the different drugs. For example, comparing placebo control A with placebo control B answers questions about the relative effectiveness of the placebo conditions but has no bearing on which drug is the most effective overall.

The a priori approach needs to be compared with perhaps the more typical alternative research scenario – *post hoc* comparisons. The latter involves an unplanned analysis of the data following their collection. While this may be a perfectly adequate process, it is nevertheless far less clearly linked with the established priorities of the research than a priori comparisons. In *post hoc* testing, there tends to be an exhaustive examination of all of the possible pairs of means – so in the example in Table A.1 all four means would be compared with each other in pairs. This gives a total of six different comparisons.

In a priori testing, it is not necessary to carry out the overall ANOVA since this merely tests whether there are differences across the various means. In these circumstances, failure of some means to differ from the others may produce non-significant findings due to conditions which are of little or no interest to the researcher. In a priori testing, the number of comparisons to be made has been limited to a small number of key comparisons. It is generally accepted that if there are relatively few a priori comparisons to be made, no adjustment is needed for the number of comparisons made. One rule of thumb is that if the comparisons are fewer in total than the degrees of freedom for the main effect minus one, it is perfectly appropriate to compare means without adjustment for the number of comparisons.

Contrasts are examined in a priori testing. This is a system of weighting the means in order to obtain the appropriate mean difference when comparing two means. One mean is weighted (multiplied by) +1 and the other is weighted −1. The other means are weighted 0. The consequence of this is that the two key means are responsible for the mean difference. The other means (those not of interest) become zero and are always in the centre of the distribution and hence cannot influence the mean difference.

There is an elegance and efficiency in the a priori comparison strategy. However, it does require an advanced level of statistical and research sophistication. Consequently, the more exhaustive procedure of the *post hoc* test (multiple comparisons test) is more familiar in the research literature. See also: **analysis of variance; Bonferroni test; contrast; Dunn's test; Dunnett's C test; Dunnett's T3 test; Dunnett's test; Dunn–Sidak multiple comparison test; omnibus test;** *post hoc* **tests**

abscissa: this is the horizontal or *x* axis in a graph. See *x* **axis**

absolute deviation: this is the difference between one numerical value and another numerical value. Negative values are ignored as we are simply measuring the distance between the two numbers. Most

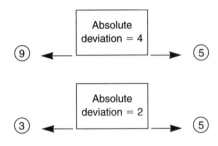

Figure A.1   *Absolute deviations*

commonly, absolute deviation in statistics is the difference between a score and the mean (or sometimes median) of the set of scores. Thus, the absolute deviation of a score of 9 from the mean of 5 is 4. The absolute deviation of a score of 3 from the mean of 5 is 2 (Figure A.1). One advantage of the absolute deviation over deviation is that the former totals (and averages) for a set of scores to values other than 0.0 and so gives some indication of the variability of the scores. See also: **mean deviation; mean, arithmetic**

acquiescence or **yea-saying response set** or **style:** this is the tendency to agree or to say 'yes' to a series of questions. This tendency is the opposite of disagreeing or saying 'no' to a set of questions, sometimes called a nay-saying response set. If agreeing or saying 'yes' to a series of questions results in a high score on the variable that those questions are measuring, such as being anxious, then a high score on the questions may indicate either greater anxiety or a tendency to agree. To control or to counteract this tendency, half of the questions may be worded in the opposite or reverse way so that if a person has a tendency to agree the tendency will cancel itself out when the two sets of items are combined.

adding: see **negative values**

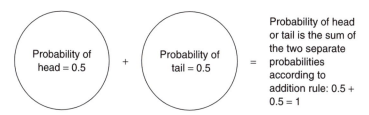

Figure A.2   *Demonstrating the addition rule for the simple case of either heads or tails when tossing a coin*

addition rule: a simple principle of probability theory is that the probability of either of two different outcomes occurring is the sum of the separate probabilities for those two different events (Figure A.2). So, the probability of a die landing 3 is 1 divided by 6 (i.e. 0.167) and the probability of a die landing 5 is 1 divided by 6 (i.e. 0.167 again). The probability of getting either a 3 or a 5 when tossing a die is the sum of the two separate probabilities (i.e. 0.167 + 0.167 = 0.333). Of course, the probability of getting any of the numbers from 1 to 6 spots is 1.0 (i.e. the sum of six probabilities of 0.167).

adjusted means, analysis of covariance: see **analysis of covariance**

agglomeration schedule: a table that shows which variables or clusters of variables are paired together at different stages of a cluster analysis. See **cluster analysis**
Cramer (2003)

algebra: in algebra numbers are represented as letters and other symbols when giving equations or formulae. Algebra therefore is the basis of statistical equations. So a typical example is the formula for the mean:

$$m = \frac{\sum X}{N}$$

In this m stands for the numerical value of the mean, X is the numerical value of a score, N is the number of scores and $\sum$ is the symbol indicating in this case that all of the scores under consideration should be added together.

One difficulty in statistics is that there is a degree of inconsistency in the use of the symbols for different things. So generally speaking, if a formula is used it is important to indicate what you mean by the letters in a separate key.

algorithm: this is a set of steps which describe the process of doing a particular calculation or solving a problem. It is a common term to use to describe the steps in a computer program to do a particular calculation. See also: **heuristic**

alpha error: see **Type I** or **alpha error**

alpha (α) reliability, Cronbach's: one of a number of measures of the internal consistency of items on questionnaires, tests and other instruments. It is used when all the items on the measure (or some of the items) are intended to measure the same concept (such as personality traits such as neuroticism). When a measure is internally consistent, all of the individual questions or items making up that measure should correlate well with the others. One traditional way of checking this is split-half reliability in which the items making up the measure are split into two sets (odd-numbered items versus

Table A.2 *Preferences for four foodstuffs plus a total for number of preferences*

	Q1: bread	Q2: cheese	Q3: butter	Q4: ham	Total
Person 1	0	0	0	0	0
Person 2	1	1	1	0	3
Person 3	1	0	1	1	3
Person 4	1	1	1	1	4
Person 5	0	0	0	1	1
Person 6	0	1	0	0	1

Table A.3 *The data from Table A.2 with Q1 and Q2 added, and Q3 and Q4 added*

	Half A: bread + cheese items	Half B: butter + ham items	Total
Person 1	0	0	0
Person 2	2	1	3
Person 3	1	2	3
Person 4	2	2	4
Person 5	0	1	1
Person 6	1	0	1

even-numbered items, the first half of the items compared with the second half). The two separate sets are then summated to give two separate measures of what would appear to be the same concept. For example, the following four items serve to illustrate a short scale intended to measure liking for different foodstuffs:

1	I like bread	*Agree Disagree*
2	I like cheese	*Agree Disagree*
3	I like butter	*Agree Disagree*
4	I like ham	*Agree Disagree*

Responses to these four items are given in Table A.2 for six individuals. One split half of the test might be made up of items 1 and 2, and the other split half is made up of items 3 and 4. These sums are given in Table A.3. If the items measure the same thing, then the two split halves should correlate fairly well together. This turns out to be the case since the correlation of the two split halves with

each other is 0.5 (although it is not significant with such a small sample size). Another name for this correlation is the split-half reliability.

Since there are many ways of splitting the items on a measure, there are numerous split halves for most measuring instruments. One could calculate the odd–even reliability for the same data by summing items 1 and 3 and summing items 2 and 4. These two forms of reliability can give different values. This is inevitable as they are based on different combinations of items.

Conceptually alpha is simply the average of all of the possible split-half reliabilities that could be calculated for any set of data. With a measure consisting of four items, these are items 1 and 2 versus items 3 and 4, items 2 and 3 versus items 1 and 4, and items 1 and 3 versus items 2 and 4. Alpha has a big advantage over split-half reliability. It is not dependent on arbitrary selections of items since it incorporates all possible selections of items.

In practice, the calculation is based on the repeated-measures analysis of variance. The data in Table A.2 could be entered into a repeated-measures one-way analysis of variance. The ANOVA summary table is to be found in Table A.4. We then calculate coefficient alpha from the following formula:

$$alpha = \frac{mean\ square\ between\ people\ -\ mean\ square\ residual}{mean\ square\ between\ people}$$

$$= \frac{0.600 - 0.200}{0.600} = \frac{0.400}{0.600} = 0.67$$

Of course, SPSS and similar packages simply give the alpha value. See **internal consistency; reliability**

Cramer (1998)

alternative hypothesis: see **hypothesis; hypothesis testing**

AMOS: this is the name of one of the computer programs for carrying out structural

Table A.4 *Repeated-measures ANOVA summary table for data in Table A.2*

	Sums of squares	Degrees of freedom	Means square
Between treatments	0.000	3	0.000 (not needed)
Between people	3.000	5	0.600
Error (residual)	3.000	15	0.200

equation modelling. AMOS stands for *A*nalysis of *Mo*ment *S*tructures. Information about AMOS can be found at the following website:

http://www.smallwaters.com/amos/index.html

See **structural equation modelling**

analysis of covariance (ANCOVA): analysis of covariance is abbreviated as ANCOVA (*an*alysis of *cov*ariance). It is a form of analysis of variance (ANOVA). In the simplest case it is used to determine whether the means of the dependent variable for two or more groups of an independent variable or factor differ significantly when the influence of another variable that is correlated with the dependent variable is controlled. For example, if we wanted to determine whether physical fitness differed according to marital status and we had found that physical fitness was correlated with age, we could carry out an analysis of covariance. Physical fitness is the dependent variable. Marital status is the independent variable or factor. It may consist of the four groups of (1) the never married, (2) the married, (3) the separated and divorced, and (4) the widowed. The variable that is controlled is called the covariate, which in this case is age. There may be more than one covariate. For example, we may also wish to control for socio-economic status if we found it was related to physical fitness. The means may be those of one factor or of the interaction of that factor with other factors. For example, we may be interested in the interaction between marital status and gender.

There is no point in carrying out an analysis of covariance unless the dependent variable is correlated with the covariate. There are two main uses or advantages of analysis of covariance. One is to reduce the amount of unexplained or error variance in the dependent variable, which may make it more likely that the means of the factor differ significantly. The main statistic in the analysis of variance or covariance is the *F* ratio which is the variance of a factor (or its interaction) divided by the error or unexplained variance. Because the covariate is correlated with the dependent variable, some of the variance of the dependent variable will be shared with the covariate. If this shared variance is part of the error variance, then the error variance will be smaller when this shared variance is removed or controlled and the *F* ratio will be larger and so more likely to be statistically significant.

The other main use of analysis of covariance is where the random assignment of cases to treatments in a true experiment has not resulted in the groups having similar means on variables which are known to be correlated with the dependent variable. Suppose, for example, we were interested in the effect of two different programmes on physical fitness, say swimming and walking. We randomly assigned participants to the two treatments in order to ensure that participants in the two treatments were similar. It would be particularly important that the participants in the two groups would be similar in physical fitness before the treatments. If they differed substantially, then those who were fitter may have less room to become more fit because they were already fit. If we found that they differed considerably initially and we found that fitness before the intervention was related to fitness after the intervention, we could control for this initial difference with analysis of covariance. What analysis of covariance does is to make the initial means on fitness exactly the same for the different treatments. In doing this it is necessary to make an adjustment to the means after the intervention. In other words, the adjusted means will differ from the unadjusted ones. The more the initial means differ, the greater the adjustment will be.

Analysis of covariance assumes that the relationship between the dependent variable and the covariate is the same in the different groups. If this relationship varies between the groups it is not appropriate to use analysis of covariance. This assumption is known as homogeneity of regression. Analysis of covariance, like analysis of variance, also assumes that the variances within the groups are similar or homogeneous. This assumption is called homogeneity of variance. See also: **analysis of variance; Bryant–Paulson simultaneous test procedure; covariate; multivariate analysis of covariance**

Cramer (2003)

analysis of variance (ANOVA): analysis of variance is abbreviated as ANOVA (*analysis of variance*). There are several kinds of analyses of variance. The simplest kind is a one-way analysis of variance. The term 'one-way' means that there is only one factor or independent variable. 'Two-way' indicates that there are two factors, 'three-way' three factors, and so on. An analysis of variance with two or more factors may be called a factorial analysis of variance. On its own, analysis of variance is often used to refer to an analysis where the scores for a group are unrelated to or come from different cases than those of another group. A repeated-measures analysis of variance is one where the scores of one group are related to or are matched or come from the same cases. The same measure is given to the same or a very similar group of cases on more than one occasion and so is repeated. An analysis of variance where some of the scores are from the same or matched cases and others are from different cases is known as a mixed analysis of variance. Analysis of covariance (ANCOVA) is where one or more variables which are correlated with the dependent variable are removed. Multivariate analysis of variance (MANOVA) and covariance (MANCOVA) is where more than one dependent variable is analysed at the same time. Analysis of variance is not normally used to analyse one factor with only two groups but such an analysis of variance gives the same

significance level as an unrelated *t* test with equal variances or the same number of cases in each group. A repeated-measures analysis of variance with only two groups produces the same significance level as a related *t* test. The square root of the *F* ratio is the *t* ratio.

Analysis of variance has a number of advantages. First, it shows whether the means of three or more groups differ in some way although it does not tell us in which way those means differ. To determine that, it is necessary to compare two means (or combination of means) at a time. Second, it provides a more sensitive test of a factor where there is more than one factor because the error term may be reduced. Third, it indicates whether there is a significant interaction between two or more factors. Fourth, in analysis of covariance it offers a more sensitive test of a factor by reducing the error term. And fifth, in multivariate analysis of variance it enables two or more dependent variables to be examined at the same time when their effects may not be significant when analysed separately.

The essential statistic of analysis of variance is the *F* ratio, which was named by Snedecor in honour of Sir Ronald Fisher who developed the test. It is the variance or mean square of an effect divided by the variance or mean square of the error or remaining variance:

$$F \text{ ratio} = \frac{\text{effect variance}}{\text{error variance}}$$

An effect refers to a factor or an interaction between two or more factors. The larger the *F* ratio, the more likely it is to be statistically significant. An *F* ratio will be larger, the bigger are the differences between the means of the groups making up a factor or interaction in relation to the differences within the groups.

The *F* ratio has two sets of degrees of freedom, one for the effect variance and the other for the error variance. The mean square is a shorthand term for the mean squared deviations. The degrees of freedom for a factor are the number of groups in that factor minus one. If we see that the degrees of freedom for a factor is two, then we know that the factor has three groups.

Traditionally, the results of an analysis of variance were presented in the form of a table. Nowadays research papers are likely to contain a large number of analyses and there is no longer sufficient space to show such a table for each analysis. The results for the analysis of an effect may simply be described as follows: 'The effect was found to be statistically significant, $F_{2, 12} = 4.72$, $p = 0.031$.' The first subscript (2) for F refers to the degrees of freedom for the effect and the second subscript (12) to those for the error. The value (4.72) is the F ratio. The statistical significance or the probability of this value being statistically significant with those degrees of freedom is 0.031. This may be written as $p < 0.05$. This value may be looked up in the appropriate table which will be found in most statistics texts such as the sources suggested below. The statistical significance of this value is usually provided by statistical software which carries out analysis of variance. Values that the F ratio has to be or exceed to be significant at the 0.05 level are given in Table A.5 for a selection of degrees of freedom. It is important to remember to include the relevant means for each condition in the report as otherwise the statistics are somewhat meaningless. Omitting to include the relevant means or a table of means is a common error among novices.

If a factor consists of only two groups and the F ratio is significant we know that the means of those two groups differ significantly. If we had good grounds for predicting which of those two means would be bigger, we should divide the significance level of the F ratio by 2 as we are predicting the direction of the difference. In this situation an F ratio with a significance level of 0.10 or less will be significant at the 0.05 level or lower $(0.10/2 = 0.05)$.

When a factor consists of more than two groups, the F ratio does not tell us which of those means differ from each other. For example, if we have three means, we have three possible comparisons: (1) mean 1 and mean 2; (2) mean 1 and mean 3; and (3) mean 2 and mean 3. If we have four means, we have six possible comparisons: (1) mean 1 and mean 2; (2) mean 1 and mean 3; (3) mean 1 and mean 4; (4) mean 2 and mean 3; (5) mean 2 and mean 4; and (6) mean 3 and mean 4. In this

Table A.5   *Critical values of F*

df for error variance	df for effect variance					
	1	2	3	4	5	∞
8	5.32	4.46	4.07	3.84	3.69	2.93
12	4.75	3.89	3.49	3.26	3.11	2.30
20	4.35	3.49	3.10	2.87	2.71	1.84
30	4.17	3.32	2.92	2.69	2.53	1.62
40	4.08	3.23	2.84	2.61	2.45	1.51
60	4.00	3.15	2.76	2.53	2.37	1.39
120	3.92	3.07	2.68	2.45	2.29	1.25
∞	3.84	3.00	2.60	2.37	2.21	1.00

situation we need to compare two means at a time to determine if they differ significantly. If we had strong grounds for predicting which means should differ, we could use a one-tailed t test. If the scores were unrelated, we would use the unrelated t test. If the scores were related, we would use the related t test. This kind of test or comparison is called a planned comparison or a priori test because the comparison and the test have been planned before the data have been collected.

If we had not predicted or expected the F ratio to be statistically significant, we should use a *post hoc* or an a posteriori test to determine which means differ. There are a number of such tests but no clear consensus about which tests are the most appropriate to use. One option is to reduce the two-tailed 0.05 significance level by dividing it by the number of comparisons to obtain the familywise or experimentwise level. For example, the familywise significance level for three comparisons is 0.0167 $(0.05/3 = 0.0167)$. This may be referred to as a Bonferroni adjustment or test. The Scheffé test is suitable for unrelated means which are based on unequal numbers of cases. It is a very conservative test in that means are less likely to differ significantly than with some other tests. Fisher's protected LSD (Least Significant Difference) test is used for unrelated means in an analysis of variance where the means have been adjusted for one or more covariates.

A factorial analysis of variance consisting of two or more factors may be a more sensitive test of a factor than a one-way analysis of variance because the error term in a factorial analysis of variance may be smaller than a one-way analysis of variance. This is because some of the error or unexplained variance in a one-way analysis of variance may be due to one or more of the factors and their interactions in a factorial analysis of variance.

There are several ways of calculating the variance in an analysis of variance which can be done with dummy variables in multiple regression. These methods give the same results in a one-way analysis of variance or a factorial analysis of variance where the number of cases in each group is equal or proportionate. In a two-way factorial analysis where the number of cases in each group is unequal and disproportionate, the results are the same for the interaction but may not be the same for the factors. There is no clear consensus on which method should be used in this situation but it depends on what the aim of the analysis is.

One advantage of a factorial analysis of variance is that it determines whether the interaction between two or more factors is significant. An interaction is where the difference in the means of one factor depends on the conditions in one or more other factors. It is more easily described when the means of the groups making up the interaction are plotted in a graph as shown in Figure A.3.

The figure represents the mean number of errors made by participants who had been deprived of either 4 or 12 hours of sleep and who had been given either alcohol or no alcohol. The vertical axis of the graph reflects the dependent variable, which is the number of errors made. The horizontal axis depicts one of the independent variables, which is sleep deprivation, while the two types of lines in the graph show the other independent variable, which is alcohol. There may be a significant interaction where these lines are not parallel as in this case. The difference in the mean number of errors between the 4 hours' and the 12 hours' sleep deprivation conditions was greater for those given alcohol than those not given alcohol. Another way of describing this interaction is to say the difference in the mean number of errors between the alcohol and the no alcohol group is greater for those deprived of 12 hours of sleep than for those deprived of 4 hours of sleep.

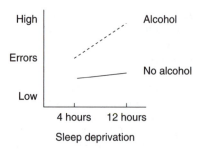

Figure A.3 *Errors as a function of alcohol and sleep deprivation*

The analysis of variance assumes that the variance within each of the groups is equal or homogeneous. There are several tests for determining this. Levene's test is one of these. If the variances are not equal, they may be made to be equal by transforming them arithmetically such as taking their square root or logarithm. See also: **Bartlett's test of sphericity; Cochran's C test; Duncan's new multiple range test; factor, in analysis of variance; F ratio; Hochberg GT2 test; mean square; repeated-measures analysis of variance; sum of squares; Type I hierarchical or sequential method; Type II classic experimental method**

Cramer (1998, 2003)

ANCOVA: see **analysis of covariance**

ANOVA: see **analysis of variance**

arithmetic mean: see **mean, arithmetic**

asymmetry: see **symmetry**

asymptotic: this describes a curve that approaches a straight line but never meets it. For example, the tails of the curve of a normal distribution approach the baseline but never touch it. They are said to be asymptotic.

attenuation, correcting correlations for: many variables in the social sciences are measured with some degree of error or unreliability. For example, intelligence is not expected to vary substantially from day to day. Yet scores on an intelligence test may vary suggesting that the test is unreliable. If the measures of two variables are known to be unreliable and those two measures are correlated, the correlation between these two measures will be attenuated or weaker than the correlation between those two variables if they had been measured without any error. The greater the unreliability of the measures, the lower the real relationship will be between those two variables. The correlation between two measures may be corrected for their unreliability if we know the reliability of one or both measures.

The following formula corrects the correlation between two measures when the reliability of those two measures is known:

$$R_c = \frac{\text{correlation between measure 1 and measure 2}}{\sqrt{\text{measure 1 reliability} \times \text{measure 2 reliability}}}$$

For example, if the correlation of the two measures is 0.40 and their reliability is 0.80 and 0.90 respectively, then the correlation corrected for attenuation is 0.47:

$$\frac{0.40}{\sqrt{0.80 \times 0.90}} = \frac{0.40}{\sqrt{0.72}} = \frac{0.40}{0.85} = 0.47$$

The corrected correlation is larger than the uncorrected one.

When the reliability of only one of the measures is known, the formula is

$$R_c = \frac{\text{correlation between measure 1 and measure 2}}{\sqrt{\text{measure 1 or measure 2 reliability}}}$$

For example, if we only knew the reliability of the first but not the second measure then the corrected correlation is 0.45:

$$\frac{0.40}{\sqrt{0.80}} = \frac{0.40}{0.89} = 0.45$$

Typically we are interested in the association or relationship between more than two variables and the unreliability of the measures of those variables is corrected by using structural equation modelling.

attrition: this is a closely related concept to drop-out rate, the process by which some participants or cases in research are lost over the duration of the study. For example, in a follow-up study not all participants in the earlier stages can be contacted for a number of reasons – they have changed address, they choose no longer to participate, etc.

The major problem with attrition is when particular kinds of cases or participants leave the study in disproportionate numbers to other types of participants. For example, if a study is based on the list of electors then it is likely that members of transient populations will leave and may not be contactable at their listed address more frequently than members of stable populations. So, for example, as people living in rented accommodation are more likely to move address quickly but, perhaps, have different attitudes and opinions to others, then their greater rate of attrition in follow-up studies will affect the research findings.

Perhaps a more problematic situation is an experiment (e.g. such as a study of the effect of a particular sort of therapy) in which drop-out from treatment may be affected by the nature of the treatment so, possibly, many more people leave the treatment group than the control group over time.

Attrition is an important factor in assessing the value of any research. It is not a matter which should be hidden in the report of the research. See also: **refusal rates**

average: this is a number representing the usual or typical value in a set of data. It is virtually synonymous with measures of central tendency. Common averages in statistics are the mean, median and mode. There is no single conception of average and every average contributes a different type of information. For example, the mode is the most common value in the data whereas the mean is the numerical average of the scores and may or may not be the commonest score. There are more averages in statistics than are immediately apparent. For example, the harmonic mean occurs in many statistical calculations such as the standard error of differences often without being explicitly mentioned as such. See also: **geometric mean**

In tests of significance, it can be quite important to know what measure of central tendency (if any) is being assessed. Not all statistics compare the arithmetic means or averages. Some non-parametric statistics, for example, make comparisons between medians.

averaging correlations: see **correlations, averaging**

axis: this refers to a straight line, especially in the context of a graph. It constitutes a reference line that provides an indication of the size of the values of the data points. In a graph there is a minimum of two axes – a horizontal and a vertical axis. In statistics, one axis provides the values of the scores (most often the horizontal line) whereas the other axis is commonly an indication of the frequencies (in univariate statistical analyses) or another variable (in bivariate statistical analysis such as a scatterplot).

Generally speaking, an axis will start at zero and increase positively since most data in psychology and the social sciences only take positive values. It is only when we are dealing with

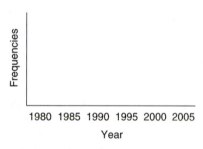

Figure A.4   *Illustrating axes*

extrapolations (e.g. in regression or factor analysis) that negative values come into play.

The following need to be considered:

- Try to label the axes clearly. In Figure A.4 the vertical axis (the one pointing up the page) is clearly labelled as Frequencies. The horizontal axis (the one pointing across the page) is clearly labelled Year.
- The intervals on the scale have to be carefully considered. Too many points on any of the axes and trends in the data can be obscured; too few points on the axes and numbers may be difficult to read.
- Think very carefully about the implications if the axes do not meet at zero on each scale. It may be appropriate to use another intersection point but in some circumstances doing so can be misleading.
- Although axes are usually presented as at right angles to each other, they can be at other angles to indicate that they are correlated. The only common statistical context in which this occurs is oblique rotation in factor analysis.

Axis can also refer to an axis of symmetry – the line which divides the two halves of a symmetrical distribution such as the normal distribution.

B

bar chart, diagram or **graph:** describes the frequencies in each category of a nominal (or category variable). The frequencies are represented by bars of different length proportionate to the frequency. A space should be left between each of the bars to symbolize that it is a bar chart not a histogram. See also: **compound bar chart; pie chart**

Bartlett's test of sphericity: used in factor analysis to determine whether the correlations between the variables, examined simultaneously, do not differ significantly from zero. Factor analysis is usually conducted when the test is significant indicating that the correlations do differ from zero. It is also used in multivariate analysis of variance and covariance to determine whether the dependent variables are significantly correlated. If the dependent variables are not significantly correlated, an analysis of variance or covariance should be carried out. The larger the sample size, the more likely it is that this test will be significant. The test gives a chi-square statistic.

Bartlett–Box F test: one of the tests used for determining whether the variances within groups in an analysis of variance are similar or homogeneous, which is one of the assumptions underlying analysis of variance. It is recommended where the number of cases in the groups varies considerably and where no

group is smaller than three and most groups are larger than five.

Cramer (1998)

baseline: a measure to assess scores on a variable prior to some intervention or change. It is the starting point before a variable or treatment may have had its influence. Pre-test and pre-test measure are equivalent concepts. The basic sequence of the research would be baseline measurement → treatment → post-treatment measure of same variable.

For example, if a researcher were to study the effectiveness of a dietary programme on weight reduction, the research design might consist of a baseline (or pre-test) of weight prior to the introduction of the dietary programme. Following the diet there may be a post-test measure of weight to see whether weight has increased or decreased over the period before the diet to after the diet.

Without the baseline or pre-test measure, it would not be possible to say whether or not weights had increased or decreased following the diet. With the research design illustrated in Table B.1 we cannot say whether the change was due to the diet or some other factor. A control group that did not diet would be required to assess this.

Baseline measures are problematic in that the pre-test may sensitize participants in some way about the purpose of the experiment or in some other way affect their behaviour. Nevertheless, their absence leads to many problems of interpretation even

Table B.1   *Illustrating baseline*

Person	Baseline/ pre-test	Treatment	Post-test
A	45 kg	DIET	42 kg
B	51 kg		47 kg
C	76 kg		69 kg
D	58 kg		52 kg
E	46 kg		41 kg

Table B.2   *Results of a study of the effects of two films on aggression*

War film	Romantic film
14	4
19	7
12	5
14	3
13	6
17	3
Mean aggression = 14.83	Mean aggression = 4.67

in well-known published research. Consequently they should always be considered as part of the research even if it is decided not to include them. Take the following simple study which is illustrated in Table B.2. Participants in the research have either seen a war film or a romantic film. Their aggressiveness has been measured afterwards. Although there is a difference between the war film and the romantic film conditions in terms of the aggressiveness of participants, it is not clear whether this is the consequence of the effects of the war film increasing aggression or the romantic film reducing aggression – or both things happening. The interpretation would be clearer with a baseline or pre-test measure. See also: **pre-test; quasi-experiments**

Bayesian inference: an approach to inference based on Bayes's theorem which was initially proposed by Thomas Bayes. There are two main interpretations of the probability or likelihood of an event occurring such as a coin turning up heads. The first is the relative frequency interpretation, which is the number of times a particular event happens over the

number of times it could have happened. If the coin is unbiased, then the probability of heads turning up is about 0.5, so if we toss the coin 10 times, then we expect heads to turn up on 5 of those 10 times or 0.50 (5/10 = 0.50) of those occasions. The other interpretation of probability is a subjective one, in which we may estimate the probability of an event occurring on the basis of our experience of that event. So, for example, on the basis of our experience of coin tossing we may believe that heads are more likely to turn up, say 0.60 of the time. Bayesian inference makes use of both interpretations of probability. However, it is a controversial approach and not widely used in statistics. Part of the reluctance to use it is that the probability of an event (such as the outcome of a study) will also depend on the subjective probability of that outcome which may vary from person to person. The theorem itself is not controversial.

Howson and Urbach (1989)

Bayes's theorem: in its simplest form, this theorem originally put forward by Thomas Bayes determines the probability or likelihood of an event A given the probability of another event B. Event A may be whether a person is female or male and event B whether they pass or fail a test. Suppose, the probability or proportion of females in a class is 0.60 and the probability of being male is 0.40. Suppose furthermore, that the probability of passing the test is 0.90 for females and 0.70 for males. Being female may be denoted as A_1 and being male A_2 and passing the test as B. If we wanted to work out what the probability (Prob) was of a person being female (A_1) knowing that they had passed the test (B), we could do this using the following form of Bayes's theorem:

$$\text{Prob}(A_1|B) = \frac{\text{Prob}(B|A_1) \times \text{Prob}(A_1)}{[\text{Prob}(B|A_1) \times \text{Prob}(A_1)] + [\text{Prob}(B|A_2) \times \text{Prob}(A_2)]}$$

where $\text{Prob}(B|A_1)$ is the probability of passing being female (which is 0.90), $\text{Prob}(A_1)$ is the probability of being female (which is 0.60), $\text{Prob}(B|A_2)$ is the probability of passing being male (which is 0.70) and $\text{Prob}(A_2)$ is the probability of being male (which is 0.40).

Substituting these probabilities into this formula, we see that the probability of someone passing being female is 0.66:

$$\frac{0.90 \times 0.60}{(0.90 \times 0.60) + (0.70 \times 0.40)} = \frac{0.54}{0.54 + 0.28} = \frac{0.54}{0.82} = 0.66$$

Our ability to predict whether a person is female has increased from 0.60 to 0.66 when we have additional information about whether or not they had passed the test. See also: **Bayesian inference**
    Novick and Jackson (1974)

beta (β) or **beta weight:** see **standardized partial regression coefficient**

beta (β) error: see **Type II** or **beta error**

between-groups or **subjects design:** compares different groups of cases (participants or subjects). They are among the commonest sorts of research design. Because different groups of individuals are compared, there is little control over a multiplicity of possibly influential variables other than to the extent they can be controlled by randomization. Between-subjects designs can be contrasted with within-subjects designs. See **mixed design**

between-groups variance or **mean square (MS):** part of the variance in the dependent variable in an analysis of variance which is attributed to an independent variable or factor. The mean square is a short form for referring to the mean squared deviations. It is calculated by dividing the sum of squares (SS), which is short for the sum of squared deviations, by the between-groups degrees of freedom. The between-groups degrees of freedom are the number of groups minus one. The sum of squares is calculated by subtracting the mean of each group from the overall or grand mean, squaring this

difference, multiplying it by the number of cases within the group and summing this product for all the groups. The between-groups variance or mean square is divided by the error variance or mean square to form the F ratio which is the main statistic of the analysis of variance. The larger the between-groups variance is in relation to the error variance, the bigger the F ratio will be and the more likely it is to be statistically significant.

between-judges variance: used in the calculation of Ebel's intraclass correlation which is worked out in the same way as the between-groups variance with the judges representing different groups or conditions. To calculate it, the between-judges sum of squares is worked out and then divided by the between-judges degrees of freedom which are the number of judges minus one. The sum of squares is calculated by subtracting the mean of each judge from the overall or grand mean of all the judges, squaring each difference, multiplying it by the number of cases for that judge and summing this product for all the judges.

between-subjects variance: used in the calculation of a repeated-measures analysis of variance and Ebel's intraclass correlation. It is the between-subjects sum of squares divided by the between-subjects degrees of freedom. The between-subjects degrees of freedom are the number of subjects or cases minus one. The between-subjects sum of squares is calculated by subtracting the mean for each subject from the overall or grand mean for all the subjects, squaring this difference, multiplying it by the number of conditions or judges and adding these products together. The greater the sum of squares or variance, the more the scores vary between subjects.

bias: occurs when a statistic based on a sample systematically misestimates the equivalent characteristic (parameter) of the population from which the samples were drawn. For example, if an infinite number of repeated samples produced too low an estimate of the population mean then the statistic would be a biased estimate of the parameter. An illustration of this is tossing a coin. This is assumed generally to be a 'fair' process as each of the outcomes heads or tails is equally likely. In other words, the population of coin tosses has 50% heads and 50% tails. If the coin has been tampered with in some way, in the long run repeated coin tosses produce a distribution which favours, say, heads.

One of the most common biases in statistics is where the following formula for standard deviation is used to estimate the population standard deviation:

$$\text{standard deviation} = \sqrt{\frac{\Sigma(X - \bar{X})^2}{N}}$$

While this defines standard deviation, unfortunately it consistently underestimates the standard deviation of the population from which it came. So for this purpose it is a biased estimate. It is easy to incorporate a small correction which eliminates the bias in estimating from the sample to the population:

$$\begin{array}{l}\text{unbiased estimate of}\\\text{population standard} \\ \text{deviation}\end{array} = \sqrt{\frac{\Sigma(X - \bar{X})^2}{N - 1}}$$

It is important to recognize that there is a difference between a biased sampling method and an unrepresentative sample, for example. A biased sampling method will result in a systematic difference between samples in the long run and the population from which the samples were drawn. An unrepresentative sample is simply one which fails to reflect the characteristics of the population. This can occur using an unbiased sampling method just as it can be the result of using a biased sampling method. See also: **estimated standard deviation**

biased sample: is produced by methods which ensure that the samples are generally systematically different from the characteristics of the population from which they are drawn. It is really a product of the method by which the sample is drawn rather than the actual characteristics of any individual sample. Generally speaking, properly randomly drawn samples from a population are the only way of eliminating bias. Telephone interviews are a common method of obtaining samples. A sample of telephone numbers is selected at random from a telephone directory. Unfortunately, although the sample drawn may be a random (unbiased) sample of people on that telephone list, it is likely to be a biased sample of the general population since it excludes individuals who are ex-directory or who do not have a telephone.

A sample may provide a poor estimate of the population characteristics but, nevertheless, is *not* unbiased. This is because the notion of bias is about systematically being incorrect over the long run rather than about a single poor estimate.

bi-directional relationship: a causal relationship between two variables in which both variables are thought to affect each other.

bi-lateral relationship: see **bi-directional relationship**

bimodal: data which have two equally common modes. Table B.3 is a frequency table which gives the distribution of the scores 1 to 8. It can be seen that the score 2 and the score 6 both have the maximum frequency of 16. Since the most frequent score is also known as the mode, two values exist for the mode: 2 and 6. Thus, this is a bimodal distribution. See also: **multimodal**

When a bimodal distribution is plotted graphically, Figure B.1 illustrates its appearance. Quite simply, two points of the histogram are the highest. These, since the data are the same as for Table B.3, are for the values 2 and 6.

Table B.3 *Bimodal distribution*

		Frequency	%	Valid %	Cumulative %
Valid	1.00	7	7.1	7.1	7.1
	2.00	16	16.2	15.2	23.2
	3.00	14	14.1	14.1	37.4
	4.00	12	12.1	12.1	49.5
	5.00	13	13.1	13.1	62.6
	6.00	16	16.2	16.2	78.6
	7.00	12	12.1	12.1	90.9
	8.00	9	9.1	9.1	100.0
	Total	99	100.0	100.0	

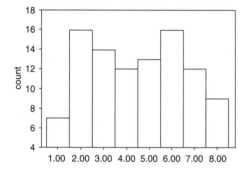

Figure B.1 *Example of a bimodal distribution*

Bimodal distributions can occur in all types of data including nominal categories (category or categorical data) as well as numerical scores as in this example. If the data are nominal categories, the two modes are the names (i.e. values) of the two categories.

binomial distribution: describes the probability of an event or outcome occurring, such as a person passing or failing or being a woman or a man, on a number of independent occasions or trials when the event has the same probability of occurring on each occasion. The binomial theorem can be used to calculate these probabilities.

binomial theorem: deals with situations in which we are assessing the probability of getting particular outcomes when there are just two values. These may be heads versus tails, males versus females, success versus failure, correct versus incorrect, and so forth. To apply the theorem we need to know the proportions of each of the alternatives in the population (though this may, of course, be derived theoretically such as when tossing a coin). P is the proportion in one category and Q is the proportion in the other category. In the practical application of statistics (e.g. as in the sign test), the two values are often equally likely or assumed to be equally likely just as in the case of the toss of a coin. There are tables of the binomial distribution available in statistics textbooks, especially older ones. However, binomials can be calculated.

In order to calculate the likelihood of getting 9 heads out of 10 tosses of a coin, $P = 0.5$ and $Q = 0.5$. N is the number of coin tosses (10). X is the number of events in one category (9) and Y is the number of events in the other category (1).

The formula for the probability of getting X objects out of N (i.e. X plus Y) in one category is

$$\text{binomial probability} = \frac{N!}{X!(Y)!} P^X Q^Y$$

$N!$ is the symbol for a factorial. The factorial of 10 is $10 \times 9 \times 8 \times 7 \times 6 \times 5 \times 4 \times 3 \times 2 \times 1 = 3,628,800$. Factorials are easily calculated on a scientific calculator although they tend to produce huge numbers which can be off-putting and difficult for those of us not used to working with exponentials. So, substituting values in the above,

$$\text{binomial probability} = \frac{10!}{9!(1)!} \times 0.5^9 \times 0.5^1$$

$$= 10 \times P^X Q^Y$$

$$= 10 \times 0.0009765625 \times 0.5$$

$$= 0.00488$$

This is the basic calculation. Remember that this gives the probability of 9 heads and 1 tail. More usually researchers will be interested in the probability, say, of 9 or more heads. In this case, the calculation would be done for 9 heads exactly as above but then a similar calculation for 10 heads out of 10. These two probabilities would then be added together to give the probability of 9 or more heads in 10 tosses.

There is also the multinomial theorem which is the distribution of several categories.

Generally speaking, the binomial theorem is rare in practice for most students and practitioners. There are many simple alternatives which can be substituted in virtually any application. Therefore, for example, the sign test can be used to assess whether the distribution of two alternative categories is equal or not. Alternatively, the single-sample chi-square distribution would allow any number of categories to be compared in terms of their frequency.

The binomial distribution does not require equal probabilities of outcomes. Nevertheless, the probabilities need to be independent so that the separate probabilities for the different events are equal to 1.00. This means, for example, that the outcomes being considered can be unequal as in the case of the likelihood of twins. Imagine that the likelihood of any birth yielding twins is 0.04 (i.e. 4 chances in 100). The probability of a non-twin birth is therefore 0.96. These values could be entered as the probabilities of P and Q in the binomial formula to work out the probability that, say, 13 out of 20 sequential births at a hospital turn out to be twins.

bivariate: involving the simultaneous analysis of two variables. Two-way chi-square, correlation, unrelated t test and ANOVA are among the inferential statistics which involve two variables. Scattergrams, compound histograms, etc., are basic descriptive methods involving a bivariate approach. Bivariate analysis involves the exploration of interrelationships between variables and, hence, possible influences of one variable on another. Conceptually, it is a fairly straightforward progression from bivariate analysis to multivariate analysis.

bivariate regression: see **simple** or **bivariate regression**

blocks: see **randomization**

blocking: see **matching**

BMDP: an abbreviation for *Bio-Medical Data Package* which is one of several widely used statistical packages for manipulating and analysing data. Information about BMDP can be found at the following website:
http://www.statsol.ie/bmdp/bmdp.htm

Bonferroni adjustment: see **analysis of variance; Bonferroni test; Dunn's test**

Bonferroni test: also known as Dunn's test, it is one test for controlling the probability of making a Type I error in which two groups are assumed to differ significantly when they do not differ. The conventional level for determining whether two groups differ is the 0.05 or 5% level. At this level the probability of two groups differing by chance when they do not differ is 1 out of 20 or 5 out of 100. However, the more groups we compare the more likely it is that two groups will differ by chance. To control for this, we may reduce the significance level by dividing the conventional significance level of 0.05 by the number of comparisons we want to make. So, if we want to compare six groups, we would divide the 0.05 level by 6 to give us a level of 0.008 (0.05/6 = 0.008). At this more conservative level, it is much less likely that we will assume that two groups differ when they do not differ. However, we are more likely to be making a Type II error in which we assume that there is no difference between two groups when there is a difference.

This test has generally been recommended as an a priori test for planned comparisons even though it is a more conservative test than some *post hoc* tests for unplanned comparisons. It is listed as a *post hoc* test in SPSS.

It can be used for equal and unequal group sizes where the variances are equal. The formula for this test is the same as that for the unrelated *t* test where the variances are equal:

$$\frac{\text{group 1 mean} - \text{group 2 mean}}{\sqrt{(\text{group 1 variance/group 1 } n) + (\text{group 2 variance/group 2 } n)}}$$

Where the variances are unequal, it is recommended that the Games–Howell procedure be used. This involves calculating a critical difference for every pair of means being compared which uses the studentized range statistic.

　　Howell (2002)

bootstrapping: bootstrapping statistics literally take the distribution of the obtained data in order to generate a sampling distribution of the particular statistic in question. The crucial feature or essence of bootstrapping methods is that the obtained sample data are, conceptually speaking at least, reproduced an infinite number of times to give an infinitely large sample. Given this, it becomes possible to sample from the 'bootstrapped population' and obtain outcomes which differ from the original sample. So, for example, imagine the following sample of 10 scores obtained by a researcher:

　　5, 10, 6, 3, 9, 2, 5, 6, 7, 11

There is only one sample of 10 scores possible from this set of 10 scores – the original sample (i.e. the 10 scores above). However, if we endlessly repeated the string as we do in bootstrapping then we would get

5, 10, 6, 3, 9, 2, 5, 6, 7, 11, 5, 10, 6, 3, 9, 2, 5, 6, 7, 11, 5, 10, 6, 3, 9, 2, 5, 6, 7, 11, 5, 10, 6, 3, 9, 2, 5, 6, 7, 11, 5, 10, 6, 3, 9, 2, 5, 6, 7, 11, 5, 10, 6, 3, 9, 2, 5, 6, 7, 11, ..., 5, 10, 6, 3, 9, 2, 5, 6, 7, 11, etc.

With this bootstrapped population, it is possible to draw random samples of 10 scores but get a wide variety of samples many of which differ from the original sample. This is simply because there is a variety of scores from which to choose now.

So long as the original sample is selected with care to be representative of the wider situation, it has been shown that bootstrapped populations are not bad population estimates despite the nature of their origins.

　　The difficulty with bootstrapping statistics is the computation of the sampling distribution because of the sheer number of samples and calculations involved. Computer programs are increasingly available to do bootstrapping calculations though these have not yet appeared in the most popular computer packages for statistical analysis. The Web provides fairly up-to-date information on this.

　　The most familiar statistics used today had their origins in pre-computer times when methods had to be adopted which were capable of hand calculation. Perhaps bootstrapping methods (and the related procedures of resampling) would be the norm had high-speed computers been available at the birth of statistical analysis. See also: **resampling techniques**

box plot: a form of statistical diagram to represent the distribution of scores on a variable. It consists (in one orientation) of a horizontal numerical scale to represent the values of the scores. Then there is a vertical line to mark the lowest value of a score and another vertical line to mark the highest value of a score in the data (Figure B.2). In the middle there is a box to indicate the 25 to the 50th percentile (or median) and an adjacent one indicating the 50th to the 75th percentile (Figure B.3).

　　Thus the lowest score is 5, the highest score is 16, the median score (50th percentile) is 11, and the 75th percentile is about 13.

　　From such a diagram, not only are these values to an experienced eye an indication of the variation of the scores, but also the

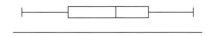

　　5　6　7　8　9　10　11　12　13　14　15　16　17

Figure B.2　*Illustration of box plot*

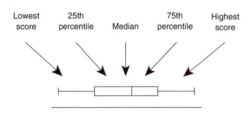

$$5\ 6\ 7\ 8\ 9\ 10\ 11\ 12\ 13\ 14\ 15\ 16\ 17$$

Figure B.3 *Interpretation of the components of a box plot*

symmetry of the distribution may be assessed. In some disciplines box plots are extremely common whereas in others they are somewhat rare. The more concrete the variables being displayed, the more useful a box plot is. So in economics and sociology when variables such as income are being tabulated, the box plot has clear and obvious meaning. The more abstract the concept and the less linear the scale of measurement, the less useful is the box plot.

Box's M test: one test used to determine whether the variance/covariance matrices of two or more dependent variables in a multivariate analysis of variance or covariance are similar or homogeneous across the groups, which is one of the assumptions underlying this analysis. If this test is significant, it may be possible to reduce the variances by transforming the scores by taking their square root or natural logarithm.

brackets (): commonly used in statistical equations. They indicate that their contents should be calculated first. Take the following equation:

$$A = B(C + D)$$

The brackets mean that C and D should be added together before multiplying by B. So,

$$
\begin{aligned}
A &= 2(3 + 4)\\
&= 2(7)\\
&= 2 \times 7\\
&= 14
\end{aligned}
$$

Bryant–Paulson simultaneous test procedure: a *post hoc* or multiple comparison test which is used to determine which of three or more adjusted means differ from one another when the F ratio in an analysis of covariance is significant. The formula for this test varies according to the number of covariates and whether cases have been assigned to treatments at random or not.

The following formula is used for a non-randomized study with one covariate where the subscripts 1 and 2 denote the two groups being compared and n is the sample size of the group:

$$
\frac{\text{adjusted mean}_1 - \text{adjusted mean}_2}{\sqrt{\left\{\begin{array}{l}\text{adjusted}\\\text{error mean}\\\text{square}\end{array}\times\left[\frac{2}{n} + \frac{(\text{covariate mean}_1 - \text{covariate mean}_2)^2}{\text{covariate error sum of squares}}\right]\right\}\Big/2}}
$$

The error term must be computed separately for each comparison.

For a randomized study with one covariate we need to use the following formula:

$$
\frac{\text{adjusted mean}_1 - \text{adjusted mean}_2}{\sqrt{\dfrac{\begin{array}{l}\text{adjusted}\\\text{error mean}\\\text{square}\end{array}\times\left[1 + \dfrac{\text{covariate between} - \text{groups mean square}}{\text{covariate error sum of squares}}\right]}{\text{number of cases in a group}}}}
$$

The error term is not computed separately for each comparison. Where the group sizes are unequal, the harmonic mean of the sample size is used. For two groups the harmonic mean is defined as follows:

$$\text{harmonic mean} = \frac{2 \times n_1 \times n_2}{n_1 + n_2}$$

Stevens (1996)

C

canonical correlation: normal correlation involves the correlation between one variable and another. Multiple correlation involves the correlation between a set of variables and a single variable. Canonical correlation involves the correlation between one set of X variables and another set of Y variables. However, these variables are not those as actually recorded in the data but abstract variables (like factors in factor analysis) known as latent variables (variables underlying a set of variables). There may be several latent variables in any set of variables just as there may be several factors in factor analysis. This is true for the X variables and the Y variables. Hence, in canonical correlation there may be a number of coefficients – one for each possible pair of a latent root of the X variables and a latent root of the Y variables.

Canonical correlation is a rare technique in modern published research. See also: **Hotelling's trace criterion; Roy's gcr; Wilks's lambda**

carryover or **asymmetrical transfer effect:** may occur in a within-subjects or repeated-measures design in which the effect of a prior condition or treatments 'carries over' onto a subsequent condition. For example, we may be interested in the effect of watching violence on aggression. We conduct a within-subjects design in which participants are shown a violent and a non-violent scene in random order, with half the participants seeing the violent scene first and the other half seeing it second. If the effect of watching violence is to make participants more aggressive, then participants may behave more aggressively after viewing the non-violent scene. This will have the effect of reducing the difference in aggression between the two conditions. One way of controlling for this effect is to increase the interval between one condition and another.

case: a more general term than participant or subject for the individuals taking part in a study. It can apply to non-humans and inanimate objects so is preferred for some disciplines. See also: **sample**

categorical (category) variable: also known as qualitative, nominal or category variables. A variable measured in terms of the possession of qualities and not in terms of quantities. Categorical variables contain a minimum of two different categories (or values) and the categories have no underlying ordering of quantity. Thus, colour could be considered a categorical variable and, say, the categories blue, green and red chosen to be the measured categories. However, brightness such as sunny, bright, dull and dark would seem *not* to be a categorical variable since the named categories reflect an underlying dimension of degrees of brightness which would make it a score (or quantitative variable).

Categorical variables are analysed using generally distinct techniques such as chi-square, binomial, multinomial, logistic regression, and log–linear. See also: **qualitative research; quantitative research**

Cattell's scree test: see **scree test, Cattell's**

causal: see **quasi-experiments**

causal effect: see **effect**

causal modelling: see **partial correlation; path analysis**

causal relationship: is one in which one variable is hypothesized or has been shown to affect another variable. The variable thought to affect the other variable may be called an independent variable or cause while the variable thought to be affected may be known as the dependent variable or effect. The dependent variable is assumed to 'depend' on the independent variable, which is considered to be 'independent' of the dependent variable. The independent variable must occur before the dependent variable. However, a variable which precedes another variable is not necessarily a cause of that other variable. Both variables may be the result of another variable.

To demonstrate that one variable causes or influences another variable, we have to be able to manipulate the independent or causal variable and to hold all other variables constant. If the dependent variable varies as a function of the independent variable, we may be more confident that the independent variable affects the dependent variable. For example, if we think that noise decreases performance, we will manipulate noise by varying its level or intensity and observe the effect this has on performance. If performance decreases as a function of noise, we may be more certain that noise influences performance.

In the socio-behavioural sciences it may be difficult to be sure that we have only manipulated the independent variable. We may have inadvertently manipulated one or more other variables such as the kind of noise we played. It may also be difficult to control all other variables. In practice, we may try to control the other variables that we think might affect performance, such as illumination. We may overlook other variables which also affect performance, such as time of day or week. One factor which may affect performance is the myriad ways in which people or animals differ. For example, performance may be affected by how much experience people have of similar tasks, their eyesight, how tired or anxious they are, and so on. The main way of controlling for these kinds of individual differences is to assign cases randomly to the different conditions in a between-subjects design or to different orders in a within-subjects design. With very small numbers of cases in each condition, random assignment may not result in the cases being similar across the conditions. A way to determine whether random assignment may have produced cases who are comparable across conditions is to test them on the dependent variable before the intervention, which is known as a pre-test. In our example, this dependent variable is performance.

It is possible that the variable we assume to be the dependent variable may also affect the variable we considered to be the independent variable. For example, watching violence may cause people to be more aggressive but aggressive people may also be inclined to watch more violence. In this case we have a causal relationship which has been variously referred to as bi-directional, bi-lateral, two-way, reciprocal or non-recursive. A causal relationship in which one variable affects but is not affected by another variable is variously known as a uni-directional, uni-lateral, one-way, non-reciprocal or recursive one.

If we simply measure two variables at the same time as in a cross-sectional survey or

Table C.1   *A contingency table with a single cell highlighted*

		Independent variable 1		
		Category A	Category B	Category C
Independent variable 2	Sample X		▨	
	Sample Y			

study, we cannot determine which variable affects the other. Furthermore, if we measure the two variables on two or more occasions as in a panel or longitudinal study, we also cannot determine if one variable affects the other because both variables may be affected by other variables. In such studies, it is more accurate and appropriate simply to refer to an association or relationship between variables unless one is postulating a causal relationship. See also: **path analysis**

ceiling effect: occurs when scores on a variable are approaching the maximum they can be. Thus, there may be bunching of values close to the upper point. The introduction of a new variable cannot do a great deal to elevate the scores any further since they are virtually as high as they can go. Failure to recognize the possibility that there is a ceiling effect may lead to the mistaken conclusion that the independent variable has no effect. There are several reasons for ceiling effects which go well beyond statistical issues into more general methodological matters. For example, if the researcher wished to know whether eating carrots improved eyesight, it would probably be unwise to use a sample of ace rifle marksmen and women. The reason is that their eyesight is likely to be as good as it can get (they would not be exceptional at shooting if it were not) so the diet of extra carrots is unlikely to improve matters. With a different sample such as a sample of steam railway enthusiasts, the ceiling effect may not occur. Similarly, if a test of intelligence is too difficult, then improvement may be impossible in the majority of people. So ceiling effects are a complex of matters and their avoidance a matter of careful evaluation of a range of issues. See also: **floor effect**

cell: a subcategory in a cross-tabulation or contingency table. A cell may refer to just single values of a nominal, category or categorical variable. However, cells can also be formed by the intersection of two categories of the two (or more) independent nominal variables. Thus, a 2×3 cross-tabulation or contingency table has six cells. Similarly, a $2 \times 2 \times 2$ ANOVA has a total of eight cells. The two-way contingency table in Table C.1 illustrates the notion of a cell. One box or cell has been filled in as grey. This cell consists of the cases which are in sample X and fall into category B of the other independent variable. That is, a cell consists of cases which are defined by the vertical column and the horizontal row it is in.

According to the type of variable, the contents of the cells will be frequencies (e.g. for chi-square) or scores (e.g. for analysis of variance).

central limit theorem: a description of the sampling distribution of means of samples taken from a population. It is an important tool in inferential statistics which enables certain conclusions to be drawn about the characteristics of samples compared with the population. The theorem makes a number of important statements about the distribution of an infinite number of samples drawn at random from a population. These to some extent may be grasped intuitively though it may be helpful to carry out an empirical investigation of the assumptions of the theory:

1 The mean of an infinite number of random sample means drawn from the population is identical to the mean of the population. Of course, the means of individual samples may depart from the mean of the population.

2　The standard deviation of the distribution of sample means drawn from the population is proportional to the square root of the sample size of the sample means in question. In other words, if the standard deviation of the scores in the population is symbolized by σ then the standard deviation of the sample means is $\sigma/\sqrt{N}$ where N is the size of the sample in question. The standard deviation of sample means is known as the standard error of sample means.

3　Even if the population is not normally distributed, the distribution of means of samples drawn at random from the population will tend towards being normally distributed. The larger the sample size involved, the greater the tendency towards the distribution of samples being normal.

Part of the practical significance of this is that samples drawn at random from a population tend to reflect the characteristics of that population. The larger the sample size, the more likely it is to reflect the characteristics of the population if it is drawn at random. With larger sample sizes, statistical techniques based on the normal distribution will fit the theoretical assumptions of the technique increasingly well. Even if the population is not normally distributed, the tendency of the sampling distribution of means towards normality means that parametric statistics may be appropriate despite limitations in the data.

With means of small-sized samples, the distribution of the sample means tends to be flatter than that of the normal distribution so we typically employ the t distribution rather than the normal distribution.

The central limit theorem allows researchers to use small samples knowing that they reflect population characteristics fairly well. If samples showed no such meaningful and systematic trends, statistical inference from samples would be impossible. See also: **sampling distribution**

central tendency, measure of: any measure or index which describes the central value in a distribution of values. The three most common measures of central tendency are the mean, the median and the mode. These three indices are the same when the distribution is unimodal and symmetrical. See also: **average**

characteristic root, value or **number:** another term for eigenvalue. See **eigenvalue, in factor analysis**

chi-square or **chi-squared** (χ^2): symbolized by the Greek letter χ and sometimes called Pearson's chi-square after the person who developed it. It is used with frequency or categorical data as a measure of goodness of fit where there is one variable and as a measure of independence where there are two variables. It compares the observed frequencies with the frequencies expected by chance or according to a particular distribution across all the categories of one variable or all the combinations of categories of two variables. The categories or combination of categories may be represented as cells in a table. So if a variable has three categories there will be three cells. The greater the difference between the observed and the expected frequencies, the greater chi-square will be and the more likely it is that the observed frequencies will differ significantly.

Differences between observed and expected frequencies are squared so that chi-square is always positive because squaring negative values turns them into positive ones (e.g. $-2^2 = 4$). Furthermore, this squared difference is expressed as a function of the expected frequency for that cell. This means that larger differences, which should by chance result from larger expected frequencies, do not have an undue influence on the value of chi-square. When chi-square is used as a measure of goodness of fit, the smaller chi-square is, the better the fit of the observed frequencies to the expected ones. A chi-square of zero indicates a perfect fit. When chi-square is used as a measure of independence, the greater the value of chi-square is the more likely it is that the two variables are related and not independent.

The more categories there are, the bigger chi-square will be. Consequently, the statistical significance of chi-square takes account of the number of categories in the analysis. Essentially, the more categories there are, the bigger chi-square has to be to be statistically significant at a particular level such as the 0.05 or 5% level. The number of categories is expressed in degrees of freedom (*df*). For chi-square with only one variable, the degrees of freedom are the number of categories minus one. So, if there are three categories, there are 2 degrees of freedom $(3 - 1 = 2)$. For chi-square with two variables, the degrees of freedom are one minus the number of categories in one variable multiplied by one minus the number of categories in the other variable. So, if there are three categories in one variable and four in the other, the degrees of freedom are 6 $[(3 - 1) \times (4 - 1) = 6]$.

With 1 degree of freedom it is necessary to have a minimum expected frequency of five in each cell to apply chi-square. With more than 1 degree of freedom, there should be a minimum expected frequency of one in each cell and an expected minimum frequency of five in 80% or more of the cells. Where these requirements are not satisfied it may be possible to meet them by omitting one or more categories and/or combining two or more categories with fewer than the minimum expected frequencies.

Where there is 1 degree of freedom, if we know what the direction of the results is for one of the cells, we also know what the direction of the results is for the other cell where there is only one variable and for one of the other cells where there are two variables with two categories. For example, if there are only two categories or cells, if the observed frequency in one cell is greater than that expected by chance, the observed frequency in the other cell must be less than that expected by chance. Similarly, if there are two variables with two categories each, and if the observed frequency is greater than the expected frequency in one of the cells, the observed frequency must be less than the expected frequency in one of the other cells. If we had strong grounds for predicting the direction of the results before the data were analysed, we could test the statistical significance of the results at the one-tailed level.

Table C.2   *Support for the death penalty in women and men*

	Yes	**No**	**Don't know**
Women	20	70	20
Men	30	50	10

Where there is more than 1 degree of freedom, we cannot tell which observed frequencies in one cell are significantly different from those in another cell without doing a separate chi-square analysis of the frequencies for those cells.

We will use the following example to illustrate the calculation and interpretation of chi-square. Suppose we wanted to find whether women and men differed in their support for the death penalty. We asked 110 women and 90 men their views and found that 20 of the women and 30 of the men agreed with the death penalty. The frequency of women and men agreeing, disagreeing and not knowing are shown in the 2 × 3 contingency table in Table C.2.

The number of women expected to support the death penalty is the proportion of people agreeing with the death penalty which is expressed as a function of the number of women. So the proportion of people supporting the death penalty is 50 out of 200 or 0.25(50/200 = 0.25) which as a function of the number of women is 27.50(0.25 × 110 = 27.50). The calculation of the expected frequency can be expressed more generally in the following formula:

$$\text{expected frequency} = \frac{\text{row total} \times \text{column total}}{\text{grand total}}$$

For women supporting the death penalty the row total is 110 and the column total is 50. The grand total is 200. Thus the expected frequency is 27.50(110 × 50/200 = 27.50).

Chi-square is the sum of the squared differences between the observed and expected frequency divided by the expected frequency for each of the cells:

$$\text{chi-square} = \frac{(\text{observed frequency} - \text{expected frequency})^2}{\text{expected frequency}}$$

This summed across cells. This value for women supporting the death penalty is 2.05:

$$\frac{(20 - 27.5)^2}{27.5} = \frac{-7.5^2}{27.5} = \frac{56.25}{27.5} = 2.05$$

The sum of the values for all six cells is 6.74 $(2.05 + 0.24 + 0.74 + 2.50 + 0.30 + 0.91 = 6.74)$. Hence chi-square is 6.74.

The degrees of freedom are $2[(2 - 1) \times (3 - 1) = 2]$. With 2 degrees of freedom chi-square has to be 5.99 or larger to be statistically significant at the two-tailed 0.05 level, which it is.

Although fewer women support the death penalty than expected by chance, we do not know if this is statistically significant because the chi-square examines all three answers together. If we wanted to determine whether fewer women supported the death penalty than men we could just examine the two cells in the first column. The chi-square for this analysis is 2.00 which is not statistically significant. Alternatively, we could carry out a 2×2 chi-square. We could compare those agreeing with either those disagreeing or those disagreeing and not knowing. Both these chi-squares are statistically significant, indicating that fewer women than men support the death penalty.

The value that chi-square has to reach or exceed to be statistically significant at the two-tailed 0.05 level is shown in Table C.3 for up to 12 degrees of freedom. See also: **contingency coefficient; expected frequencies; Fisher (exact probability) test; log–linear analysis; partitioning; Yates's correction**

Cramer (1998)

classic experimental method, in analysis of variance: see **Type II, classic experimental** or **least squares method in analysis of variance**

cluster analysis: a set of techniques for sorting variables, individuals, and the like, into groups on the basis of their similarity to each

Table C.3 *The 0.05 probability two-tailed critical values of chi-square*

df	X^2	df	X^2
1	3.84	7	14.07
2	5.99	8	15.51
3	7.82	9	16.92
4	9.49	10	18.31
5	11.07	11	19.68
6	12.59	12	21.03

other. These groupings are known as clusters. Really it is about classifying things on the basis of having similar patterns of characteristics. For example, when we speak of families of plants (e.g. cactus family, rose family, and so forth) we are talking of clusters of plants which are similar to each other. Cluster analysis appears to be less widely used than factor analysis, which does a very similar task. One advantage of cluster analysis is that it is less tied to the correlation coefficient than factor analysis is. For example, cluster analysis sometimes uses similarity or matching scores. Such a score is based on the number of characteristics that, say, a case has in common with another case.

Usually, depending on the method of clustering, the clusters are hierarchical. That is, there are clusters within clusters or, if one prefers, clusters of clusters. Some methods of clustering (divisive methods) start with one all-embracing cluster and then break this into smaller clusters. Agglomerative methods of clustering usually start with as many clusters as there are cases (i.e. each case begins as a cluster) and then the cases are brought together to form bigger and bigger clusters. There is no single set of clusters which always applies – the clusters are dependent on what ways of assessing similarity and dissimilarity are used. Clusters are groups of things which have more in common with each other than they do with other clusters.

There are a number of ways of assessing how closely related the entities being entered into a cluster analysis are. This may be referred to as their similarity or the proximity. This is often expressed in terms of correlation coefficients but these only indicate high covariation, which is different from precise

Table C.4   *Squared Euclidean distances and the sum of the squared*
Euclidean distances for facial features

Feature	Person I	Person 2	Difference	Difference^2
Nose size	4	4	0	0
Bushiness of eyebrows	3	I	2	4
Fatness of lips	4	2	2	4
Hairiness	I	4	−3	9
Eye spacing	5	4	I	I
Ear size	4	I	−3	9
				Sum = 27

matching. One way of assessing matching would be to use squared Euclidean distances between the entities. To do this, one simply calculates the difference between values, squares each difference, and then sums the square of the difference. This is illustrated in Table C.4 for the similarity of facial features for just *two* of a larger number of individuals entered into a cluster analysis. Obviously if we did the same for, say, 20 people, we would end up with a 20 × 20 matrix indicating the amount of similarity between every possible pair of individuals – that is, a proximity matrix. The pair of individuals in Table C.4 are not very similar in terms of their facial features.

Clusters are formed in various ways in various methods of cluster analysis. One way of starting a cluster is simply to identify the pair of entities which are closest or most similar to each other. That is, one would choose from the correlation matrix or the proximity matrix the pair of entities which are most similar. They would be the highest correlating pair if one were using a correlation matrix or the pair with the lowest sum of squared Euclidean distances between them in the proximity matrix. This pair of entities would form the nucleus of the first cluster. One can then look through the matrix for the pair of entities which have the next highest level of similarity. If this is a completely new pair of entities, then we have a brand-new cluster beginning. However, if one member of this pair is in the cluster first formed, then a new cluster is not formed but the additional entity is added to the first cluster making it a three-entity cluster at this stage.

According to the form of clustering, a refined version of this may continue until all of the entities are joined together in a single grand cluster. In some other methods, clusters are discrete in the sense that only entities which have their closest similarity with another entity which is already in the cluster can be included. Mostly, the first option is adopted which essentially is hierarchical clustering. That is to say, hierarchical clustering allows for the fact that entities have varying degrees of similarity to each other. Depending on the level of similarity required, clusters may be very small or large. The consequence of this is that this sort of cluster analysis results in clusters within clusters – that is, entities are conceived as having different levels of similarity. See also: **agglomeration schedule; dendrogram; hierarchical agglomerative clustering**

Cramer (2003)

cluster sample: cluster sampling employs only limited portions of the population. This may be for a number of reasons – there may not be available a list which effectively defines the population. For example, if an education researcher wished to study 11 year old students, it is unlikely that a list of all 11 year old students would be available. Consequently, the researcher may opt for approaching a number of schools each of which might be expected to have a list of its 11 year old students. Each school would be a cluster.

In populations spread over a substantial geographical area, random sampling is enormously expensive since random sampling maximizes the amount of travel and consequent expense involved. So it is fairly common to employ cluster samples in which the larger geographical area is subdivided into representative clusters or sub-areas. Thus, large towns, small towns and rural areas might be identified as the clusters. In this way, characteristics of the stratified sample may be built in as well as gaining the advantages of reduced geographical dispersion of participants or cases. Much research is only possible because of the use of a limited number of clusters in this way.

In terms of statistical analysis, cluster sampling techniques may affect the conceptual basis of the underlying statistical theory as they cannot be regarded as random samples. Hence, survey researchers sometimes use alternative statistical techniques from the ones common in disciplines such as psychology and related fields.

clustered bar chart, diagram or **graph:** see **compound bar chart**

Cochran's C test: one test for determining whether the variance in two or more groups is similar or homogeneous, which is an assumption that underlies the use of analysis of variance. The group with the largest variance is divided by the sum of variances of all the groups. The statistical significance of this value may be looked up in a table of critical values for this test.

Cramer (1998)

Cochran's Q test: used to determine whether the frequencies of a dichotomous variable differ significantly for more than two related samples or groups.

Cramer (1998)

coefficient of alienation: indicates the amount of variation that two variables do *not*

have in common. If there is a perfect correlation between two variables then the coefficient of alienation is zero. If there is no correlation between two variables then the coefficient of alienation is one. To calculate the coefficient of alienation, we use the following formula:

$$\text{coefficient of alienation} = 1 - r^2$$

Where r^2 is the squared correlation coefficient between the two variables. So if we know that the correlation between age and intelligence is -0.2 then

$$\text{coefficient of alienation} = 1 - (-0.2)^2$$
$$= 1 - 0.04 = 0.96$$

In a sense, then, it is the opposite of the coefficient of determination which assesses the amount of variance that two variables have in common.

coefficient of determination: an index of the amount of variation that two variables have in common. It is simply the square of the correlation coefficient between the two variables:

$$\text{coefficient of determination} = r^2$$

Thus, if the correlation between two variables is 0.4, then the coefficient of determination is $0.4^2 = 0.16$.

The coefficient of determination is a clearer indication of the relationship between two variables than the correlation coefficient. For example, the difference between a correlation coefficient of 0.5 and one of 1.0 is not easy for newcomers to statistics to appreciate. However, converted to the corresponding coefficients of determination of 0.25 and 1.00, then it is clear that a correlation of 1.00 (i.e. coefficient of determination = 1.0) is four times the magnitude as one of 0.5 (coefficient of determination = 0.25) in terms of the amount of variance explained.

Table C.5 gives the relationship between the Pearson correlation (or point biserial

Table C.5 *The relationship between correlation, coefficient of determination and percentage of shared variance*

Correlation	1.0	0.9	0.8	0.7	0.6	0.5	0.4	0.3	0.2	0.1	0.0
Coefficient of determination	1.00	0.81	0.64	0.49	0.36	0.25	0.16	0.09	0.04	0.01	0.00
Shared variance	100%	81%	64%	49%	36%	25%	16%	9%	4%	1%	0%

or phi coefficients for that matter) and the coefficient of determination. The percentage of shared variance is also given. This table should help understand the meaning of the correlation coefficient values. See **coefficient of alienation**

coefficient of variation: it would seem intuitive to suggest that samples with big mean scores of, say, 100 are likely to have larger variation around the mean than samples with smaller means such as 5. In order to indicate relative variability adjusting the variance of samples for their sample size, we can calculate the coefficient of variation. This is merely the standard deviation of the sample divided by the mean score. (Standard deviation itself is an index of variation, being merely the square root of variance.) This allows comparison of variation between samples with large means and small means. Essentially, it scales down (or possibly up) all standard deviations as a ratio of a single unit on the measurement scale.

Thus, if a sample mean is 39.0 and its standard deviation is 5.3, we can calculate the coefficient of variation as follows:

$$\text{coefficient of variation} = \frac{\text{standard deviation}}{\text{mean}}$$

$$= \frac{5.3}{39.0} = 0.14$$

Despite its apparent usefulness, the coefficient of variation is more common in some disciplines than others.

Cohen's d: one index of effect size used in meta-analysis and elsewhere. Compared with using Pearson's correlation for this purpose, it lacks intuitive appeal. The two are readily converted to each other. See **meta-analysis**

cohort: a group of people who share the same or similar experience during the same period of time such as being born or married during a particular period. This period may vary in duration.

cohort analysis: usually the analysis of some characteristic from one or more cohorts at two or more points in time. For example, we may be interested in how those in a particular age group vote in two consecutive elections. The individuals in a cohort need not be the same at the different points in time. A study in which the same individuals are measured on two or more occasions is usually referred to as a panel or prospective study.

Glenn (1977)

cohort design: a design in which groups of individuals pass through an institution such as a school but experience different events such as whether or not they have been exposed to a particular course. The groups have not been randomly assigned to whether or not they experience the particular event so it is not possible to determine whether any difference between the groups experiencing the event and those not experiencing the event is due to the event itself.

Cook and Campbell (1979)

Table C.6   *Percentage intending to vote for
different cohorts and periods
with age in brackets*

		Year of measurement (period)		
		1980	1990	2000
Year of birth	1950	60 (30)	70 (40)	
(cohort)	1960		50 (30)	60 (40)

cohort effect: may be present if the behaviour of one cohort differs from that of another. Suppose, for example, we asked people their voting intentions in the year 1990 and found that 70% of those born in 1950 said they would vote compared with 50% of those born in 1960 as shown in Table C.6. We may consider that this difference may reflect a cohort effect. However, this effect may also be due to an age difference in that those born in 1960 will be younger than those born in 1950. Those born in 1960 will be aged 30 in the year 1990 while those born in 1950 will be aged 40. So this difference may be more an age effect than a cohort effect.

To determine whether this difference is an age effect, we would have to compare the voting intentions of the two cohorts at the same age. This would mean finding out the voting intention of these two groups at two other periods or times of measurement. These times could be the year 1980 for those born in 1950 who would then be aged 30 and the year 2000 for those born in 1960 who would then be 40. Suppose, of those born in 1950 and asked in 1980, we found that 60% said they would vote compared with 60% of those born in 1960 and asked in 2000 as shown in Table C.6. This would suggest that there might also be an age effect in that older people may be more inclined to vote than younger people. However, this age effect could also be a time of measurement or period effect in that there was an increase in people's intention to vote over this period.

If we compare people of the same age for the two times we have information on them, we see that there appears to be a decrease in their voting intentions. For those aged 30, 60% intended to vote in 1980 compared with 50% in 1990. For those aged 40, 70% intended

to vote in 1990 compared with 60% in 2000. However, this difference could be more a cohort effect than a period effect.

Menard (1991)

collinearity: a feature of the data which makes the interpretation of analyses such as multiple regression sometimes difficult. In multiple regression, a number of predictor (or independent) variables are linearly combined to estimate the criterion (or dependent variable). In collinearity, some of the predictor or independent variables correlate extremely highly with each other. Because of the way in which multiple regression operates, this means that some variables which actually predict the dependent variable do not appear in the regression equation, but other predictor variables which appear very similar have a lot of impact on the regression equation. Table C.7 has a simple example of a correlation matrix which may have a collinearity problem. The correlations between the independent variables are the major focus. Areas where collinearity may have an effect have been highlighted. These are independent variables which have fairly high correlations with each other. In the example, the correlation matrix indicates that independent variable 1 correlates at 0.7 with independent variable 4. Both have got (relatively) fairly high correlations with the dependent variable of 0.4 and 0.3. Thus, both are fairly good predictors of the dependent variable. If one but not the other appears as the significant predictor in multiple regression, the researcher should take care not simply to take the interpretation offered by the computer output of the multiple regression as adequate. Another solution to collinearity problems is to combine the highly intercorrelated variables into a single variable which is then used in the analysis. The fact that they are highly intercorrelated means that they are measuring much the same thing. The best way of combining variables is to convert each to a z score and sum the z scores to give a total z score.

It is possible to deal with collinearity in a number of ways. The important thing is that

Table C.7   *Examples of high intercorrelations which may make collinearity a problem*

	Independent variable 2	Independent variable 3	Independent variable 4	Independent variable 5	Dependent variable
Independent variable 1	0.3	0.2	⓪.7	0.1	0.4
Independent variable 2		⓪.8	0.3	0.2	0.2
Independent variable 3			0.2	0.1	0.2
Independent variable 4				0.3	0.3
Independent variable 5					0.0

the simple correlation matrix between the independent variables and the dependent variable is informative about which variables ought to relate to the dependent variable. Since collinearity problems tend to arise when the predictor variables correlate highly (i.e. are measuring the same thing as each other) then it may be wise to combine different measures of the same thing so eliminating their collinearity. It might also be possible to carry out a factor analysis of the independent variable to find a set of factors among the independent variables which can then be put into the regression analysis.

combination: in probability theory, a set of events which are not structured by order of occurrence is called a combination. Combinations are different from permutations, which involve order. So if we get a die and toss it six times, we might get three 2s, two 4s and a 5. So the combination is 2, 2, 2, 4, 4, 5. So combinations are less varied than permutations since there is no time sequence order dimension in combinations. Remember that order is important. The following two permutations (and many others) are possible from this combination:

4, 2, 4, 5, 2, 2
———————————→

or

5, 2, 4, 2, 4, 2
———————————→

See also: **permutation**

combining variables: one good and fairly simple way to combine two or more variables to give total scores for each case is to turn each score on a variable into a z score and sum those scores. This means that each score is placed on the same unit of measurement or standardized.

common variance: the variation which two (or more) variables share. It is very different from error variance, which is variation in the scores and which is not measured or controlled by the research method in a particular study. One may then conceptually describe error variance in terms of the Venn diagram (Figure C.1). Each circle represents a different variable and where they overlap is the common variance or variance they share. The non-overlapping parts represent the error variance. It has to be stressed that the common and error variances are as much a consequence of the study in question and are not really simply a characteristic of the variables in question.

An example which might help is to imagine people's weights as estimated by themselves as one variable and their weights as estimated by another person as being the other variable. Both measures will assess weight up to a point but not completely accurately. The extent to which the estimates agree across a sample between the two is a measure of the common or shared variance; the extent of the disagreement or inaccuracy is the error variance.

communality, in factor analysis: the total amount of variance a variable is estimated to share with all other variables in a factor

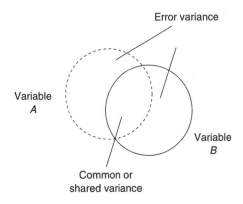

Figure C.1 *A Venn diagram illustrating the difference between common variance and error variance*

analysis. The central issue is to do with the fact that a correlation matrix normally has 1.0 through one of the diagonals indicating that the correlation of a variable with itself is always 1.0. In factor analysis, we are normally trying to understand the pattern of association of variables with other variables, not the correlation of a variable with itself. In some circumstances, having 1.0 in the diagonal results in the factor analysis being dominated by the correlations of individual variables with themselves. If the intercorrelations of variables in the factor analysis are relatively small (say correlations which are generally of the order 0.1 to 0.4), then it is desirable to estimate the communality using the methods employed by principal axis factoring. This is because the correlations in the diagonal (i.e. the 1.0s) swamp the intercorrelations of the variables with the other variables. Communalities are essentially estimated in factor analysis by initially substituting the best correlation a variable has with another variable in place of the correlation of the variable with itself. An iterative process is then employed to refine the communality estimate. The communality is the equivalent of squaring the factor loadings of a variable for a factor and summing them. There will be one communality estimate per factor. In principal component analysis communality is always 1.00, though the term communality is not fully appropriate in that context. In principal axis factoring it is almost invariably less than 1.00 and usually substantially

less. To understand communality better, it is useful to compare the results of a principal components analysis with those of a principal axis analysis of the same data. In the former, you are much more likely to find factors which are heavily loaded on just one variable. The differences between these two forms of factor analysis are small when the correlation matrix consists of high intercorrelations.

compound bar chart: a form of bar chart which allows the introduction of a second variable to the analysis. For example, one could use a bar chart to indicate the numbers of 18 year olds going to university to study one of four disciplines (Figure C.2). This would be a simple bar chart. In this context, a compound bar chart might involve the use of a second variable gender. Each bar of the simple bar chart would be differentiated into a section indicating the proportion of males and another section indicating the proportion of females. In this way, it would be possible to see pictorially whether there is a gender difference in terms of the four types of university course chosen. In a clustered bar chart, the bars for the two genders are placed side by side rather than stacked into a single column so that it is possible to see the proportions of females going to university, males going to university, females not going to university, and males not going to university more directly.

Compound bar charts work well only when there are small numbers of values for each of the variables. With many values the charts become too complex and trends more difficult to discern.

compound frequency distributions: see **frequency distribution**

computational formulae: statistical concepts are largely defined by their formulae. Concepts such as standard deviation are difficult to understand or explain otherwise.

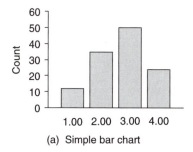

(a) Simple bar chart

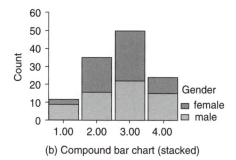

(b) Compound bar chart (stacked)

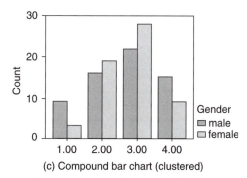

(c) Compound bar chart (clustered)

Figure C.2 *Simple and two types of compound bar chart*

Such formulae are not always the most easily calculated by hand or using a calculator. So more easily calculated versions of the formulae have been derived from the basic defining formulae. These are known as computational formulae. They have the disadvantage of obscuring what the basic concept is since their purpose is to minimize arithmetic labour. Consequently, they are probably best disregarded by those trying to learn statistical concepts as such, especially if it is intended to do all calculations using a standard statistical package on a computer.

concurrent validity: the extent to which a measure is related to another measure which it is expected to be related to and which is measured at the same time. For example, a measure of intelligence will be expected to be related to a measure of educational achievement which is assessed at the same time. Individuals with higher intelligence will be expected to show higher educational achievement. See also: **predictive validity**

condition: in experiments, a condition refers to the particular circumstances a particular group of cases or participants experience. Conditions are the various alternative treatments for the independent variables. If the experiment has only an experimental group and a control group, there are two conditions (which are the same as the different levels of treatment for the independent variable). Where the study is more complex, the number of conditions goes up commensurately. Thus, in a $2 \times 2 \times 2$ analysis of variance there would be eight different conditions – two for each variable giving $2 \times 2 \times 2 = 8$. Sometimes the different conditions for a particular independent variable are mentioned. Thus, in a study of the effects of a drug, the treatments would perhaps be 5 mg, 3 mg, 1 mg and 0 mg. See also: **levels of treatment**

conditional probability: the probability of any event occurring can be affected by another event. For example, the likelihood of being knocked over by a car on any day might be 0.0002. However, what if one decides to spend the entire day in bed? In these circumstances, the probability of being knocked down by a car would probably go down to 0.00000 – or smaller. In other words, a probability can be substantially affected by consideration of the particular antecedent conditions applying. So the chances of choking to death probably greater when eating bony fish than when eating tomato soup. Hence, it is misleading to report general probabilities of a particular event occurring if factors (conditions) which greatly change the likelihood are present.

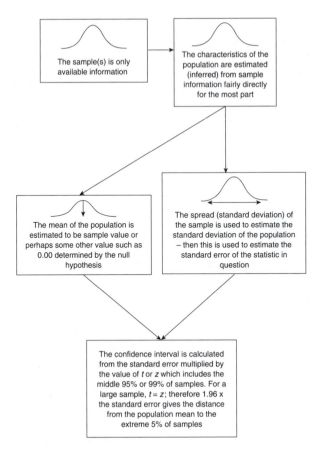

Figure C.3   *Flowchart for confidence intervals*

confidence interval: an approach to assessing the information in samples which gives the interval for a statistic covering the most likely samples drawn from the population (estimated from the samples).

Basically, the sample characteristics are used as an estimate of the population characteristics (Figure C.3). The theoretical distribution of samples from this estimated population is then calculated. The 95% confidence interval refers to the interval covering the statistic (e.g. the mean) for the 95% most likely samples drawn from the population (Figure C.4). Sometimes the confidence interval given is for the 99% most likely samples. The steps are:

- Usually the population value is estimated to be the same as the sample statistic. This

does not have to be the case, however, and any value could be used as the population value.
- The variability of the available sample(s) is used to estimate the variability of the population.
- This estimated population variability is then used to calculate the variability of a particular statistic in the population. This is known as the standard error.
- This value of the standard error is used in conjunction with the sample size(s) to calculate the interval of the middle 95% of samples drawn from that estimated population.

The concept of confidence intervals can be applied to virtually any statistic. However, it is probably best understood initially in

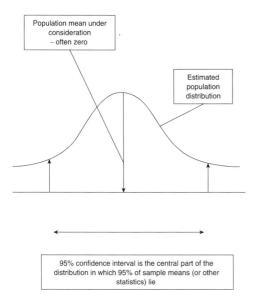

Figure C.4   *Illustrating feature of the confidence interval*

confidence interval for a measure of dogmatism is 22 to 24 then this is less evidently meaningful. See **confidence interval of the mean; margin of error; standard error of the regression coefficient**

confidence interval of the mean: indicates the likely variability in samples given the known characteristic of the data. Technically, it gives the spread of the 95% (or sometimes 99%) most likely sample means drawn from the population estimated from the known characteristics of the research sample. If one knows the likely spread of sample means then it is possible to interpret the importance and implications of the means of the data from the sample(s) researched in the study. One problem with the concept of confidence interval is that it is difficult to put into everyday language without distorting its mathematical reality. When the confidence interval is wide, our sample is likely to be a poor guide to the population value.

An alternative way of looking at confidence intervals is to define them as the sample of means that are *not* significantly different statistically from a particular population mean. By definition, then, the 95% confidence interval is the range of the middle 95% of sample means: 47.5% above the mean and 47.5% below the mean. Obviously it is assumed that the distribution is symmetrical. This is illustrated in Figure C.5.

Most commonly in the single-sample study, the mean of the population is estimated as being the same as the mean of the known sample from that population. When comparing two sample means (e.g. as with the *t* test) the population mean would be set according to the null hypothesis as being zero (because if the null hypothesis is true then the difference between the two samples will be zero). In this case, if the confidence interval does *not* include zero then the hypothesis is preferred to the null hypothesis.

Consider a public opinion survey in which a sample, say, of 1000 people have been asked their age. Provided that the sample is a random sample from the population, then the

terms of the confidence interval of the mean – probably the most common statistic though any statistic will have a confidence interval.

Confidence intervals are often promoted as an alternative to point estimates (conventional significance testing). This is to overstate the case since they are both based on the same hypothesis testing approach. Confidence intervals are set values (95%, 99%). Consequently they may not be as informative as the exact values available for point estimates using computers. (The equivalent drawback is true of point estimates when critical values are employed in hand calculations.)

Confidence intervals are also claimed to allow greater understanding of the true importance of trends in the data. This is basically because the confidence interval is expressed in terms of a range on the original scale of measurement (i.e. the measurement scale on which the calculations were based). Again this is somewhat overstated. Unless the confidence refers to something which is of concrete value in assessing the magnitude of the trend in the data, then there is not that much gain. For example, if we know that the 95% confidence interval for height is 1.41 to 1.81 metres then this refers to something that is readily understood. If we know that the

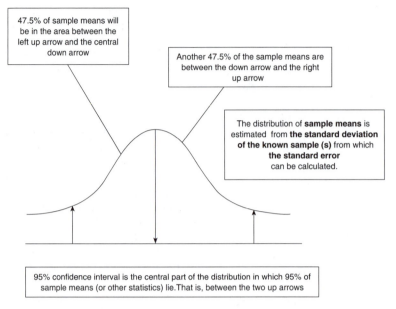

47.5% of sample means will be in the area between the left up arrow and the central down arrow

Another 47.5% of the sample means are between the down arrow and the right up arrow

The distribution of **sample means** is estimated from **the standard deviation of the known sample (s)** from which **the standard error** can be calculated.

95% confidence interval is the central part of the distribution in which 95% of sample means (or other statistics) lie. That is, between the two up arrows

Figure C.5   *Illustrating the 95% confidence interval for the mean*

characteristics of the sample are generally our best estimate of the characteristics of that population in the absence of any other information. However, given that we know that random samples can and do depart from the population characteristics, we need to be aware that the sample probably reflects the population characteristics less than precisely. The confidence interval of the mean stipulates the range of values of sample means likely from the population. This, of course, is to base our estimate on the characteristics of the sample about which we have information.

Say the mean age of a sample of 1000 individuals for example is known as ($m = 34.5$) and the standard deviation of age is 3.6; then the confidence intervals are relatively easily calculated. Assume we want to know the 95% confidence interval of age. We can estimate the population mean age at 34.5 (our best estimate from the sample information). We then use the estimated standard deviation of the sample to calculate the estimated standard error of samples of a particular size (1000 in this case). The formula for estimated standard error is merely the estimated standard deviation/square root of sample size. So the standard error in this case is

$$\text{standard error} = \frac{3.6}{\sqrt{1000}} = \frac{3.6}{17.321} = 0.21$$

For large samples, 1.96 standard errors above and below the population mean cut off the middle 95% of the distribution. (This is because the distribution is the same as for the z distribution.) For smaller sample sizes, this figure increases somewhat but can be obtained from the t distribution. So if the standard error is 0.21 then the 95% confidence interval is a distance of

$$0.21 \times 1.96 = 0.412$$

from the mean. The estimated mean age is 34.5 so the 95% confidence interval is 34.5 minus 0.412 to 34.5 plus 0.412. That is, the 95% confidence interval is 34.088 to 34.912 years.

This indicates that the researcher should be confident that the mean age of the population from which the sample came is close to 34.5 as the vast majority of the likely samples have means very close to this. If the confidence interval were 25.0 to 44.5 years then there would obviously be considerable uncertainty as to the typical age in the population.

Normally research samples are much smaller so instead of using the z value of

Table C.8 *Example of values of* t *to calculate the 95% and 99% confidence intervals*

	N = 6	N = 10	N = 15	N = 30	N = 50	N = 100	N = 1000
95%	2.57	2.26	2.13	2.04	2.01	1.98	1.96
99%	4.03	3.25	2.98	2.74	2.68	2.63	2.58

1.961 we need to use the appropriate z value which is distributed by degrees of freedom (usually the sample size minus one). Tables of the t distribution tell us the number of standard errors required to cover the middle 95% or middle 99% of sample means. Table C.8 gives the 95% and the 99% values of the t distribution for various degrees of freedom.

Broadly speaking, the confidence interval is the opposite of the critical value in significance testing. In significance testing, we identify whether the sample is sufficiently different from the population in order to place it in the extreme 5% of sample means. In confidence intervals, we estimate the middle 95% of sample means which are not significantly different from the population mean.

There is not just one confidence interval but a whole range of them depending on what value of confidence (or non-significance) is chosen and the sample size.

confirmatory factor analysis: a form of factor analysis concerned with testing hypotheses about or models of the data. Because it involves assessing how well theoretical notions about the underlying structure of data actually fit the data, confirmatory factor analysis ideally builds on developed theoretical notions within a field. For example, if it is believed that loneliness is composed of two separate components – actual lack of social contact and emotional feelings of not being close to others – then we have a two-component model of loneliness. The question is how well this model accounts for data on loneliness. So we would expect to be able to identify which items on a loneliness questionnaire are measuring these different aspects of loneliness. Then using confirmatory factor analysis, we could test how well this two-component model fits the data. A

relatively poor fit of the model to the data might indicate that we need to consider that a third component may be involved – perhaps something as simple as geographical isolation. This new model could be assessed against the data in order to see if it achieves a better fit. Alternatively, one might explore the possibility that there is just one component of loneliness, not two.

Perhaps because of the stringent intellectual demands of theory and model development, much confirmatory factor analysis is merely the confirmation or otherwise of the factor structure of data as assessed using exploratory factor analysis. If the factors established in exploratory factor analysis can be shown to fit a data set well then the factor structure is confirmed.

Although there are alternative approaches, typically confirmatory factor analysis is carried out with a structural equation modelling software such as LISREL or EQS. There are various indices for determining the degree of fit of a model to the data. See also: **structural equation modelling**

Cramer (2003)

confounding variable: a factor which may affect the dependent and independent variables and confuse or confound the apparent nature of the relationship between the independent and dependent variables. In most studies, researchers aim to control for these confounding variables. In any study there is potentially an infinite variety of possible confounding variables. See **partial correlation; semi-partial correlation coefficient**

constant: a value that is the same in a particular context. Usually, it is a term (component) of a statistical formula which maintains a fixed value for all cases in the analysis. In a regression equation, the intercept and the regression coefficients are constants for a particular set of cases and variables in so far that they remain the same. The values of the variables, however, are not constant as they will vary. See also: **criteria variable; predictor variable**

construct validity: the extent to which a measure assesses the construct that it is intended or supposed to measure. For example, we would expect a measure of the construct of how anxious you were at a particular moment would vary appropriately according to how anxious you were. So you would expect this measure to show greater anxiety before an exam than a few hours after it. If a measure does not appear to show construct validity, the measure may be invalid or our ideas about the construct may be wrong or both.

contingency coefficient: a sort of correlation coefficient applied to cross-tabulation tables. For such cross-tabulation tables involving just two variables (e.g. Table C.9), the chi-square test can be used to compare samples in order to assess whether the distributions of frequencies in the samples are different. But it is equally an indication of how related the two variables are. Table C.9 indicates how the same contingency table can be reformulated in alternative ways. As can be seen, what is conceived as a sample is not crucial. If there is a zero or non-significant value of chi-square, then the samples are not different in terms of the distributions in the different categories. If the value of chi-square is significant, this is an indication that the samples differ in their distributions of the categories. This also means that there is a correlation between the two variables. See also: **correlation**

Another way of putting this is that there is a correlation between the variable 'sample' and another variable 'category'. In other

Table C.9 *A contingency table expressed in three different forms*

	High jumpers	Long jumpers	Hurdlers
Males	27	33	15
Females	12	43	14

	Sample 1	Sample 2	Sample 3
Males	27	33	15
Females	12	43	14

	High jumpers	Long jumpers	Hurdlers
Sample 1	27	33	15
Sample 2	12	43	14

words, there is not a great difference between a test of differences and a correlation. Chi-square is often referred to a test of association. The problem with using chi-square as a test of association or correlation is that its numerical values differ greatly from the -1 through 0 to $+1$ range characteristic of, say, the Pearson correlation coefficient. Pearson offered a simple formula by which a chi-square value could be converted into a correlation coefficient known as the contingency coefficient. This is simply

$$\text{contingency coefficient} = \sqrt{\frac{\chi^2}{\chi^2 + N}}$$

N is the total number of frequencies in the contingency table and χ^2 is the value of chi-square for the table. The significance of the contingency coefficient is the same as the constituent chi-square value.

The contingency coefficient simply does not match the Pearson correlation coefficient as it cannot take negative values and its upper bound is always less than 1.00.

Cramer (1998)

contingency or **cross-tabulation table:** usually shows the frequency of cases according to two or more categorical variables. Examples of such tables are to be found in

Tables C.2 and C.9. A table displaying two variables is called a two-way table, three variables three-way, and so on. It is so called because the categories of one variable are contingent on or tabulated across the categories of one or more other variables. This table may be described according to the number of categories in each variable. For example, a 2×2 table consists of two variables which each have two categories. A 2×3 table has one variable with two categories and another variable with three categories. See also: **Cramer's V; log–linear analysis; marginal totals**

continuity correction: see **Yates's correction**

continuous data: scores on a variable that could be measured in minutely incremental amounts if we had the means of measuring them. Essentially it is a variable which has many different values. For example, height is continuous in that it can take an infinite number of different values if we have a sufficiently accurate way of measuring it. Other data cannot take many different values and may just take a number of discrete values. For example, sex only has two values – male and female.

contrast: a term used to describe the planned (a priori) comparisons between specific pairs of means in analysis of variance. See also: **a priori tests; analysis of variance; *post hoc* tests; trend analysis in analysis of variance**

control condition or **group:** a comparison condition which is as similar as possible to the principal condition or treatment under study in the research – except that the two conditions differ in terms of the key

variable. In most disciplines, the control conditions consist of a group of participants who are compared with the treatment group. Without the control group, there is no obvious or unambiguous way of interpreting the data obtained. In experimental research, equality between the treatment group and control group is usually achieved by randomization.

For example, in a study of the relative effectiveness of Gestalt therapy and psychoanalysis, the researchers may assign at random participants to the Gestalt therapy treatment and others to the psychoanalysis treatment condition. Any comparisons based on these data alone simply compare the outcomes of the two types of therapy condition. This actually does not tell us if either is better than no treatment at all. Typically, control groups receive no treatment. It is the outcomes in the treatment group compared with the control group which facilitate interpretation of the value of treatment. Compared with the control group, the treatment may be better, worse or make no difference.

In research with human participants, control groups have their problems. For one thing it is difficult to know whether to put members of the control group through no procedure at all. The difficulty is that they do not receive the attention they would if they were, say, brought to the laboratory and closely studied. Similarly, if the study was of the effects of violent videos, what should be the control condition? No video? A video about rock climbing? Or what? Each of the listed alternatives has different implications. See also: **quasi-experiments; treatment group**

controlling: usually refers to eliminating the influence of covariates or third variables. Our research may suggest that there is a relationship between variable A and variable B. However, it may be that another variable(s) is also correlated with variable A and variable B. Because of this, it is possible that the relationship between variable A and variable B is the consequence of variable C. Controlling involves eliminating the influence of variable

C from the correlation of variable *A* and variable *B*. This may be achieved through the use of the partial correlation coefficient though there are other ways of controlling for variable *C*. Without controlling, it is not possible to assess what the strength of the relationship of variable *A* and variable *B* would be without any influence of variable *C*. Controlling sometimes refers to the use of a control group. See also: **controlling; partial correlation**

convenience sample or **sampling:** a sample or method of sampling in which cases are selected because of the convenience of accessing them and not because they are thought to be representative of the population. Unless some form of representative or random sampling has been employed, most samples are of this nature.

convergent validity: the extent to which a measure is related to other measures which have been designed to assess the same construct. For example, a measure of anxiety would be expected to be related to other measures of anxiety.

coordinates: the position a case has on two or more axes is its coordinates. This is much as geographical location may be defined by the coordinates of latitude and longitude. In statistics, an example of coordinates would be the lines of a scatterplot. These allow the precise position of an individual case on the two variables to be pinpointed.

correlated groups or **measures design:** see **within-subjects design**

correlated groups or **samples:** see **matching; within-subjects design**

correlation or **correlation coefficient:** an index of the linear or straight line relationship between two variables which can be ordered. Correlations can be either positive or negative. A positive correlation indicates that high scores on one variable go with high scores on the other variable. A negative correlation means that high scores on one variable go with low scores on the other variable. The size of a correlation can vary from a minimum of -1.00 through 0 to a maximum of 1.00. The bigger the size of the correlation, regardless of whether it is positive or negative, the stronger the linear relationship between the two variables. A correlation of 0 or close to 0 means that there is either no or no linear relationship between the two variables. There may, however, be a curvilinear relationship between the two variables. Consequently, when the correlation is 0 or close to 0, it is useful to draw a scatter diagram which is a graph of the relationship between the two variables.

Correlations which differ substantially from 0 are statistically significant. The bigger the correlation, regardless of its sign, the more likely it is to be statistically significant. The bigger the sample, the more likely it is that a correlation will be significant. Very small correlations may be statistically significant provided that the sample is big enough.

There are various kinds of correlations. The most widely used is Pearson's product moment correlation coefficient. This name is usually shortened to Pearson's correlation and is symbolized as *r*. It can be calculated by multiplying the standardized scores of the two variables to obtain their 'product'. These products are then summed and divided by the number of cases minus one to give the mean population estimate of the products. A product moment is the expected or mean value of a product of two variables. A Pearson's correlation is the same as a standardized regression coefficient. It is used to determine the linear relationship between two variables which are normally distributed. Pearson's correlation can be strongly affected by extreme scores or outliers. Consequently, if the scores are not normally distributed, the scores can be ranked and a Pearson's correlation carried out on these ranked scores. This

Table C.10   *Correlations, percentage of*
shared variance and minimum
size of sample for the two-tailed
0.05 statistical significance

Correlation	Percentage of shared variance	Size of sample
1.00	100	3
0.90	81	6
0.80	64	9
0.70	49	11
0.60	36	15
0.50	25	22
0.40	16	26
0.30	9	44
0.20	4	97
0.10	1	400
0.00	0	

type of correlation is known as Spearman's rank order correlation coefficient. This name is usually shortened to Spearman's correlation or rho and is symbolized with the Greek letter ρ. A Pearson's correlation between a dichotomous variable (such as sex) and a normally distributed variable may be called the point–biserial correlation. A Pearson's correlation between two dichotomous variables is called phi.

Squaring a Pearson's correlation gives the coefficient of determination. This provides a clearer indication of the meaning of the size of a correlation as it gives the proportion of the variance that is shared between two variables. For example, a correlation of 0.50 means that the proportion of the variance shared between the two variables is 0.25 ($0.50^2 = 0.25$). These proportions are usually expressed as a percentage, which in this case, is 25% ($0.25 \times 100\% = 25\%$). The percentage of shared variance for 11 correlations which each differ by 0.10 is shown in Table C.10.

We can see that as the size of the correlation increases, the percentage of shared variance becomes disproportionately larger. Although a correlation of 0.60 is twice as large as a correlation of 0.30, the percentage of variance accounted for is four times as large.

Correlations of 0.80 or above are usually described as being large, strong or high and may be found for the same variable (such as depression) measured on two occasions two weeks apart. Correlations of 0.30 or less are

normally spoken of as being small, weak or low and are typically found for different variables (such as depression and social support). Correlations between 0.30 and 0.80 are typically said to be moderate or modest and are usually shown for similar measures (such as marital support and marital satisfaction).

Also shown in this table is the minimum size that the sample needs to be for a Pearson's correlation to be statistically significant at the two-tailed 0.05 level. As the correlations become smaller, the size of the sample that is required to reach this level of statistical significance increases. For example, a very weak correlation of 0.10 will be statistically significant at this level with a sample of 400 or more.

The statistical significance of the correlation can be calculated by converting it into a *t* value using the following formula (though there are tables readily available or significance may be obtained from computer output):

$$t = \sqrt{r \times \frac{N-2}{1-r^2}}$$

The statistical significance of the *t* value can be looked up in a table of its critical values against the appropriate degrees of freedom which are the number of cases (*N*) minus one.

Other types of correlations for two variables which are rank ordered are Kendall's tau *a*, tau *b* and tau *c*, Goodman and Kruskall's gamma and tau, and Somer's *d*.

Measures of association for categorical variables include the contingency coefficient, Cramér's *V* and Goodman and Kruskal's lambda. See also: **simple** or **bivariate regression; unstandardized partial regression coefficient**

Cramer (1998)

correlation line: a straight line drawn through the points on a scatter diagram of the standardized scores of two variables so that it best describes the linear relationship between these variables. If the scores were not standardized, this would simply be the regression line.

The vertical axis of the scatter diagram is used to represent the standardized values of one variable and the horizontal axis the standardized values of the other variable. To draw this line we need two points. The mean of a standardized variable is zero. So one point is where the mean of one variable intersects with the mean of the other variable. To work out the value of the other point we multiply the correlation between the two variables by the standardized value of one variable, say that represented by the horizontal axis, to obtain the predicted standardized value of the other variable. Where these two values intersect forms the second point. See also: **standardized score; Z score**

correlation matrix: a symmetrical table which shows the correlations between a set of variables. The variables are listed in the first row and first column of the table. The diagonal of the table shows the correlation of each variable with itself which is 1 or 1.00. (In factor analysis, these values in the diagonal may be replaced with communalities.) Because the information in the diagonal is always the same, it may be omitted. The values of the correlations in the lower left-hand triangle of the matrix are the mirror image of those in the upper right-hand triangle. Because of this, the values in the upper right-hand triangle may be omitted.

correlations, averaging: when there is more than one study which has reported the Pearson's correlation between the same two variables or two very similar variables, it may be useful to compute a mean correlation for these studies to indicate the general size of this relationship. This procedure may be carried out in a meta-analysis where the results of several studies are summarized. If the size of the samples was exactly the same, we could simply add the correlations together and divide by the number of samples. If the size of the samples are not the same but similar, this procedure gives an approximation of

the average correlation because the different sample sizes are not taken into account. The more varied the size of the samples, the grosser this approximation is.

The varying size of the samples is taken into account by first converting the correlation into a z correlation. This may be done by looking up the appropriate value in a table or by computing it directly using the following formula where $\log_e$ stands for the natural logarithm and r for Pearson's correlation:

$$Z_r = 0.5 \times \log_e [(1 + r)/(1 - r)]$$

This z correlation needs to be weighted by multiplying it by the number of cases in the sample minus three. The weighted z correlations are added together and divided by the sum for each sample of its size minus three. This value is the average z correlation which needs to be converted back into a Pearson's correlation. This can be done by looking up the value in the appropriate table or using the following formula:

$$r = (2.718^2 \times z_r - 1)/(2.718^2 \times z_r + 1)$$

The calculation of the average Pearson's correlation is given in Table C.11 for three correlations from different-sized samples. Note that Pearson's correlation is the same as the z correlation for low values so that when the values of the Pearson's correlation are low a good approximation of the average correlation can be obtained by following the same procedure but using the Pearson's correlation instead of the z correlation. The average z correlation is 0.29 which changed into a Pearson's correlation is 0.28.

Cramer (1998)

correlations, testing differences: normally, we test whether a correlation differs significantly from zero. However, there are circumstances in which we might wish to know whether two different correlation coefficients differ from each other. For example, it would be interesting to know whether the correlation between IQ and income for men is different from the correlation between IQ and

Table C.11 *Averaging Pearson's correlations*

Sample	r	z_r	Size (N)	N − 3	$z_r \times (N − 3)$
1	0.38	0.40	33	30	$0.40 \times 30 = 12.00$
2	0.29	0.30	53	50	$0.30 \times 50 = 15.00$
3	0.20	0.20	43	40	$0.20 \times 40 = 8.00$
Sum				120	35.00
Mean z_r					$35.00/120 = 0.29$
Mean r	0.28				

income for women. There are various tests to determine whether the values of two correlations differ significantly from each other. Which test to use depends on whether the correlations come from the same or different samples and, if they come from the same sample, whether one of the variables is the same.

The z test determines whether the correlation between the two variables differs between two unrelated samples. For example, the z test is used to see whether the correlation between depression and social support differs between women and men.

The Z_2^* test assesses whether the correlation between two different variables in the same sample varies significantly. For instance, the Z_2^* test is applied to determine whether the correlation between depression at two points differs significantly from the correlation between social support at the same two points.

The T_2 test ascertains whether the correlations in the same sample which have a variable in common differ significantly. For example, the T_2 test is employed to find out whether the correlation between social support and depression varies significantly from that between social support and anxiety.

Cramer (1998)

count: another word for frequency or total number of something, especially common in computer statistical packages. In other words, it is a tally or simply a count of the number of cases in a particular category of the variable(s) under examination. In this context, a count would give the number of people with blue eyes, for example. Generally speaking, counts need statistics which are appropriate to nominal (or category or categorical) data such as chi-square. See also: **frequency**

When applied to a single individual, the count on a variable may be equated to a score (e.g. the number of correct answers an individual gave to a quiz).

counterbalanced designs: counterbalancing refers to one way of attempting to nullify the effects of the sequence of events. It uses all (or many) of the various possible sequences of events. It is appropriate in related (matched) designs where more than one measure of the same variable is taken at different points in time. Imagine a related designs experiment in which the same group of participants is being studied in the experimental and control conditions. It would be common practice to have half of the participants serve in the experimental condition first and the other half in the control condition first (see Table C.12).

In this way, all of the possible orders of running the study have been used. This is a very simple case of a group of designs called the Latin Square design which allow participants to serve in a number of different conditions while the number of different orders in which the conditions of the study are run is maximized.

There are a number of ways of analysing these data including the following:

- Combine the two experimental conditions (group 1 + group 2) and the two control

Table C.12 *Example of a simple,
counterbalanced design*

Group 1	Experimental condition first	Control condition second

$\longrightarrow$

Group 2	Control condition first	Experimental condition second

$\longrightarrow$

conditions (group 1 + group 2). Then there is just an experimental and control condition to compare with a related *t* test or similar technique.

- The four conditions could be compared using two-way analysis of variance (mixed design). Keeping the data in the order of Table C.12, then differences between the experimental and control treatment will be indicated by a significant interaction. Significant main effects would indicate either a general difference between group 1 and group 2, or an order effect if it is between first and second. This approach is probably less satisfactory than the next given the problems of interpreting main effects in ANOVA.
- Alternatively, the table could be rearranged so that the two experimental conditions are in the first column and the two control groups are in the second column. This time, the main effect comparing the experimental condition with the control condition would indicate an effect of condition. An interaction indicates that order and condition are having a combined effect.

These different approaches differ in terms of their directness and statistical sophistication. Each makes slightly different assumptions about the nature of the data. The main difference is that some allow the issue of order effects to be highlighted whereas others ignore order effects assuming that the counterbalancing has been successful.

Another context in which it is worth considering counterbalancing is when samples of individuals are being measured twice on the same variable. For example, the researcher may be interested in changes of children's IQs over time. To give exactly the same IQ test twice would encourage the claim that practice effects are likely to lead to increases in IQ at the second time of measurement. By using two different versions (forms) of the test this criticism may be reduced. As the two different versions may vary slightly in difficulty, it would be wise to give version A to half of the sample first followed by version B at the second administration, and also give version B first to the other half of the sample followed by version A. Of course, this design will not totally negate the criticism of practice effects. There are more complex designs in which some participants do not receive the first version of the test which may be helpful in dealing with this issue.

In counterbalanced designs, practicalities will sometimes intervene since there may be too many different orders to be practicable. Partial counterbalancing may be the only practical solution. See also: **matching**

covariance: the variance that is shared between two variables. It is the sum of products divided by the number of cases minus one. The product is the deviation of a score from the mean of that variable multiplied by the deviation of the score from the mean of the other variable for that case. In other words, covariance is very much like variance but is a measure of the variance that two different variables share. The formal formula for the covariance is

$$\text{covariance}_{[X \text{ with } Y]} = \frac{\sum (X - \bar{X})(Y - \bar{Y})}{N}$$

Cramer (1998)

covariance, analysis of: see **analysis of covariance**

covariate: a variable that is related to (usually) the dependent variable. Since the covariate is correlated with the other variable, it is very easy for the effects of the covariate to be confused with the effects of the other variable. Consequently, the covariate is usually controlled for statistically where this is a problem. Hence, controlling for the covariant is an important feature of procedures such as analysis of covariance and hierarchical multiple regression. See also: **analysis of covariance**

Cramer's V: also known as Cramer's phi. This is a correlation coefficient applied to a contingency or cross-tabulation table. As such, it is similar in application to the contingency coefficient. It can be used for any two-variable contingency table. For a 2×2 contingency table, Cramer's V gives exactly the same value as the phi coefficient.

The formula for the statistic is

$$\text{Cramer's } V = \sqrt{\frac{x^2}{N \times (S - 1)}}$$

Where x^2 is the chi-square value for the table, N is the total number of cases in the table, and S is the smaller of the number of columns or the number of rows. Applying the procedure to the data in Table C.13 which has a x^2 value of 12.283, a total N of 139, and the smaller of the number of rows or columns is 2:

$$\text{Cramer's } V = \sqrt{\frac{12.283}{139 \times (2-1)}} = \sqrt{\frac{12.283}{139 \times 1}}$$

$$= \sqrt{0.0884} = 0.297$$

Treating this as roughly analogous to Pearson's correlation coefficient, the value of Cramer's V suggests a modest correlation between leisure activity and nationality. There is an associated probability level but it is recommended that Cramer's V is calculated using a computer statistical package. See also: **correlation**

Cramer (1998)

criterion variable: the variable whose values are being predicted or understood on the basis of information about related variables. So, if a

Table C.13 *A contingency table showing relationship between nationality and favourite leisure activity*

	Sport	Social	Craft
Australian	29	16	19
British	14	22	39

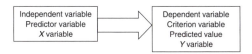

Figure C.6 *Synonyms for independent and criterion variable*

researcher wishes to predict the recidivism of an offender, the criterion variable would be a measure of recidivism. In other words, the criterion variable is the dependent variable of this analysis (Figure C.6). The predictor variable might be use of illegal drugs. See also: **logistic regression; regression equation**

The criterion variable is also known as the dependent variable though this is a more general term which does not have the implication of prediction.

critical values: in tests of significance such as the t test, F ratio, etc., certain values of t or F form the lower boundary for a particular significance level. These are the values which are tabulated in tables of significance. So, from tables of the t distribution, with degrees of freedom of 10 and a two-tailed significance of 0.05 (i.e. 5%), the minimum value of t to be significant at this level is 2.228. It clearly simplifies assessing statistical significance if important levels of significance are provided for each size of sample. Conventional statistical tables found in statistics textbooks are really tables of such critical values. However, with the widespread use of powerful computer programs it is more common to have available from the printout the exact statistical significance of the same statistical tests. On balance, it is probably better in general to report the exact significance than the critical values since these indicate extreme differences much smaller than available tables of critical values can. See also: **analysis of variance; chi-square; critical values; trend analysis in analysis of variance**

Cronbach's alpha reliability: see **alpha reliability**

cross-lagged correlations: the pattern of correlations between two variables which are both measured at two separate points in time. It is consequently often employed in the analysis of panel studies. Imagine the two variables are the amount of TV viewed and aggressiveness. These could be measured when a child is 8 years old and again when the child is 15 years old. So really we have four variables: aggression age 8, aggression age 15, viewing age 8 and viewing age 15. There are a number of correlation coefficients that could be calculated:

- Aggression age 8 with viewing age 8
- Aggression age 15 with viewing age 15
- Aggression age 8 with aggression age 15
- Viewing age 8 with viewing age 15
- Aggression age 8 with viewing age 15
- Aggression age 15 with viewing age 8

The first two correlations are regular correlation coefficients measured at a single point in time. The third and fourth correlations are lagged correlations since there is a time lag in collecting the first and second measures. The fifth and sixth correlations are cross-lagged correlations. This means that there is a time lag in their collection but also the correlation crosses over to the other variable as well as being lagged.

The point of this is that it may help assess whether or not there is a causal relationship between TV viewing and aggression. The correlation between aggression age 8 and viewing age 8 does not establish a causal link. It could be that TV viewing causes the child to be aggressive but it could equally be that

aggressive children just choose to watch more TV. However, what if we found that there was a stronger correlation between aggression at age 15 and viewing at age 8 than there was between aggression at age 8 and viewing at age 8? This would tend to suggest that viewing at age 8 was causing aggression at age 15. By examining the strengths of the various correlations, some researchers claim to be able to gain greater confidence on issues of causality.

cross-lagged panel correlation analysis: a method which tries to ascertain the temporal predominance or order of two variables which are known to be related to one another. For example, we may be interested in knowing what the temporal relationship is between mental health and social support. There are four possible temporal relationships. One relationship is that greater support precedes or leads to greater mental health. Another relationship is that greater mental health precedes or brings about greater support. A third relationship is that both support and mental health affect each other. A fourth relationship is that the apparent relationship between the two variables is spurious and is due to one or more other variable which is related to the two variables.

The two variables need to refer to the same period of time and to be measured at least at two points in time as depicted in Figure C.7. If the cross-lagged correlation between support at time 1 and mental health at time 2 is significantly more positive than the cross-lagged correlation between mental health at time 1 and support at time 2, this difference implies that greater support precedes or brings about greater mental health. If the cross-lagged correlation between mental health at time 1 and support at time 2 is significantly more positive than the cross-lagged correlation between support at time 1 and mental health at time 2, this difference implies that greater mental health precedes or brings about greater support. If there is no significant difference between the cross-lagged correlations (one or both of which must be significant), the relationship between

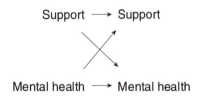

Time 1   Time 2

Figure C.7   *A two-wave two-variable panel design*

Table C.14   *Example of a cumulative frequency table*

Age range	Cumulative frequency
5 year olds	12
5–6 year olds	32
5–7 year olds	46
5–8 year olds	57
5–9 year olds	62
5–10 year olds	71
5–11 year olds	71

the two variables is either reciprocal or spurious. These interpretations depend on there being no significant difference between the synchronous correlations at time 1 and 2 and the two auto- or test–retest correlations.

It is generally recommended that a more appropriate method of analysing this kind of design is structural equation modelling.

Kenny (1975); Rogosa (1980)

cross-sectional design or study: a study where measures have been obtained at a cross-section of, or single point in, time. In such studies it is not possible to infer any changes over time or the causal nature of any relationship between the variables. For example, if we had a sample of individuals which varied in age from 18 to 75 and we found that older people were more conservative in their political views, we could not conclude that people become more conservative as they

become older, because it could be that the older group underwent experiences which made them more conservative which may not be the case for the younger group.

cross-tabulation or **cross-tabulation tables:** see **contingency table; log–linear analysis; marginal totals**

cube or **cubed:** in statistics used to refer to a number multiplied by itself three times. For example, 2.7 cubed is written as 2.7^3 and means $2.7 \times 2.7 \times 2.7 = 19.683$. Another way of putting it is to say 2.7 to the power of 3. It is also 2.7 to the exponent of 3. It is occasionally met with in statistical calculations though not the common ones.

cumulative frequencies: frequencies which accumulate by incorporating earlier values in the range. So in a class of children whose ages range from 5 to 11 years, a cumulative frequency distribution would be 5 year olds; 5 and 6 year olds; 5, 6 and 7 year olds; and so forth. So it answers the question how many children are there up to age 8 years? A frequency table would tell you the number of 8 year olds.

From Table C.14 the number of 6 year olds is 20 (i.e. 32 − 12). Also in this table, it should be noted that there are no 11 year olds (since the cumulative frequency does not increase over the final two categories). The cumulative frequency can also be expressed as cumulative percentage frequencies.

It is possible to have a bar chart which accumulates in this fashion. See also: **Kolmogorov–Smirnov test for one sample**

curvilinear relationship: mostly in the social sciences the relationships between two variables are assumed to be linear or straight line in form. However, relationships can take

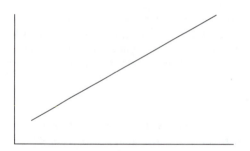

Figure C.8   *Linear relationship*

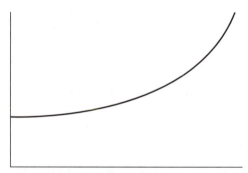

Figure C.9   *Curvilinear relationship*

the form of curved lines – that is, the best fitting line through the points of the scattergram between two variables is a curved shape such as a U-shape or an inverted U-shape. Figure C.8 shows a linear relationship and Figure C.9 shows a curvilinear relationship.

Just as with a linear relationship, the closeness of the points to the curved line is the important factor in determining the size of the correlation: the more the spread, the lower the correlation.

The usually recommended correlation coefficient for curvilinear data is eta, which is related to ANOVA. See also: **correlation; eta**

D

data: (plural of datum) the information or facts about something. Statistics employ data which have in some way been expressed in a numerical form as frequencies or scores. One crucial step in the successful application of statistics is to understand and recognize the difference between score data and nominal or categorical data. Score data collect information from each case or participant in the form of a numerical value which indicates the quantity of a characteristic. Nominal data involve the assignment of individuals to categories. The number of individuals placed in each category is known as the frequency. Statistical analysis of nominal data is largely the analysis of these frequencies.

deciles: like percentiles except are the cut-off points for the bottom 10%, 20%, 30%, etc., of scores. Hence, the fifth decile or the 50% decile is the score which separates the lowest 50% of scores from higher ones. A decile is presented as a specific score though sometimes it is an estimated value, not an actual value. See also: **percentiles**

decimal places (number of): decimals are attractive since they add an appearance of precision. Unfortunately, given the nature of much of the data in many disciplines, this precision is spurious or more apparent than real. It is a matter of judgement, but for data

collected on whole-number scales, it is usually sufficient to report statistics such as the mean or standard deviation to two decimal places at the most, and one decimal place will suffice in most circumstances. With data collected with a greater degree of accuracy (i.e. involving decimals), the reporting of means and standard deviations to one more decimal place than in the data is again probably sufficient accuracy.

Calculations, of course, should proceed using as many decimals as the means of calculation permits. Computers and calculators can be safely left to work out decimals appropriately. Systematic rounding errors can occur in hand calculations if too few decimal places are used, which produce misleading outcomes. A minimum of three more decimal places than present in the data would seem a very safe rule of thumb.

decimal places (rounding): see **rounding decimal places**

decimals: a convenient way of writing fractions or fractions of numbers without using the fraction notation. Fractions are simply parts of whole numbers such as a half, a fifth, a tenth, a seventeenth, a hundredth and a thousandth – or two-fifths or three-fifths and so forth. The simplest way of writing fractions is $\frac{2}{5}$ or $\frac{11}{25}$ though this is not used generally in

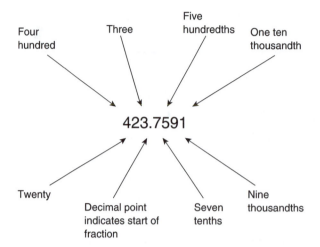

Figure D.I   *The components of a decimal number*

statistics. For many purposes this sort of notation is fine. The difficulty with it is that one cannot directly add fractions together.

Decimals are a notational system for expressing fractions of numbers as tenths, hundredths, thousands, etc., which greatly facilitates the addition of fractions. In the decimal system, there are whole numbers followed by a dot which is then followed by the fraction:

$$17.5$$

In the above number, 17 is the whole number, the dot . indicates the beginning that a fraction will follow and the number after the dot indicates the size of the fraction.

The first number after the dot is the number of tenths that there are. In the above example we therefore have five tenths which is $\frac{5}{10}$ which simplifies to $\frac{1}{2}$ or a half.

In the following number we have two numbers after the dot or decimal point:

$$160.25$$

In this example, the whole number is 160 and the fraction after the decimal point . is 25. The first number 2 is the number of tenths. The second number 5 is the number of hundredths. In other words, there are two tenths

and five hundredths. Put more simply, the 25 after the decimal place is the number of hundredths since two tenths $(\frac{2}{10})$ is the same thing as twenty hundredths $(\frac{20}{100})$. A decimal of 0.25 corresponds to 25 hundredths which is a quarter.

The following number has three numbers after the decimal point:

$$14.623$$

Therefore we have 14 and $\frac{6}{10}$ and $\frac{2}{100}$ plus something else. The final 3 refers to the number of thousandths that we have. Thus, in full $14.623 = 14$ and $\frac{6}{10}$ and $\frac{2}{100}$ and $\frac{3}{1000}$. This is actually the same as 14 and $\frac{623}{1000}$.

The system goes on to the number of ten thousandths, the number of hundred-thousandths, millionths and beyond.

Figure D.1 illustrates the components of the decimal number 423.7591.

The addition and subtraction of decimals are far simpler than the addition and subtraction of other forms of fractions. Thus, $0.53 + 0.22$ can be directly added together to become 0.75. Similarly with subtraction: $0.53 - 0.22 = 0.31$. Because we are adding fractions, sometimes the fraction will be bigger than one. So $0.67 + 0.92 = 1.59$.

See also: **decimal places (number of); rounding decimal places**

degrees of freedom: a difficult concept which has a bearing on many of the basic inferential statistical techniques. Statistical estimates based on samples often contain redundant information which if included may lead to a systematic bias in the estimate. For example, when calculating the variance or standard deviation of a sample in order to estimate the population characteristics, we know both the scores in the sample and the sample mean. The sample mean is used to estimate the population mean. However, this mean is also used in the estimation of the variance or standard deviation of the population. Take the following set of scores:

$$2, 5, 7, 9$$

The mean of this sample is $23/4 = 5.75$.

Imagine that we wish to calculate the variance based on this sample. It is basically the square of each of the deviations from the mean. So we take $(2 - 5.75)^2$, $(5 - 5.75)^2$, $(7 - 5.75)^2$, etc., but a problem emerges when we come to the score of 9. It actually contains no new information. Since we know that the sample mean is 5.75 then knowing the first three scores allows us to know that the final score has to be 9. No other number will fit. So, the final number actually provides no information that has not already been accounted for. In this case there would be three degrees of freedom since the final score is fixed by the mean and the other three scores.

The calculation method for degrees of freedom varies according to what is being estimated and it is not possible to give general rules which easily apply to any calculation. Nevertheless, where degrees of freedom have to be calculated, it is usually a simple matter. Generally speaking, degrees of freedom are only an issue in relation to hand calculation of statistical tests because tables of critical values are often distributed according to the degrees of freedom. Computer calculations rarely if ever require reference to such tables by the user. See also: **analysis of variance; chi-square; estimated standard deviation; t distribution, t test for unrelated samples; variance estimate**

De Moivre's distribution: another term for a normal distribution. See also: **normal distribution**

dendrogram: a graphical representation of the results of a cluster analysis in which lines are used to indicate which variables or clusters are paired at which stage of the analysis.

denominator: in a fraction such as $\frac{4}{7}$ or $\frac{3}{17}$ the denominator is the number at the bottom – that is, 7 in the first example and 17 in the second. The numerator is the number at the top. See also: **numerator**

dependent groups or **samples:** see **within-subjects design**

dependent variable: a variable that is assumed to 'depend' on, be affected by, or related to the value of one or more independent variables. See also: **criterion variable; multiple regression; regression equation**

descriptive statistics: a wide variety of techniques that allow us to describe the general characteristics of the data we collect. The central tendency (typical score) may be assessed by the mean, median or mode. The shape or spread of the distribution of scores can be presented graphically (using histograms, for example) and the spread can be given as the range, standard deviation or variance. They are key to and essential in knowing the nature of the data collected. They are too easily overlooked by those impressed by the complexity of inferential statistics.

Although descriptive statistics seem to be much simpler than inferential statistics, they are essential to any data analysis. A common mistake on the part of novices in statistics is to disregard the descriptive analysis in favour of the inferential analysis. The consequence of this is that the trends in the data are not understood or overlooked and the results of the inferential statistical analysis appear meaningless. A thorough univariate and bivariate examination of the data is an initial and key step in analysing any data. See also: **exploratory data analysis**

design: see **between-subjects design; cross-sectional design** or **study; factorial design; longitudinal design** or **study; non-experimental design** or **study; true experiment; within-subjects design**

determinant, of a matrix: a value associated with a square matrix which is calculated from it. It is denoted by two vertical lines on either side of the letter which represents it such as |**D**|. The determinant of a correlation matrix may vary between 0 and 1. When it is 1, all the correlations in the matrix are 0. This is known as an identity matrix in which the main or leading diagonal of the matrix (going from top left to bottom right) consists of ones and the values above and below it of zeros. When the determinant is zero, there is at least one linear dependency in the matrix. This means that one or more columns can be formed from other columns in the matrix. This can be done by either transforming a column (such as multiplying it by a constant) or forming a linear combination (such as subtracting one column from another). Such a matrix may be called ill-conditioned.

deviation: the size of the difference between a score and the mean (usually) of the set of scores to which it belongs. Deviation is calculated to include the sign – that is, the deviation of a score of 6 from the mean of 4 is 2, whereas the deviation of a score of 2 from the

mean of 4 is −2 See also: **absolute deviation; difference score**

dichotomous variable: a variable having only two values. Examples include sex (male and female being the values), employment status (employed and non-employed being the two values) and religion (Catholic and non-Catholic being the values in the study). There is no assumption that the two values are equally frequent.

One reason for treating dichotomous variables as a special case is that they can be treated as simple score variables. So, if we code male as 1 and female as 2, these are values on the variable femaleness. The bigger the score, the more female the individual is. In this way, a dichotomous variable can be entered into an analysis which otherwise requires scores.

It also explains that there is a close relationship between some research designs that are generally seen as looking at mean differences and those which seek correlations between variables. The *t* test is commonly applied to designs where there are an experimental group and a control group which are compared on a dependent variable measured as scores. However, if we consider the independent variable here (group) then it is easy to see that it can be coded 1 for the control group and 2 for the experimental group. If that is done, the 1s and 2s (the independent variable) can be correlated with the scores (the dependent variable). This Pearson correlation coefficient gives exactly the same probability value as does the *t* test applied to the same data.

This is important since it allows any nominal variable to be recoded as a number of dichotomous variables. For example, if participants are given a choice of, say, six geographical locations for their place of birth, it would be possible to recode this single variable as several separate variables. So if Northern England is one of the geographical locations, people could be scored as being from Northern England or not. If another category is South West England then all participants could then be scored as being from South West England or not. These are essentially dummy variables.

difference score: in related designs in which individuals are measured twice, for example, a difference score is simply the difference between that individual's score on one variable and their score on another variable. Difference scores can take positive or negative values. See also: **deviation**

directional hypothesis: see **hypothesis**

directionless tests: (a) a test of significance which is two tailed (see **significant**); (b) more likely to refer to a test of significance which can only yield absolute values and hence is not capable of testing for direction. Examples of this include chi-square (for bigger than 2×2 tables) and the F ratio.

discriminant function analysis: identifies the pattern of variables which differentiates a group of cases from other groups of cases. For example, imagine the research issue is the childhood and family factors which differentiate criminal adolescents from their peers. The obvious strategy is to collect information about, say:

1   The extent of father's nurturant behaviour
2   Family income
3   Mother's IQ

It would be a simple matter to determine whether delinquents differ from their non-delinquent peers by using the unrelated t test or ANOVA on each variable to see whether there is a significant difference on nurturant behaviour between the two groups, then family income, and then mother's IQ. Up to a point this is fine. Unfortunately it does nothing to establish what are the really important factors distinguishing the groups and what is the best pattern for differentiating between the various groups. Discriminant function analysis attempts to rectify these difficulties with the simpler approach.

In discriminant function analysis there is a dependent or criterion variable (the particular group to which an individual actually belongs) and a set of independent or predictor or discriminating variables (things which might differentiate between the groups involved). A discriminant function is a weighted combination of variables which optimizes the ability of the predictors to differentiate between the groups of cases. So a discriminant function might be

$$\text{discriminant (function) score} = \text{constant} + b_1 x_1 + b_2 x_2 + b_3 x_3 + b_4 x_4 + b_5 x_5 + b_6 x_6$$

Wilks's lambda is used to indicate the contribution of each of the discriminating variables to the separation of the groups. The smaller lambda is the greater the discriminating power of the predictor variable. The discriminant function is made up by a weighted combination of scores on different variables. The bs in the above formula are the weights, and the xs the scores an individual has on particular measures. So in the above example there are six predictor variables. This is essentially little different from the formula for multiple regression, except we are predicting which group a person with a particular pattern will belong to rather than what score that person will get on the dependent variable. As with multiple regressions, regression weights may be expressed in unstandardized or standardized form. When expressed in standardized form, the relative impact of the different variables on the classification of individuals to the different groups can be seen much more clearly from what are known as standardized discriminant coefficients.

If there are more than two groups to differentiate, the number of discriminant functions increases. This is normally the number of groups minus one but can be smaller if the number of independent (predictor or discriminating) variables is less.

The centroid is the average score on the discriminant function of a person who is classified in a particular group. For a two-group discriminant function analysis there are two centroids. Quite clearly, there has also got to be cut-off points which sort out which group the individual should belong to on the basis of the discriminant function. This is midway between the two centroids if the group sizes are equal but weighted towards one if they are not.

There is also the important matter of how well the discriminant function sorts the cases into their known groups. Sometimes this may be referred to as the classification table, confusion matrix or prediction table. It tabulates the known distribution of groups against the predicted distribution of individuals between the groups based on the independent variables. The better the fit between the actual groups and predicted groups, the better the discriminant function.

Discriminant function analysis is easily conducted using a standard computer package such as SPSS. Despite this, its use is surprisingly rare in many disciplines. See also: **hierarchical** or **sequential entry; Hotelling's trace criterion; multivariate normality; Roy's gcr; stepwise entry; Wilks's lambda**

Cramer (2003)

discriminant validity: the extent to which a measure of one construct is less strongly related to measures of other constructs than measures of the same one. For example, we would expect measures of anxiety to be less strongly related to measures of intelligence than other measures of anxiety – that is, if our measure of anxiety is valid.

dispersion, measure of: a measure or index of the spread or dispersion of values in a sample. The three most common measures of dispersion are the range, the variance and the standard deviation.

distribution: the pattern of characteristics (e.g. variable values). That is, the way in which characteristics (values) of a variable are distributed over the sample or population. Hence, the distribution of scores in a sample is merely a tally or graph which shows the pattern of the various values of the score. The

distribution of gender, for example, would be merely the number or proportion of males and females in the sample or population. See **normal distribution**

distribution-free tests: generally used to denote non-parametric statistical techniques. They are distribution free in the sense that no assumptions are made about the distribution of the data in the population from which the samples are drawn. Parametric tests assume normality (normal distribution) and symmetry which may make them inappropriate in extreme cases of non-normality of asymmetry. See **non-parametric tests; ranking tests**

drop-out rate: see **attrition**

dummy coding: a method for defining a dummy variable in which membership of a category is coded as 1 and non-membership as 0. It is so called because the zero does not specify, or is dumb to, the membership of other categories.

Cohen and Cohen (1983)

dummy variable: a common procedure, where data have been collected as a complex category (nominal/categorical/qualitative) variable, is to employ dummy variables in order to be able to analyse the variable using regression and other techniques. Imagine the following categories of a variable measuring occupation:

Construction work
Forestry work
Office work
Medical work
Other

Classed as a single variable, this occupation variable is not readily turned into numerical scores for the obvious reason that it is a nominal variable. The different jobs can be turned into dummy variables by creating several dichotomous or binary variables. So, for example, construction work could be turned into a dummy variable by simply coding 0 if the respondent was not in construction work and 1 if the respondent was in construction work. Forestry work similarly would be coded as 0 if the respondent was not in forestry and 1 if the respondent was in forestry work.

There is no requirement that every possible dummy variable is created from a nominal variable. Once the dummy variables have been coded as 0 or 1 (any other pair of values would do in most circumstances), they can be entered in correlational techniques such as Pearson's correlation coefficient (see **phi coefficient** and **point–biserial correlation coefficient**) or especially regression and multiple regression. If entering the dummy variables into multiple regression, one would restrict the number of dummy variables to one less than the number of categories in the category variable. This is to avoid the situation in which variables may be strongly collinear in the regression analysis. Strong collinearity is a problem for the proper interpretation of predictions in multiple regression. A simple example might help explain why we restrict the number of dummy variables to the number of categories minus one. Take the variable gender which has the values male and female. We could turn this into two dummy variables. One for male in which being male is coded 1 and not being male is coded 0, and another dummy variable for female in which being female is coded 1 and not being male is coded 0. There would be a perfect (negative) correlation between the two. Entered into a multiple regression, only one of these dummy variables would emerge as being predictive and the other would not emerge as predictive. This is a consequence of the collinearity.

Dummy variables provide a useful means of entering what is otherwise nominal data into powerful techniques such as multiple regression. Some confidence is needed to manipulate data in this way but dummy variables are simple to produce and the benefits of employing them considerable. See also: **analysis of variance; dichotomous variable; effect coding; multiple regression**

Duncan's new multiple range test: a *post hoc* or multiple comparison test which is used to determine whether three or more means differ significantly in an analysis of variance. It may be used regardless of whether the overall analysis of variance is significant. It assumes equal variance and is approximate for unequal group sizes. It is a stepwise or sequential test which is similar to the Newman–Keuls method, procedure or test in that the means are first ordered in size. However, it differs in the significance level used. For the Newman–Keuls test the significance level is the same for however many comparisons there are, while for Duncan's test it becomes more lenient the more comparisons there are. Consequently, differences are more likely to be significant for this test.

The significance level is $1 - (1 - \alpha)^{r-1}$ where r is the number of steps the two means are apart in the ordered set of means. For two adjacent means, r is 2, for two means separated by a third mean r is 3, for two means separated by two other means r is 4, and so on. For an α or significance level of 0.05, the significance level for Duncan's test is 0.05 when r is 2 $[1 - (1 - 0.05)^{2-1} = 1 - 0.95^1 = 1 - 0.95 = 0.05]$. It increases to 0.10 when r is 3 $[1 - (1 - 0.05)^{3-1} = 1 - 0.95^2 = 1 - 0.90 = 0.10]$, to 0.14 when r is 4 $[1 - (1 - 0.05)^{4-1} = 1 - 0.95^3 = 1 - 0.86 = 0.14]$, and so on.

For the example given in the entry for the Newman–Keuls method, the value of the studentized range is 3.26 when r is 2, 3.39 when r is 3, and 3.47 when r is 4. These values can be obtained from a table which is available in some statistics texts such as the source below. Apart from the first value which is the same as that for the Newman–Keuls method, these values are smaller, which means that the difference between the two means being compared does not have to be as large as it does for the Newman–Keuls method when r is more than 2 to be statistically significant. For the example given in the entry for the Newman–Keuls method, these differences are 5.97 when r is 3 (3.39 × 1.76 = 5.97) and 6.11 when r is 4 (3.47 × 1.76 = 6.11) compared with 7.11 and 7.97 for the Newman–Keuls method respectively.

Kirk (1995)

Dunn's test: the same as the Bonferroni *t* test. It is an a priori or multiple comparison test used to determine which of three or more means differ significantly from one another in an analysis of variance. It controls for the probability of making a Type I error by reducing the 0.05 significance level to take account of the number of comparisons made. It can be used with groups of equal or unequal size.

Dunn–Sidak multiple comparison test: an a priori or multiple comparison test used to determine which of three or more means differ significantly from one another in an analysis of variance. It controls for the probability of making a Type I error by reducing the 0.05 significance level to take account of the number of comparisons made. It assumes equal variances but can be used with groups of equal or unequal size. It is a slight modification of Dunn's or the Bonferroni *t* test. This revision makes it very slightly more powerful than this latter test, which practically may make little difference. For Dunn's test the familywise or experimentwise significance level is calculated by dividing the conventional 0.05 level by the number of comparisons to be made. So with three comparisons this significance level is 0.0167 (0.05/3 = 0.0167). For the Dunn–Sidak test the comparison level is computed with the following formula where *C* is the number of comparisons:

$$1 - (1 - 0.05)^{1/C}$$

For three comparisons this level is 0.0170 [$1 - (1 - 0.05)^{1/3} = 1 - 0.95^{1/3} = 1 - 0.9830 = 0.0170$]. The difference between these two significance levels is only 0.0003. The difference between the two significance levels becomes progressively smaller the greater the number of comparisons being made.
  Kirk (1995)

Dunnett's C test: an a priori or multiple comparison test used to determine whether the mean of a control condition differs from that of two or more experimental conditions in an analysis of variance. It can be used for equal and unequal group sizes where the variances are unequal. This test takes account of the increased probability of making a Type I error the more comparisons that are made.
  Toothaker (1991)

Dunnett's T3 test: an a priori or multiple comparison test used to determine whether the mean of a control condition differs from that of two or more experimental conditions in an analysis of variance. It can be used for equal and unequal group sizes where the variances are unequal. This test takes account of the increased probability of making a Type I error the more comparisons that are made. It is a modification of Tamhane's *T2* multiple comparison test.
  Toothaker (1991)

Dunnett's test: an a priori or multiple comparison test used to determine whether the mean of a control condition differs from that of two or more experimental conditions in an analysis of variance. It can be used for equal and unequal group sizes where the variances are equal. The formula for this test is the same as that for the unrelated *t* test where the variances are equal:

$$\frac{\text{group 1 mean} - \text{group 2 mean}}{\sqrt{(\text{group 1 variance/group 1 } n) + (\text{group 2 variance/group 2 } n)}}$$

However, the probability level of this *t* test has been reduced to take account of the increased probability of making a Type I error the more comparisons that are made. Dunnett's *C* or *T3* test should be used when the variances are unequal.
  Kirk (1995)

E

Ebel's intraclass correlation: see **between-judges variance**

ecological validity: the extent to which a study can be seen as representing the 'real-life' phenomenon it is designed to investigate. For example, the way couples handle their differences when asked to do so in a laboratory may be different from the way they would do this outside of this setting in their everyday lives. In these circumstances, ecological validity is poor.

effect: the influence of one variable on another variable (though this may be zero). A common phrase is to discuss 'the effect of variable X on variable Y'. The term may be used in the sense of a causal effect in which changes in one variable result directly or cause changes in the other. However, more generally the term is used to refer to the extent of the relationship of one variable with another – that is, simply their mathematical relationship with no implications of social science causality. Experimental effect refers to the influence of the independent variable on the dependent variable in an experiment.

effect coding: a method for coding nominal variables in which the two categories or groups to be identified are coded as 1 and − 1 respectively and any other categories or groups as 0. It is so called because it determines the effect of the groups or treatments being compared. It is used in multiple regression.

Cohen and Cohen (1983)

effect size: a term used in meta-analysis and more generally to indicate the relationship between two variables. The normal implication of the term effect size is that it indicates the size of the difference between the means of the conditions or groups on the dependent variable. Such an approach does not readily allow direct comparisons between studies using different measuring instruments and so forth. Consequently effect size is normally reported as a more standardized index such as Cohen's d. Alternatively, and probably much more usefully, effect size can be expressed in terms of a Pearson's correlation coefficient. This is more intuitively understood by researchers with modest statistical knowledge. The point–biserial correlation and eta may be used to calculate correlation coefficients where the independent variable is in the form of a small number of nominal categories. Where both variables are scores, then Pearson's correlation is the appropriate statistic. In this way, correlation coefficients which are comparable with each other may be obtained for the vast majority of studies. The effect size expressed in this way, since it is a correlation coefficient, gives the proportion of variance explained by the two variables if the coefficient is squared. See coefficient of determination. See also: **meta-analysis**

eigenvalue, in factor analysis: the amount (not percentage) of variance accounted for by the variables on a factor in a factor analysis. It is the sum of the squared correlations or loadings between each variable and that factor. The magnitude of a factor and its 'significance' are assessed partly from the eigenvalue. See also: **Kaiser's (Kaiser–Guttman) criterion; scree test, cattell's**

endogenous variable: a variable in a path analysis which is assumed to be explained by one or more other variables in the analysis. As a consequence it has one or more arrows leading either directly or indirectly to it from other variables.

EQS: (pronounced like the letter X) the name of one of the computer programs for carrying out structural equation modelling. The name seems to be an abbreviation for *equation systems*. Information about EQS can be found at the following website:
http://www.mvsoft.com/index.htm
See also: **structural equation modelling**

error: the variation in scores which the researcher has failed to control or measure in a particular study. Once it is measured as an identifiable variable it ceases to be error. So variations in the scores on a measure which are the consequence of time of day, for example, are error if the researcher does not appreciate that they are due to variations in time of day and includes time of day as a variable in the study. Error may be due to poor research design or methodology, but it is not a mistake in the conventional sense. The objective of the

researcher needs to be to keep error to a minimum as far as possible. Error makes the interpretation of trends in the data difficult since the greater the error, the greater the likely variation due to chance or unknown factors. Many factors lead to increased error – poor measurement techniques such as unclear or ambiguous questions and variations in the instructions given to participants, for instance.

error mean square: the term used in analysis of variance for dividing the effect mean square to obtain the F ratio. It is the error sum of squares divided by the error degrees of freedom. The smaller this term is in relation to the effect mean square, the bigger the F ratio will be and the more likely that the means of two or more of the groups will be statistically significant.

error sum of squares: the sum of squares in an analysis of variance which remains after the sum of squares for the other effects has been removed. It represents the variance which remains to be explained and so may be referred to as the residual sum of squares. See also: **analysis of variance**

error variance: see **within-groups variance**

estimated standard deviation: an estimate of the 'average' amount by which scores vary from the mean of scores. It is the likely standard deviation of the population of scores. It is based on the characteristics of a known sample from that population. The formula for calculating the estimated standard deviation differs from that of the standard deviation in that it features a correction for bias in the estimate. This simply reduces the sample size (N) by one, which then produces an unbiased estimate. So for the sample of scores 3, 7 and 8, the formula and calculation of estimated standard deviation is

$$\text{estimated standard deviation} = \sqrt{\frac{\Sigma(X - \bar{X})^2}{N - 1}}$$

where X is a score, $\bar{X}$ is the mean score, and N is the number of scores. Thus

$$\text{estimated standard deviation} = \sqrt{\frac{(3 - 6)^2 + (7 - 6)^2 + (8 - 6)^2}{3 - 1}}$$

$$= \sqrt{\frac{-3^2 + 1^2 + 2^2}{2}} = \sqrt{\frac{9 + 1 + 4}{2}}$$

$$= \sqrt{\frac{14}{2}} = \sqrt{7} = 2.65$$

Thus, the value of the estimated standard deviation is 2.65 units. So the average score in the population differs from the mean of 6 by 2.65. The average, however, is not calculated conventionally but this is a helpful way to look at the concept. However, since there are a number of ways of calculating averages in statistics (e.g. harmonic mean, geometric mean) then we should be prepared for the unusual. The estimated standard deviation is basically the square root of the average squared deviation from the mean.

Computer packages often compute the estimated standard deviation but nevertheless and confusingly call it the standard deviation. Since generally the uses of standard deviation are in inferential statistics, we would normally be working with the estimated standard deviation anyway because research invariably involves samples. Hence, the unavailability of standard deviation in some packages is not a problem. As long as the researcher understands this and reports standard deviation appropriately as estimated when it is, few difficulties arise.

estimated variance: see **variance estimate, estimated population variance** or **sample variance**

estimation: when we cannot know something for certain then sometimes it is useful to estimate its value. In other words, have a good guess or an educated guess as to its value. This is an informed decision really rather than a guess. In statistics the process of estimation is commonly referred to as statistical inference. In this, the most likely population value is calculated or estimated based on the available information from the research sample(s). Without estimation, research on samples could not be generalized beyond the individuals or cases that the research was conducted on. The process of estimation sometimes does employ some complex calculations (as in multiple regression), but for the most part there is a simple relationship between the characteristics of a sample and the estimated characteristics of the population based on this sample.

eta (η): usually described as a correlation coefficient for curvilinear data for which linear correlation coefficients such as Pearson's product moment correlation are not appropriate. This is a little misleading as eta gives exactly the same numerical value as Pearson's correlation when applied to perfectly linear data. However, if the data are *not* ideally fitted by a straight line then there will be a disparity. In this case, the value of eta will be bigger (never less) than the corresponding value of Pearson's correlation applied to the same data. The greater the disparity between the linear correlation coefficient and the curvilinear correlation coefficient, the less linear is the underlying relationship.

Eta requires data that can be presented as a one-way analysis of variance. This means that there is a dependent variable which takes the form of numerical scores. The independent variable takes one of a number of different categories. These categories may be ordered (i.e. they can take a numerical value and, as such, represent scores on the independent variable). Alternatively, the categories of the independent variable may simply be nominal categories which have no underlying order.

Data suitable for analysis using eta can be found in Table E.1 and Table E.2. They clearly contain the same data. The first table could be directly calculated as a Pearson's correlation coefficient. The correlation coefficient is 0.81. The data in the other table are obviously amenable to a one-way analysis of variance. The value of eta can be calculated from the analysis of variance summary table since it is merely the following:

$$eta = \sqrt{\frac{\text{between sum of squares}}{\text{total sum of squares}}}$$

Table E.1 *Data with four categories of the independent variable*

Independent variable	Dependent variable
1	3
1	4
1	2
1	5
1	4
2	3
2	6
2	7
2	5
3	7
3	6
3	4
3	8
3	9
3	8
4	12
4	12
4	11
4	10
4	6

Table E.3 gives the analysis of variance summary table for the data in Table E.2 as well as the calculation of eta for that table. The analysis of variance is a basic one-way Analysis of Variance. Not every aspect of the summary table is used to calculate eta – we do not use the within subjects (i.e. error) sum of squares. We find that the value of eta is 0.83 compared with 0.81 for Pearson's correlation. Thus, there is virtually no departure from linearity since the 'curvilinear' eta is only marginally larger than the linear correlation.

Table E.2 *The data (from Table E.1) put in the form of one-way ANOVA*

Category of Independent Variable			
Category 1	Category 2	Category 3	Category 4
3	3	7	12
4	6	6	12
2	7	4	11
5	5	8	10
4		9	6
		8	

Table E.3 *Analysis of variance summary table for data in Table E.2*

Source of variance	Sum of squares	Degrees of freedom	Mean square
Between groups	118.050	3	39.350
Within or Error	54.750	16	
Total	172.800		

The calculation of eta should be more routine than it is in current practice. In many disciplines it is rarely considered. However, its calculation is easy on statistical computer packages with data entered in a form suitable for calculating Pearson's correlation (unrelated ANOVA). It gives an indication of non-linearity when compared with Pearson's correlation. It is important to stress again that although our example deals with a linear independent variable, nevertheless this is not a requirement. So the independent variable may be nominal categories. With nominal data, the test of linearity is obviously inapplicable.

$$eta \text{ for above} = \sqrt{\frac{118.050}{172.800}} = \sqrt{0.683} = 0.83$$

As we interpret the value of eta more or less as a Pearson's correlation coefficient then a correlation of 0.83 indicates a strong relationship between the independent variable and the dependent variable. In light of the fact that the linear relationship is almost as strong, we would hesitate to describe the relationship as curvilinear in this example as the departure from linearity is small. See also: **curvilinear relationship**

Excel: a widely available spreadsheet program for handling data which has good facilities for graphics and offers some basic but useful statistical procedures.

exogenous variable: a variable in a path analysis which is not explained by any other variables in the analysis but which explains one or more other variables. As a consequence, it has one or more arrows leading from it but none leading to it.

expected frequencies: the counts or frequencies expected if the null hypothesis were true (or it is what is based on the statistical model in some forms of analysis). Most commonly met in relation to the chi-square test. If there is just one sample of scores (one-sample or one-way chi-square) the expected frequencies are based either on known distributions or on the probabilities expected by chance under the null hypothesis. In a two-way chi-square, the expected frequencies are based on the null hypothesis of no difference or relationship between samples. The expected frequencies are the distribution obtained by combining the samples proportionately to give a single population estimate. See **chi-square** for the calculation of expected frequencies.

experiment: see also: **condition; treatment group**

experimental conditions: see **quasi-experiment**

experimental design or **study:** see **between-subjects design; factorial design; longitudinal design** or **study; true experiment; within-subjects design**

experimental effect: see **effect**

experimental group: see **dichotomous variable; treatment group**

experimental manipulation: see **fixed effects**

experimentwise error rate: see **analysis of variance; familywise error rate**

exploratory data analysis: a philosophy and strategy of research which puts the primary focus of the researcher on using the data as the starting point for understanding the matter under research. This is distinct from the use of data as a resource for checking the adequacy of theory. Classical or conventional approaches to data analysis are driven by a desire to examine fairly limited hypotheses empirically but, as a consequence, may ignore equally important features of the data which require understanding and explanation. In conventional approaches, the focus is on using techniques such as the *t* test, ANOVA, and so forth, in order to establish the credibility of the model developed by the researcher largely prior to data collection.

In exploratory data analysis, the emphasis is on maximizing the gain from the data by making more manifest the process of describing and analysing the obtained data in their complexity. Many of the techniques used in exploratory data analysis would be regarded as very basic statistical plots, graphs and tables – simple descriptive statistics. Exploratory data analysis does not require the powerful inferential statistical techniques common to research. The reason is that inferential statistical techniques may be seen as testing the adequacy of hypotheses that have been developed by other methods.

The major functions of exploratory data analysis are as follows:

1   To ensure maximum understanding of the data by revealing their basic structure.
2   To identify the nature of the important variables in the structure of the data.
3   To develop simple but insightful models to account for the data.

In exploratory data analysis, anomalous data such as the existence of outliers are not regarded as a nuisance but something to be explained as part of the model. Deviations from linearity are seen as crucial aspects to be explained rather than a nuisance. See also: **descriptive statistics**

exploratory factor analysis: refers to a number of techniques used to determine the way in which variables group together but it is also sometimes applied to see how cases group together. The latter may be called *Q* analysis, methodology or technique, to distinguish it from the former which may be referred to as *R* analysis, methodology or technique. Variables which are related or which group together should correlate highly with the same factor and not correlate highly with other factors. If the variables seem to be measuring or sampling aspects of the same underlying construct, they may be aggregated to form a single variable which is a composite of these variables. For example, questions which seek to measure how anxious people are may form a factor. If this is the case, the answers to these questions may be combined to produce a single index or score of anxiety.

In a factor analysis there are as many factors as variables. The first factor explains the greatest amount of the variance that is shared by the variables in that analysis. The second factor explains the next greatest amount of the remaining variance that is shared by the variables. Subsequent factors explain progressively smaller amounts of the shared variance. The amount of variance explained by a factor is called the eigenvalue, which may also be called the characteristic or latent root.

As the aim of factor analysis is to determine whether the variables can be explained in terms of a number of factors which are smaller than the number of variables, there needs to be some criterion to decide the number of factors which explains a substantial amount of the variance. Various criteria have been proposed. One of the most widely used is the Kaiser or Kaiser–Guttman criterion. Factors which have an eigenvalue of more than one are considered to explain a worthwhile amount of variance as this represents the amount of variance a variable would have on average. This criterion may result in too few factors when there are few variables and too many factors when there are many factors, although these numbers have not been specified. It may be considered a minimum criterion below which a factor cannot possibly be statistically significant. An alternative method for determining the number of factors is Cattell's scree test. This test plots the eigenvalues of the factors. The scree starts where there appears to be a sharp break in the size of the eigenvalues. At this point the size of the eigenvalue will tend to be small and appears to decrease in a linear or straight line function for subsequent factors. Factors before the scree tend to decline in substantial steps of variance explained. The number of the factor at the start of the scree is the number of factors that are considered to explain a useful amount of the variance.

Often, these factors are then rotated so that some variables will correlate highly with a factor while others will correlate lowly with it, making it easier to interpret the meaning of the factors. There are various methods of rotation. One kind of rotation is to ensure that the factors are uncorrelated with or independent of one another. Factors that are unrelated to one another can be visually depicted as being at right angles to one another. Consequently, this form of rotation is often referred to as orthogonal rotation as opposed to oblique rotation in which the factors are allowed to lie at an oblique angle to one another. The correlations of the variables on a factor can be aggregated together to form a score for that factor – these are known as factor scores. The advantage of orthogonal rotation is that as the scores on one factor are unrelated to those on other factors, the information provided by one factor is not similar to the information provided by other factors. In other words, this information is not redundant. This is not the case with oblique rotation where the scores on one factor may be related to scores on other factors. The more highly related the factors are, the more similar the information is for those factors and so the more redundant it is. The advantage of oblique rotation is that it is said to be a more accurate reflection of the correlations of the variables. Factors which are related to one another may be entered into a new factor analysis to form second-order or higher order factors. This is possible because oblique factors are correlated with each other and so can generate a correlation matrix. Orthogonal factors are not correlated so their correlations cannot generate further factors.

The meaning of a factor is usually interpreted in terms of the variables which correlate highly with it. The higher the correlation, regardless of its sign, the more that factor reflects that variable. To aid interpretation of its meaning, a factor should have at least three variables which correlate substantially with it. Variables may correlate highly with two or more factors, which suggests that these variables represent two or more factors. When aggregating variables together to form a single index for a factor, it is preferable to include only those variables which correlate highly with that factor and to exclude variables which correlate lowly with it or correlate

highly with one or more other factor. In this way, the index can be seen as being a clearer representation of that factor.

It is usual to report the amount of variance that is explained by orthogonal factors. This is normally done in terms of the percentage of variance accounted for by those factors. It is not customary to describe the amount of variance explained by oblique factors as some of the variance will be shared with other factors. The stronger the oblique factors are correlated, the greater the shared variance will be.

Cramer (2003)

exponent: a symbol or number written above and to the right of another symbol or number to indicate the number of times that a quantity should be multiplied by itself. For example, the exponent 3 in the expression 2^3 indicates that the quantity 2 should be multiplied by itself three times, $2 \times 2 \times 2$. The exponent 2 in the expression R^2 indicates that the quantity R is multiplied by itself twice. The exponent J in the expression C^J indicates that the quantity C should be multiplied by itself the number of times that J represents. See also: **logarithm**

exponential: see **natural** or **Napierian logarithm**

external validity: the extent to which the findings of a study can be applied more generally to other samples, settings and times. If the findings are specific to a contrived research situation, then they are said to lack external validity. See also: **randomization**

F

F ratio: the effect mean square divided by the error mean square in an analysis of variance.

$$F = \frac{\text{effect mean square}}{\text{error mean square}}$$

It is used to determine whether one or more means or some combination of means differ significantly from each other. The bigger the ratio is, the more likely it is to be statistically significant. Tables for the value that the F ratio has to be or to exceed are available in many statistical texts. Some of these values are shown in the entry on **analysis of variance**. The significance levels of the values obtained for analysis of variance are usually provided by statistical programs which compute this test.

The F ratio in multiple regression can be expressed in terms of the following formula:

$$F = \frac{R^2 \text{ change/number of predictors in that change}}{(1 - R^2)/(N - \text{number of predictors} - 1)}$$

R^2 is the squared multiple correlation between the criterion and all the predictors that have been entered into the multiple regression at that stage. Consequently, $1 - R^2$ is the error or remaining variance. R^2 change is the difference in R^2 between all the predictors that have been entered into the multiple regression and the predictor or predictors that have been entered into the last step of the multiple regression. In other words, R^2 change is the variance accounted for by the predictor(s) in the last stage. These two sets of variance are divided by their degrees of freedom. For R^2 change it is the number of predictors involved in that change. For $1 - R^2$ it is the number of cases in the sample (N) minus the number of predictors that have been entered including those in the last step minus one. See also: **between-groups variance**

Cramer (1998)

F test for equal variances in unrelated samples: one test for determining whether the variance in two groups of unrelated scores is equal or similar and does not differ significantly. This may be of interest in itself. It needs to be determined if a t test is to be used to see whether the means of those two groups differ because which version of the t test is to be used depends on whether the variances are equal or not. The F test is the larger variance divided by the smaller one:

$$F \text{ test} = \frac{\text{larger variance}}{\text{smaller variance}}$$

The value that F has to be or to exceed to be statistically significant at the 0.05 level is found in many statistics texts. This test has

Table F.1   *The 0.05 critical values for the F test*

df for smaller variance	df for larger variance					
	10	20	30	40	50	∞
10	3.72	3.42	3.31	3.26	3.22	3.08
20	2.77	2.46	2.35	2.29	2.25	2.09
30	2.51	2.20	2.07	2.01	1.97	1.79
40	2.39	1.99	1.94	1.80	1.75	1.64
50	2.32	1.94	1.87	1.74	1.70	1.55
∞	2.05	1.71	1.57	1.48	1.43	1.00

two degrees of freedom (*df*), one for the larger variance and one for the smaller variance. These degrees of freedom are one minus the number of cases in that group. The critical value that *F* has to be or to exceed for the variances to differ significantly at the 0.05 level is given in Table F.1 for a selection of degrees of freedom.

This test is suitable for normally distributed data.

face validity: the extent to which a measure appears to be measuring what it is supposed to be measuring. For example, a measure of self-reported anxiety may have face validity if the items comprising it seem to be concerned with aspects of anxiety.

factor: see **analysis of variance; higher order factors; principal axis factoring; scree test, Cattell's**

factor analysis: see **Bartlett's test of sphericity; confirmatory factor analysis; eigenvalue, in factor analysis; exploratory factor analysis; factor loading; factorial validity; iteration; Kaiser's (Kaiser–Guttman) criterion; oblique rotation; Q analysis; principal components analysis; R analysis; scree test, Cattell's; simple solution; varimax rotation, in factor analysis**

factor, in analysis of variance: a variable which consists of a relatively small number of levels or groups which contain the values or scores of a measured variable. This variable is sometimes called an independent variable as this variable is thought to influence the other variable which may be referred to as the dependent variable. There may be more than one factor in such an analysis.

factor, in factor analysis: a composite variable which consists of the loading or correlation between that factor and each variable making up that factor. Factor analysis is used to determine the extent to which a number of related variables can be grouped together into a smaller number of factors which summarize the linear relationship between those variables.

factor loading: a term used in factor analysis. A factor loading is a correlation coefficient (Pearson's product moment) between a variable and a factor (which is really a cluster of variables). Loadings can take positive and negative values between − 1 and + 1. They are interpreted more or less as a correlation coefficient would be. So if a variable has a factor loading of 0.8 on factor *A*, then this means that it is strongly correlated with factor *A*. If a variable has a strong negative correlation of − 0.9, then this means that the variable needs to be reversed in order to understand what it is about the variable which relates to factor *A*. A factor loading of zero approximately means that the variable has no relationship with the factor.

Each variable has a different factor loading on each of the different factors. The pattern of variables which have high loadings on a factor (taken in conjunction with those which do not load on that factor) is the basis for interpreting the meaning of that factor. In other words, if there are similarities between the variables which get high loadings on a particular factor, the nature of the similarity is the starting point for identifying what the factor is.

Table F.2   *Factorials*

N	0	1	2	3	4	5	6	7	8	9	10	11
N!	0	1	2	6	24	120	720	5040	40,320	362,880	3,628,800	39,916,800

factor rotation: see **oblique** and **orthogonal rotation**

factorial: the factorial of 6 is denoted as 6! and equals $6 \times 5 \times 4 \times 3 \times 2 \times 1 = 720$ while the factorial of 4 is denoted 4! and equals $4 \times 3 \times 2 \times 1 = 24$. Thus, a factorial is the number multiplied by all of the whole numbers lower than itself down to one (Table F.2). The factorial of 1 is 1 and the factorial of 0 is also 1. It has statistical applications in calculating the Fisher exact probability test and permutations and combinations. Unfortunately, factorials rapidly exceed the capabilities of calculators and their use can be difficult as a consequence. One solution is to look for terms which can be cancelled, so 6!/5! which is $(6 \times 5 \times 4 \times 3 \times 2 \times 1)/(5 \times 4 \times 3 \times 2 \times 1)$ simply cancels out to 6.

See **Fisher (exact probability) test**

factorial analysis of variance: see **analysis of variance**

factorial design: a design which investigates the relationship between two or more factors on the scores of one or more other measured variables. There are two main advantages in studying two or more factors together. The first is that error or unexplained variance in the measured variables may be explained by some of the other factors or their interactions, thereby reducing it. This provides a more sensitive test of that factor. The second advantage is that the interaction between the factors can be examined. See also: **interaction**

factorial validity: sometimes used to refer to whether the variables making up a measure have been shown to group together as a unitary factor through the statistical technique of factor analysis. A measure may be said to be factorially valid or to have factorial validity if the variables comprising it have been demonstrated to cluster together in this way.
Nunnally and Bernstein (1994)

familywise error rate: the probability or significance level for a finding when a family or number of tests or comparisons are being made on the data from the same study. It is also known as the experimentwise error rate. When determining whether a finding is statistically significant, the significance level is usually set at 0.05 or less. If more than one finding is tested on a set of data, the probability of those findings being statistically significant increases the more findings or tests of significance that are made. The following formula can be used for determining the familywise error rate significance level or a (alpha) where the tests are independent:

$$1 - (1 - \alpha)^{\text{number of comparisons}}$$

For example, if three tests are conducted using the 0.05 alpha level the familywise error rate is about 0.14:

$$1 - (1 - 0.05)^3 = 1 - 0.95^3 = 1 - 0.8574 = 0.1426$$

There are various ways of controlling for this familywise error rate. Some of the tests for doing so are listed under multiple comparison tests. One of the simplest is the Bonferroni test where the 0.05 level is divided by the number of tests being made. So, if three tests are being conducted, the appropriate significance level is 0.0167 ($0.05/3 = 0.0167$) though this is reported as 0.05. See also: **analysis of variance**

first-order partial correlation: see **zero-order correlation**

Table F.3 *Contingency table to illustrate calculation of 2 × 2 Fisher exact test with letter symbols added to ease calculation*

	Men	**Women**	
Employed	$a = 6$	$b = 2$	$W = a + b = 8$
Not employed	$c = 1$	$d = 4$	$X = c + d = 5$
	$Y = a + c = 7$	$Z = b + d = 6$	$N = 13$

Fisher (exact probability) test: a test of significance (or association) for small contingency tables. Generally known is the 2 × 2 contingency table version of the test but there is also a 2 × 3 contingency table version available. As such, it is an alternative technique to the chi-square in these cases. It can be used in circumstances in which the assumptions of chi-square such as minimal numbers of expected frequencies are not met. It has the further advantage that exact probabilities are calculated even in the hand calculation, though this advantage is eroded by the use of power statistical packages which provide exact probabilities for all statistics. The major disadvantage of the Fisher (exact probability) test is that it involves the use of factorials which can rapidly become unwieldy with substantial sample sizes. The calculation of a simple 2 × 2 Fisher test on the data in Table F.3 begins as follows:
Fisher exact probability

$$\text{Fisher exact probability} = \frac{W!X!Y!Z!}{N!a!b!c!d!}$$

$$= \frac{8!5!7!6!}{13!6!2!1!4!}$$

Taking the factorial values from Table F.2, this is

$$\frac{40{,}320 \times 120 \times 5040 \times 720}{6{,}227{,}020{,}800 \times 720 \times 2 \times 1 \times 24} = 0.082$$

This value (0.082) is the probability of getting precisely the outcome to be found in Table F.3 – that is, the data. This is just one component of the calculation. In order to calculate the significance of the Fisher exact test one must also calculate the probability of the more extreme outcomes while maintaining the marginal totals as they are in Table F.3. Table F.4 gives all of the possible tables – the table starts with the cases that are more extreme than the data and finishes with the tables that are more extreme in the *opposite* direction. Not all values are possible in the top left-hand side cell if the marginal totals are to be retained. So, for example, it is not possible to have 8, 1 or 0 in the top left-hand cells.

We can use the probabilities calculated using the formula above to calculate the Fisher exact probabilities. It is simply a matter of adding the appropriate probabilities together:

- One-tailed significance is assessed by adding together the probability for the data themselves (0.082) with any more extreme probabilities in the same direction (there is only one such table – the first one which has a probability of 0.005). Consequently, in this case, the one-tailed significance is 0.082 + 0.005 = 0.087. This is not statistically significant in our example.
- Two-tailed significance is not simply twice the one-tailed significance. This gives too high a value as the distribution is not symmetrical. One needs to find all of the extreme tables in the opposite direction from the actual data which also have a probability equal to or smaller than that for the data. The probability for the data themselves is 0.082. As can be seen, the only table in the opposite direction with an equal or smaller probability is the final table. This has a probability of 0.016. To obtain the two-tailed probability one simply adds this value to the one-tailed probability value. This is 0.087 + 0.016 = 0.103. This is not statistically significant at the 5% level.

Table F.4 *All of the possible outcomes of a study which maintain the marginal totals of Table F.3*

7	1
0	5

$p = 0.005$ – this is the only more extreme case than the data in the same direction as the data

6	2
1	4

$p = 0.082$ – this is the same table as for the data

5	3
2	3

$p = 0.326$

4	4
3	2

$p = 0.408$

3	5
4	1

$p = 0.163$

2	6
5	0

$p = 0.016$ – this is the only more extreme case in the opposite direction to the data

One important thing to remember about the Fisher exact probability test is that the number obtained (in this case 0.082) is the significance level – it is *not* a chi-square value which has to be looked up in tables. While a significance level of 0.082 is not statistically significant, of course, it does suggest a possible trend. See also: **factorial**

Fisher's LSD (Least Significant Difference) or protected test: a *post hoc* or multiple comparison test which is used to determine which of three or more means differ from one another when the F ratio in an analysis of variance is significant. It is essentially an unrelated *t* test in which the significance level has not been adjusted for the number of comparisons being made. As a consequence its use is generally not recommended. The formula for this test is the same as that for the unrelated *t* test where the variances are equal:

$$t = \frac{\text{group 1 mean} - \text{group 2 mean}}{\sqrt{(\text{group 1 variance/group 1 } n) + (\text{group 2 variance/group 2 } n)}}$$

A version of this test is also used to ascertain which of three or more adjusted means differ from one another when the F ratio in an analysis of covariance is significant. This test has the following formula:

$$t = \frac{\text{adjusted group 1 mean} - \text{adjusted group 2 mean}}{\sqrt{\dfrac{\text{adjusted}}{\substack{\text{mean}\\\text{square}\\\text{error}}} \times \left[\dfrac{1}{n_1} + \dfrac{1}{n_2} + \dfrac{(\text{covariate group 1 mean} - \text{covariate group 2 mean})^2}{\text{covariate error sum of squares}}\right]}}$$

See **analysis of variance**
    Howell (2002); Huitema (1980)

Fisher's z transformation: the logarithmic transformation of Pearson's correlation coefficient. Its common use is in the *z* test which compares the size of two correlation coefficients from two unrelated samples. (This is obviously different from the more conventional test of whether a single correlation coefficient differs from zero.) Without

Table F.5   *r to z transformation*

r	z	r	z
0.00	0.00	0.60	0.69
0.10	0.10	0.70	0.87
0.20	0.20	0.80	1.10
0.30	0.31	0.90	1.47
0.40	0.42	1.00	3.00
0.50	0.55		

the transformation, the distribution of differences between the two correlation coefficients becomes very skewed and unmanageable.

This transformation may be found by looking up the appropriate value in a table or by computing it directly using the following formula where $\log_e$ stands for the natural logarithm and r for Pearson's correlation:

$$z_r = 0.5 \times \log_e [(1 + r)/(1 - r)]$$

The values of Pearson's correlation vary from 0 to ± 1 as shown in Table F.5 and the values of the z correlation from 0 to about ± 3 (though, effectively, infinity).

fixed effects: the different levels of an experimental treatment (experimental manipulation) in many studies are merely a small selection from a wide range of possible levels. Generally speaking, the researcher chooses a small number of different levels for the treatment on the basis of some reasoned argument about what is appropriate, practical and convenient. That is, the levels are fixed by the researcher. This is known as the fixed effects model. It merely indicates that the different treatments are fixed by the researchers. The alternative is the random effects model in which the researcher selects the different levels of the treatment used by a random procedure. So, the range of possible treatments has to be identified and the selection made randomly from this range. Fixed effects are by far the most common approach in the various social sciences. As all of the common statistical techniques assume fixed rather than random effects, there is little

point in deviating from the fixed effects approach in terms of planning one's own research. It is difficult to find examples of the use of the random effects model in many disciplines. Nevertheless, advanced textbooks in statistics cover the appropriate procedures. See also: **random effects model**

floor effect: occurs when scores on the dependent variable are so low that the introduction of an experimental treatment cannot depress the scores of participants any further. This, if it is not recognized, might be taken as a sign that the experimental treatment is ineffective. This is not the case. For example, if children with educational difficulties are given a multiple-choice spelling test, it is likely that their performances are basically random so that they score at a chance level. For these children, the introduction of time pressure, stress or some other deleterious factor is unlikely to reduce their performance. This is because their performances on the test are at the chance level anyway. It is the opposite of a ceiling effect. The reasons for floor effects are diverse. They can be avoided by careful development of the measuring instruments and by careful review of the appropriate research participants.

frequency: the number of times a particular event or outcome occurs. Thus, the frequency of women in a sample is simply the total number of women in the sample. The frequency of blue-eyed people is the number of people with blue eyes. Generally in statistics we are referring to the number of cases with a particular characteristic. An alternative term, most common in statistical packages, is count. This highlights the fact that the frequency is merely a count of the number of cases in a particular category.

Data from individuals sometimes may be collected in the form of frequencies. This might cause the novice some confusion. For example, a score may be based on the frequency or number of eye blinks a participant does in a 10-minute period. This is really a score since it indicates the rate of blinking in a 10-minute period for each participant. Those with little knowledge or experience of statistics may find frequencies hard to differentiate from scores. This is because in order to decide whether the number 23 is a score or a frequency one needs to know how the number 23 was arrived at.

Data collected in the form of frequencies in nominal categories (categorical or category data) are analysed using tests such as chi-square. See also: **Bayesian inference; count; marginal totals**

frequency curve: a graphical frequency distribution applied to a continuous (or near continuous) score. It consists of an axis of frequency and an axis corresponding to the numerical value of the scores (Figure F.1). Since the steps on the value axis are small, the frequency distribution is fitted well by using a curved line rather than a succession of blocks. The term frequency polygon is sometimes met to describe the line that connects the points of a frequency curve. The most famous frequency curve in statistics is the bell-shaped, normal distribution.

frequency distribution: a table or diagram giving the frequencies of values of any given variable. For qualitative variables this is the number of times each of the categories occurs (e.g. depressive, schizophrenic and paranoid) whereas for quantitative variables this is the number of times each different score (or range of scores) occurs. The importance of a frequency distribution is simply that it allows the researcher to see the general characteristics of a particular variable for the cases or participants in the research. The frequency distribution may reveal important characteristics such as asymmetry, normality, spread, outliers, and so forth, in the case of score data. For qualitative data, it may help reveal

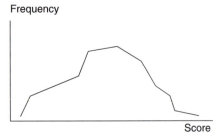

Frequency

Score

Figure F.1   *Frequency curve*

categories which are very frequent or so infrequent that it becomes meaningless to analyse them further.

Frequency distributions may be presented in a number of different forms: simple frequency distributions which are merely frequencies, percentage frequency distributions in which the frequencies are expressed as a percentage of the total of frequencies for that variable, cumulative frequencies, and even probability curves in which the frequencies are expressed as a proportion of the total (i.e. expressed as a proportion or probability out of one).

While frequency distributions reflect the distribution of a single variable, there are variants on the theme which impose a second or third variable. These are compound frequency distributions (more often compound bar charts or compound histograms).

frequency polygon: see **frequency curve**

Friedman two-way analysis of variance test: determines if the mean ranks of three or more related samples or groups differ significantly. It is a non-parametric test which is used on ranked data. The test statistic approximates a chi-square distribution where the degrees of freedom are the number of groups minus one.

Cramer (1998)

G

Gabriel simultaneous test procedure: a *post hoc* or multiple comparison test which is used to determine which of three or more means differ from one another in an analysis of variance. It is used with groups which have equal variances. It is based on the studentized maximum modulus rather than the studentized range. The studentized maximum modulus is the maximum absolute value of the group means which is divided by the standard error of the means.

  Kirk (1995)

Games–Howell multiple comparison procedure: a *post hoc* or multiple comparison test which is used to determine which of three or more means differ from one another when the F ratio in an analysis of variance is significant. It was developed to deal with groups with unequal variances. It can be used with groups of equal or unequal size. It is based on the studentized range statistic. See also: **Tamhane's T2 multiple comparison test**

  Howell (2002); Kirk (1995)

Gaussian distribution: another term for a normal distribution. See **normal distribution**

geometric mean: the nth root of the product of n scores. So the geometrical mean of 2, 9, and 12 is

$$\sqrt[3]{2 \times 9 \times 12} = \sqrt[3]{216} = 6.0$$

The geometric mean of 3 and 6 is

$$\sqrt[2]{3 \times 6} = \sqrt[2]{18} = 4.24$$

The geometric mean has no obvious role in basic everyday statistical analysis. It is important, though, since it emphasizes that there are more meanings of the concept of mean than the arithmetic mean or average. See also: **average**

general factor: in factor analysis, a general factor is one on which *all* of the variables in the analysis load to a significant degree. If there is a general factor, it will inevitably be the largest factor in terms of variance explained (eigenvalue) and consequently the first factor to emerge in the analysis.

Goodman and Kruskal's gamma (γ): a measure of association for ranked or ordinal data. It can range from -1 to $+1$ just like a correlation coefficient. It takes no account of the number of ranks for the two variables or cases which have the same or tied ranks. See also: **correlation**

  Cramer (1998); Siegal and Castellan (1988)

Table G.1 *Number of females and males passing or failing a test*

	Pass	Fail	Row total
Females	108	12	120
Males	56	24	80
Column total	164	36	200

Goodman and Kruskal's lambda (λ): a measure of the proportional increase in accurately predicting the outcome for one categorical variable when we have information about a second categorical variable, assuming that the same prediction is made for all cases in a particular category. For example, we could use this test to determine how much our ability to predict whether students pass or fail a test is affected by knowing their sex.

We can illustrate this test with the data in Table G.1 which show the number of females and males passing or failing a test.

If we had to predict whether a particular student had passed the test disregarding whether they were female or male, our best bet would be to say they had passed as most of the students passed (164 out of 200). If we did this we would be wrong on 36 occasions. How would our ability to predict whether a student had passed be increased by knowing whether they were male or female? If we predicted that the student had passed and we also knew that they were female we would be wrong on 12 occasions, whereas if they were male we would be wrong on 24 occasions. If we knew whether a student was female or male we would be wrong on 36 occasions. This is the same number of errors as we would make without knowing the sex of the student, so the proportional increase knowing the sex of the student is zero. The value of lambda varies from 0 to 1. Zero means that there is no increase in predictiveness whereas one indicates that there is perfect prediction without any errors.

This test is asymmetric in that the proportional increase will depend on which of the two variables we are trying to predict. For this case, lambda is about 0.15 if we reverse the prediction in an attempt to predict the sex of the student on the basis of whether they have passed or failed the test. The test

assumes that the same prediction is made for all cases in a particular row or column of the table. For example, we may assume that all females have passed or that all males have failed. Goodman and Kruskal's tau presumes that the predictions are randomly made on the basis of their proportions in the row and column totals. See also: **correlation**

Cramer (1998); Siegal and Castellan (1988)

Goodman and Kruskal's tau (τ): a measure of the proportional increase in accurately predicting the outcome of one categorical variable when we have information about a second categorical variable where it is assumed that the predictions are based on the their overall proportions.

We can illustrate this test with the data in Table G.1 (under the entry for Goodman and Kruskal's lambda) where we may be interested in finding out how much our ability to predict whether a person has passed or failed a test is increased by our knowledge of whether they are female or male. If we predicted whether a person had passed on the basis of the proportion of people who had passed disregarding whether they were female or male, we would be correct for 0.82 ($164/200 = 0.82$) of the 164 people who had passed, which is for 134.48 of them ($0.82 \times 164 = 134.48$). If we did this for the people who had failed, we would be correct for 0.18 ($36/200 = 0.18$) of the 36 people who had failed, which is for 6.48 of them ($0.18 \times 36 = 6.48$). In other words, we would have guessed incorrectly that 59.04 of the people had passed ($200 - 134.48 - 6.48 = 59.04$) which is a probability of error of 0.295 ($59.04/200 = 0.295$).

If we now took into account the sex of the person, we would correctly predict that the person had passed the test

for 0.90 ($108/120 = 0.90$) of the 108 females who had passed, which is for 97.20 of them ($0.90 \times 108 = 97.20$),

for 0.70 ($56/80 = 0.70$) of the 56 males who had passed, which is for 39.20 of them ($0.70 \times 56 = 39.20$), for 0.10 (12/120 = 0.10) of the 12 females who had failed, which is for 1.20 of them (0.10 × 12 = 1.20), and

for 0.30 (24/80 = 0.30) of the 24 males who had failed, which is for 7.20 of them (0.30 × 24 = 7.20).

In other words, we would have guessed incorrectly that 55.20 of the people had passed (200 − 97.20 − 39.20 − 1.20 − 7.20 = 55.20). Consequently, the probability of error of prediction is 0.276 (55.20/200 = 0.276). The proportional reduction in error in predicting whether people had passed knowing whether they were female or male is 0.064 [(0.295 − 0.276)/0.295 = 0.064].

Cramer (1998)

goodness-of-fit test: gives an indication of the closeness of the relationship between the data actually obtained empirically and the theoretical distribution of the data based on the null hypothesis or a model of the data. These can be seen in the chi-square test and log–linear analysis respectively. In chi-square the empirically observed data and the expected data under the null hypothesis are compared. The smaller the value of chi-square the better is the goodness of fit to the theoretical model based on the null hypothesis. In log–linear analysis, chi-square is used to test the closeness of the empirically observed data and a complex model based on interactions and main effects. So a goodness-of-fit test assesses the correspondence between the actual data and a theoretical account of that data that can be specified numerically. See also: **chi-square**

grand: as in grand mean and grand total. This is a somewhat old-fashioned term from when the analysis of variance, for example, would be routinely hand calculated. It refers to the overall characteristics of the data – not the characteristics of individual cells or components of the analysis.

grand mean: see **between-groups variance**

graph: a diagram which illustrates the relationship between variables, usually two variables. Scattergrams are a typical example of a graph in statistics.

grouped data: usually refers to the process by which a range of values are combined together especially to make trends in the data more apparent. So, for example, weights in the range 40–49 kg could be combined into one group, weights in the range 50–59 kg into the second group, weights in the range 60–69 kg into the third group, and so forth. There is a loss of information by doing so since a person who weighs 68 kg is placed in the same group as a person who weighs 62 kg despite the fact that their weights do differ. Grouping is most appropriate for graphical presentations of data. The purpose of grouping is basically to clarify trends in the distribution of data. Too many data points with fairly small samples can help disguise what the major features of the data are. Grouping smooths out some of these difficulties.

Grouping is sometimes used in the collection of data. For example, one commonly sees age being assessed in terms of age bands when participants are asked their age group, such as 20–29 years, 30–39 years, etc. There is no statistical reason for collecting data in this form. Indeed, there is an obvious case for collecting information such as age as actual age. Modern computer analyses of data can recode information in non-grouped form readily into groups if this is required.

There are special formulae for the rapid calculation of statistics such as the mean from grouped data. These had advantages in the days of hand calculation but they have less to offer nowadays.

H

harmonic mean: the harmonic mean of 3 and 6 is

$$\frac{2}{\frac{1}{3}+\frac{1}{6}} = \frac{2}{0.333 + 0.167} = \frac{2}{0.5} = 4$$

The harmonic mean of 3, 6 and 7 is

$$\frac{3}{\frac{1}{3}+\frac{1}{6}+\frac{1}{7}} = \frac{3}{0.333 + 0.167 + 0.143} = \frac{3}{0.643} = 4.67$$

In other words, the harmonic mean is the number of scores, divided by the sum of $1/X$ for each score.

The harmonic mean is rarely directly calculated as such in statistics. It is part of the calculation of the unrelated t test, for example. See also: **average**

Hartley's test or F_{max}: one test used to determine whether the variances of three or more groups are similar (i.e. homogeneous) when the number of cases in each group is the same or very similar. It is the largest variance divided by the smallest variance. The degrees of freedom for this F ratio are the number of groups for the numerator. For the denominator they are the number of cases in a group minus one or, where the group sizes differ slightly, the number of cases in the most numerous group minus one.

heterogeneity: the state of being of incomparable magnitudes. It is particularly applied

to variance. Heterogeneity of variance is a phrase that indicates that two variances are very dissimilar from each other. This means in practice that, since they are so very different, it is misleading to try to combine them to give a better estimate of the population variance, for example. The usual criterion is that the two variances need to be significantly different from each other using such tests as the F ratio, Levene's test or the Bartlett–Box F test.

heteroscedasticity: most notably an issue in connection with correlation and regression which uses the least squares method of fitting the best fitting straight line between the data points. The variation of the data points of the scattergram vertically can differ at different points of the scattergram. For some points on the horizontal of the scattergram there may be a large amount of variation of the points, for other points on the horizontal of the scattergram there may be little variation. Such variation at different points tends to make the fit of the best fitting straight line rather poor or less than ideal (though not consistently so in any direction). Tests of heteroscedasticity are available so that appropriate corrections can be made.

Heteroscedasticity is shown in Figure H.1. This is a scattergram of the relationship between two variables X and Y. If we take the first data point along the horizontal axis and look at the four scores indicated above that point, we can see that these data points vary in their score on the vertical Y axis but this

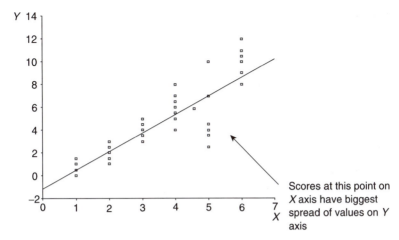

Figure H.1 *Illustrating heteroscedasticity*

variation is relatively small (2 units on the vertical axis). They all are at position 1 on the horizontal axis. Look at the scores at data point 5 on the horizontal axis. Obviously all of these points are 6 on the horizontal axis but they vary from 2 to 10 on the vertical axis. Obviously the variances at positions 1 and 5 on the horizontal axis are very different from each other. This is heteroscedasticity. See also: **multiple regression; regression equation**

heuristic: this term has several different meanings. It may be used as an adjective or a noun. A general meaning is finding out or discovering. Another meaning is to find out through experience. A third meaning is a process or method which leads to a solution. See also: **algorithm**

hierarchical agglomerative clustering: one of the more widely used methods of cluster analysis in which clusters of variables are formed in a series or hierarchy of stages. Initially there are as many clusters as variables. At the first stage, the two variables that are closest are grouped together to form one cluster. At the second stage, either a third variable is added or agglomerated to the first

cluster containing the two variables or two other variables are grouped together to form a new cluster, whichever is closest. At the third stage, two variables may be grouped together, a third variable may be added to an existing group of variables or two groups may be combined. So, at each stage only one new cluster is formed according to the variables, the variable and cluster or the clusters that are closest together. At the final stage all the variables are grouped into a single cluster.
    Cramer (2003)

hierarchical or **sequential entry:** a method in which predictors are entered in an order or sequence which is determined by the analyst in statistical techniques such as logistic regression, multiple regression, discriminant function analysis and log–linear analysis.

hierarchical method in analysis of variance: see **Type I, hierarchical** or **sequential method in analysis of variance**

hierarchical multiple regression: see **covariate; multiple regression**

higher order factors: these emerge from a factor analysis of the correlations between the first or first-order factors of a factor analysis of variables. This is only possible when the factors are rotated obliquely (i.e. allowed to correlate). So long as the factors in a higher order factor analysis are rotated obliquely, further higher order factor analyses may be carried out. Except where the analysis involves numerous variables, it is unlikely that more than one higher order factor analysis will be feasible. See also: **exploratory factor analysis**

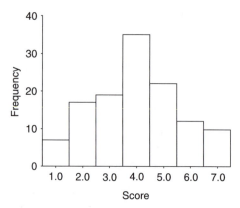

Figure H.2   *Histogram*

higher order interactions: involve relationships between more than two factors or variables. For example, the interaction between the three variables of gender, social class and age would constitute a higher order interaction.

histogram: used to present the distribution of scores in diagram form. They use rectangular bars to illustrate the frequency of a particular score or range of scores. Because scores are based on numerical order, the bars of a histogram will touch (unless there is zero frequency for a particular bar). Unlike a bar chart, the bars cannot be readily rearranged in terms of order without radically altering the interpretation of the data. A typical histogram is to be found in Figure H.2. This diagram is interpreted generally by looking at the numerical frequency scale along the vertical axis if there is one or simply the heights of the histogram bars.

There is an important point to bear in mind if one is using scores in short ranges such as ages 20–29, 30–39, 40–49 years etc. These ranges should be identical in width otherwise there is a complication. For example, if the researcher classified in the above data as 20–29 years, 30–39 years, 40–49 years and above 50–79 years, then one should examine the area of the bar and not its height as the width of the bar should be greater if the age range is greater. However, this is commonly not done by researchers.

Although histograms are common in the media in general and are used by non-statisticians, it is important not to regard them as having little or no place in sophisticated statistical analyses. Quite the contrary: time spent examining univariate data (and bivariate data) using histograms, compound bar charts, and the like, may reveal unexpected features of the data. For example, it may be that scores on a variable appear to be in two distinct groups on a histogram. This sort of information would not be apparent from the most complex of statistical analyses without using these simple graphical techniques.

Hochberg GT2 test: a *post hoc* or multiple comparison test which is used to determine which of three or more means differ from one another in an analysis of variance. It is used with groups which have equal variances. It is based on the studentized maximum modulus rather than the studentized range. The studentized maximum modulus is the maximum absolute value of the group means which is divided by the standard error of the means.

Toothaker (1991)

homogeneity: the state of being uniform or similar especially in terms of extent when applied to statistics. Hence, homogeneity of variance means that the variances of two or more sets of scores are highly similar (or not statistically dissimilar). Homogeneity of regression similarly means that the regression coefficients between two variables are similar for different samples.

Some statistical techniques (e.g. the *t* test, the analysis of variance) are based on the assumption that the variances of the samples are homogeneous. There are tests for homogeneity of variances such as the *F* ratio test. If it is shown that the variances of two samples of scores are not homogeneous, then it is inappropriate to use the standard version of the unrelated *t* test. Another version is required which does not combine the two variances to estimate the population variance. This alternative version is available in a few textbooks and in a statistical package such as SPSS.

homogeneity of regression: the regression coefficients being similar or homogeneous in an analysis of covariance or multivariate analysis of covariance for the different categories or groups of an independent variable. The results of such an analysis are difficult to interpret if the regression coefficients are not homogeneous because this means that the relationship between the covariate and the dependent variable is not the same across the different groups. One of the assumptions of this type of analysis is that the regression coefficients need to be homogeneous. See also: **analysis of covariance**

homogeneity of variance: the variances of two or more groups of scores being similar or homogeneous. Analysis of variance assumes that the variances of the groups are similar. These variances are grouped together to form the error mean square or variance estimate. If the variance of one or more of the groups is considerably larger than that of the others, the larger variance will increase the size of the error variance estimate which will reduce the chance of the *F* ratio being significant. The means of the groups with the smaller variances may differ from each other but this difference is hidden by the inclusion of the groups with the larger variances in the error variance estimate. If the variances are dissimilar or heterogeneous, they may be made more similar by transforming the scores through procedures such as taking their square root. If there are only two groups, a *t* test may be used in which the variances are treated separately. See also: **analysis of variance**

Hotelling's trace criterion: a test used in multivariate statistical procedures such as canonical correlation, discriminant function analysis and multivariate analysis of variance to determine whether the means of the groups differ on a discriminant function or characteristic root. See also: **Wilks's lambda**
Tabachnick and Fidell (2001)

hypergeometric distribution: a probability distribution which is based on sampling without replacement where once a particular outcome has been selected it cannot be selected again.

hypothesis: a supposition or suggestion about the possible nature of the facts. It is generally regarded as the starting point for further investigation. Nevertheless, some research is purely exploratory without any formally expressed hypotheses. In such studies data are explored in order to formulate ideas about the nature of relationships.

It should be noted that the researcher's hypothesis and the statistical hypothesis are not necessarily the same thing. Statistical hypotheses are made up of the null hypothesis of no relationship between two variables and the alternative hypothesis of a relationship between the two variables. Failure of the null hypothesis merely indicates that it is more plausible that the relationship between the two variables is *not* the result of chance than it is the result of chance. Hence, the researcher's hypothesis may be preferred in these circumstances but there may be other equally plausible hypotheses which cannot be explained on the basis of chance either.

At the very least a hypothesis expresses a relationship between two variables such as 'Social support will be negatively related to depression' or 'Those with high support will be less depressed than those with low support.' It is usual to express the direction of the expected relationship between the variables as illustrated here because the researcher typically expects the variables to be related in a particular way. Hypotheses may be non-directional in the sense that a relationship between the variables is expected but the direction of that relationship is not specified. An example of such a hypothesis is 'Social support will be related to depression.' In some areas of research it may not be possible to specify the direction of the hypothesis. For example, people who are depressed may be more likely to seek and to receive support or they may be those individuals who have not received sufficient support. In such circumstances a non-directional hypothesis may be proposed.

With a true experimental design it is preferable to indicate the causal direction of the relationship between the two variables such as 'Greater social support will lead to less depression' if at all possible. See **exploratory data analysis; hypothesis testing**

hypothesis testing: generally speaking, this is a misnomer since much of what is described as hypothesis testing is really null-hypothesis testing. Essentially in null-hypothesis testing, the plausibility of the idea that there is zero difference or zero relationship between two measures is examined. If there is a reasonable likelihood that the trends in the obtained data could reflect a population in which there is no difference or no relationship, then the hypothesis of a relationship or a difference is rejected. That is, the findings are plausibly explained by the null hypothesis which suggests that chance factors satisfactorily account for the trends in the obtained data.

Research which deals with small samples (i.e. virtually all modern research) suffers from the risk of erroneous interpretations of any apparent trends in the data. This is because samples are intrinsically variable. Hypothesis testing generally refers to the Neyman–Pearson strategy for reducing the risk of faulty interpretations of data. Although this approach is generally the basis of much statistics teaching, it has always been a controversial area largely because it is taken to establish more than it actually does. In the Neyman–Pearson approach, the alternative hypothesis of a relationship between two variables is rigorously distinguished from the null hypothesis (which states that there is *no* relationship between the same two variables). The reason for concentrating on the null hypothesis is that by doing so some fairly simple inferences can be made about the population which the null hypothesis defines. So according to the null hypothesis, the population distribution should show no relationship between the two variables (by definition). Usually this means that their correlation is 0.00 or there is 0.00 difference between the sample means. It is assumed, however, that other information taken from the sample such as the standard deviation of the scores or any other statistic adequately reflects the characteristics of the population.

Hypothesis testing then works out the likely distribution of the characteristics of all samples taken from this theoretical population defined by the null hypothesis and aspects of the known sample(s) studied in the research. If the actual sample is very different from the population as defined by the null hypothesis then it is unlikely to come from the population as defined by the null hypothesis. (The conventional criterion is that samples which come in the extreme 5% are regarded as supporting the hypothesis; the middle 95% of samples support the null hypothesis.) If a sample does not come from the population as defined by the null hypothesis, then the sample must come from a population in which the null hypothesis is false. Hence, the more likely it is that the alternative hypothesis is true. In contrast, if the sample(s) studied in the research is typical of the vast majority of samples which would be obtained if the null hypothesis were true, then the more the actually obtained sample leads us to prefer the null hypothesis.

One difficulty with this lies in the way that the system imposes a rigid choice between the hypothesis and the null hypothesis based solely on a simple test of the likelihood that the data obtained could be explained away as a chance variation if the null hypothesis were true. Few decisions in real life would be made on the basis of such a limited number of considerations and the same is true in terms of research activity. The nature of scientific and intellectual endeavour is that ideas and findings are scrutinized and checked. Hence, the test of the null hypothesis is merely a stage in the process and quite a crude one at that – just answering the question of how well the findings fit the possibility that chance factors alone might be responsible. Of course, there are any number of other reasons why a hypothesis or null hypothesis may need consideration even after statistical significance testing has indicated a preference between the hypothesis and null hypothesis. For example, inadequate methodology including weak measurement may be responsible. See also: **significant**

I

icicle plot: one way of graphically presenting the results of a cluster analysis in which the variables to be clustered are placed horizontally with each variable separated by a column. The number of clusters is presented vertically, starting with the final cluster and ending with the first cluster. A symbol, such as X, is used to indicate the presence of a variable as well as the link between variables and clusters in the columns between the variables.

identification: the extent to which there is sufficient information to estimate the parameters of a model in structural equation modelling. In a just-identified model there is just enough information to identify or estimate all the parameters of the model. Such models always provide a perfect fit to the data. In an under-identified model there is not sufficient information to estimate all the parameters of the model. In an over-identified model there is more than enough information to identify all the parameters of the model and the fit of different over-identified models may be compared.

ill-conditioned matrix: see **determinant**

independent-samples t test: see **t test for unrelated samples**

independent variable: a variable thought to influence or affect another variable. This other variable is sometimes referred to as a dependent variable as its values are thought to depend on the corresponding value of the independent variable. See also: **analysis of variance; between-groups variance; dependent variable; multiple regression; regression equation**

inferential statistics: that branch of statistics which deals with generalization from samples to the population of values. It involves significance testing. The other main sort of statistics is descriptive statistics which involve the tabulation and organization of data in order to demonstrate their main characteristics.

infinity: basically the largest possible number. Infinity can by definition always be exceeded by adding one. It is usually symbolized as ∞. The concept is of little practical importance in routine statistical analyses.

integer: a whole number such as 1, 50 or 209. Fractions and decimals, then, are not integers.

interaction: a situation in which the influence of two or more variables does not operate in a simple additive pattern. This occurs when the relationship between two variables changes markedly when the values of another variable(s) are taken into account. For example, the relationship between gender and depression may vary according to marital status. Never married women may be less depressed than never married men whereas married women may be more depressed than married men. In other words, whether women are more depressed than men depends on the third variable of depression. It is not possible to account for depression on the basis of the separate influences of gender and marital status, in this case. Particular combinations of the values of the variable gender and of the variable marital status tend to produce especially high or especially low depression levels. So, for example, women are more depressed than men when they are married and less depressed when they have never been married. In this case there is an interaction between gender and marital status on depression.

The presence or absence of an interaction may be more readily understood if the relevant statistic for the different groups is displayed in a graph such as that in Figure I.1. In this figure marital status is represented as two points on the horizontal axis while gender is represented by two types of lines. Which variable is represented by the horizontal axis and which variable is represented by the lines does not matter. The vertical axis is used to represent the relevant statistic. In this case it is mean depression score. There is no interaction when the two lines in the graph are more or less parallel to one another. There is an interaction when the two lines are not parallel as is the case here. Whether this interaction is statistically significant depends on the appropriate statistical test being applied, which in this case would be a 2 × 2 analysis of variance. See also: **analysis of variance; factorial design; log–linear analysis; main effect; multiple regression**

intercept: in a simple or bivariate regression, the intercept is the point at which the regression line intercepts or cuts across the

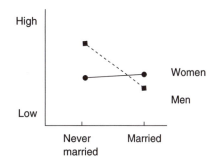

Figure I.1 *A group showing an interaction*

vertical axis when the value of the horizontal axis is zero. The vertical or *y* axis represents the criterion variable while the horizontal or *x* axis represents the predictor variable. The cut point is usually symbolized as *a* in the regression equation.

More generally, the intercept is the parameter in a regression equation which is the expected or predicted value of the criterion variable when all the predictor variables are zero. It is often referred to as the constant in a regression analysis. See also: **slope; unstandardized partial regression coefficient**

interjudge (coder, rater) reliability: the extent to which two or more judges, coders or raters are consistent or similar in the way they make judgements about identical information. These measures include Cohen's kappa coefficient for categorical variables and Ebel's intraclass correlation for noncategorical variables. For example, does teacher A rate the same children as intelligent as teacher B does? See also: **reliability**

internal consistency: the extent to which the items making up a scale are related to one another. The most widely used test is Cronbach's alpha reliability or α. Essentially, it should vary from 0 to 1. Measures with an alpha of 0.75 or more are considered to be internally consistent. The more similar the items, the higher alpha is likely to be. Scales

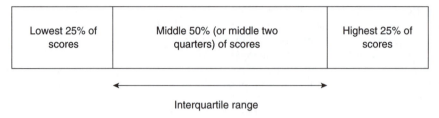

| Lowest 25% of scores | Middle 50% (or middle two quarters) of scores | Highest 25% of scores |

Interquartile range

Figure I.2   *Interquartile range*

with more items are also more likely to have higher alpha values. An alpha with a negative value may be obtained if items have not been appropriately recoded. For example, if high scores are being used to indicate greater anxiety but there are some items which have been worded so that high scores represent low anxiety, then these items need to be recoded. See also: **alpha reliability, Cronbach's**

internal validity: the extent to which a research design allows us to infer that a relationship between two variables is a causal one or that the absence of a relationship indicates the lack of a causal relationship. The implication is that the interpretation is valid in the context of the research situation but may simply not apply to non-research settings. That is, the findings have no external validity. See also: **randomization**

interquartile range: the range of the middle 50% of scores in a distribution. It is obtained by dividing the scores, in order, into four distinct quarters with equal numbers of scores in each quarter (Figure I.2). If the largest and smallest quarters are discarded, the interquartile range is the range of the remaining 50% of the scores. See also: **quartiles; range**

interval or **equal interval scale** or **level of measurement:** one of several different types of measurement scale – nominal, ordinal and ratio are the others. An interval scale is a

measure in which the adjacent intervals between the points of the scale are of equal extent and where the measure does not have an absolute zero point. It is thought that psychological characteristics such as intelligence or anxiety do not have an absolute zero point in the sense that no individual can be described as having no intelligence or no anxiety. A measure of such a construct may consist of a number of items. For example, a measure of anxiety may consist of 10 statements or questions which can be answered in terms of, say, 'Yes' or 'No'. If these two responses are coded as 0 or 1, the minimum score on this measure is 0 and the maximum 10. The intervals between the adjacent possible scores of this measure are of the same size, namely 1. So, the size of the interval between a score of 2 and a score of 3 is the same as that between a score of 3 and a score of 4. Let us assume that higher scores indicate higher anxiety. Because a score of 0 does not represent the absence of anxiety, we cannot say that a person who has a score of 8 is twice as anxious as someone with a score of 4. Measures which have an absolute zero point and equal intervals, such as age, are known as ratio levels of measurement or scales because their scores can be expressed as ratios. For example, someone aged 8 is twice as old as someone aged 4, the ratio being 8:4. It has been suggested that interval and ratio scales, unlike ordinal scales, can be analysed with parametric statistics. Some authors argue that in practice it is neither necessary nor possible to distinguish between ordinal, interval and ratio scales of measurement in many disciplines. Instead they propose a dichotomy between nominal measurement and score measurement. See also: **measurement; ratio level of measurement; score**

intervening variable: a variable thought to explain the relationship between two other variables in the sense that it is caused by one of them and causes the other. For example, there may be a relationship between gender and pay in that women are generally less well paid than men. Gender itself does not immediately affect payment but is likely to influence it through a series of intermediate or intervening variables such as personal, familial, institutional and societal expectations and practices. For instance, women may be less likely to be promoted which in turn leads to lower pay. Promotion in this case would be an intervening variable as it is thought to explain at least the relationship between gender and pay. Intervening variables are also known as mediating variables.

intraclass correlation, Ebel's: estimates the reliability of the ratings or scores of three or more judges. There are four different forms of this correlation which can be described and calculated with analysis of variance.

If the ratings of the judges are averaged for each case, the appropriate measure is the interjudge reliability of all the judges which can be determined as follows:

$$\frac{\text{between-subjects variance} - \text{error variance}}{\text{between-subjects variance}}$$

If only some of the cases were rated by all the judges while other cases were rated by one of the other judges, the appropriate measure is the interjudge reliability of an individual judge which is calculated as follows:

$$\frac{\text{between-subjects variance} - \text{error variance}}{\text{between-subjects variance} + [\text{error variance} \times (\text{number of judges} - 1)]}$$

The above two measures do not determine if a similar rating is given by the judges but only if the judges rank the cases in a similar way. For example, judge A may rate case A as 3 and case B as 6 while judge B may rate case A as 1 and case B as 5. While the rank order of the two judges is the same in that both judges rate case B as higher than case A, none

of their ratings are the same. Measures which take account of the similarity of the ratings as well as the similarity of their rank order may be known as interjudge agreement and include a measure of between-judges variance. There are two forms of this measure which correspond to the two forms of interjudge reliability.

If the ratings of the judges are averaged for each case, the appropriate measure is the interjudge agreement of all the judges which can be determined as follows:

$$\frac{\text{between-subjects variance} - \text{error variance} - \text{between-judges variance}}{\text{between-subjects variance}}$$

If only some of the cases were rated by all the judges while other cases were rated by one of the other judges, the appropriate measure is the interjudge reliability of an individual judge which is calculated as follows:

$$\frac{\text{between-subjects variance} - \text{error variance} - \text{between-judges variance}}{\text{between-subjects variance} + [(\text{error} + \text{between-judges variance}) \times (\text{number of judges} - 1)]}$$

Tinsley and Weiss (1975)

iteration: not all calculations can be fully computed but can only be approximated to give values that can be entered into the equations to make a better estimate. Iteration is the process of doing calculations which make better and better approximations to the optimal answer. Usually in iteration processes, the steps are repeated until there is little change in the estimated value over successive iterations. Where appropriate, computer programs allow the researcher to stipulate the minimum improvement over successive iterations at which the analysis ceases. Iteration is a common feature of factor analysis and log–linear analysis as prime examples.

Generally speaking, because of the computational labour involved, iterative processes are rarely calculated by hand in statistical analysis.

J

joint probability: the probability of having two distinct characteristics. So one can speak of the joint probability of being male *and* rich, for example.

just-identified model: a term used in structural equation modelling to describe a model in which there is just sufficient information to estimate all the parameters of the model. This model will provide a perfect fit to the data and will have no degrees of freedom. See also: **identification**

K

Kaiser's or Kaiser–Guttman criterion: a criterion used in factor analysis to determine the number of factors or components for consideration and possible rotation. It may be regarded as a minimal test of statistical significance of the factor. The criterion is that factors with eigenvalues of greater than 1.00 should be retained or selected for rotation. An eigenvalue is the amount of variance that is explained or accounted for by a factor. The maximum amount of variance that a variable in a factor analysis can have is 1.00. So, the criterion of 1.00 means that the factors selected will explain the variance equal to that of at least one variable on average. It has been suggested that this criterion may select too many factors when there are many variables and too few factors when there are few variables. Consequently, other criteria have been proposed for determining the optimum number of factors to be selected, such as Cattell's scree test. See also: **exploratory factor analysis**

kappa (κ) coefficient, Cohen's: an index of the agreement between two judges in categorizing information. It can be extended to apply to more than two judges. The proportion of agreement between two judges is assessed while taking into account the proportion of agreement that may simply occur by chance. It can be expressed in terms of the following formula:

$$\frac{\text{observed proportion of agreement} - \text{chance-expected proportion of agreement}}{1 - \text{chance-expected proportion of agreement}}$$

which can be re-expressed in frequencies:

$$\frac{\text{observed frequency of agreement} - \text{chance-expected frequency of agreement}}{\text{number of cases} - \text{chance-expected frequency of agreement}}$$

Kappa can vary from –1 to 1. A kappa of 0 indicates agreement equal to chance levels. A negative kappa indicates a less than chance agreement and a positive kappa a greater than chance agreement. A kappa of 0.70 or more is usually considered to be an acceptable level of agreement or reliability.
Siegal and Castellan (1988)

Kendall's partial rank correlation coefficient: a measure of partial association for ordinal variables in which one or more other ordinal variables may be partialled out or controlled. Its calculation is similar to that of partial correlation except that Kendall's rank correlation tau b is used instead of Pearson's correlation coefficient in the formula.

Kendall's rank correlation or tau (τ): a measure of the linear association between two ordinal variables. A negative value means that lower ranks on one variable are associated with higher ranks on the other variable. A positive value means that higher ranks on one variable go together with higher ranks on the other variable. A zero or close to zero value means that there is no linear association between the two variables.

There are three forms of this measure called tau *a*, tau *b* and tau *c*.

Tau *a* should be used when there are no ties or tied ranks. It can vary from –1 to 1. It can be calculated with the following formula:

$$\frac{\text{number of concordant pairs} - \text{number of discordant pairs}}{\text{total number of pairs}}$$

A concordant pair is one in which the first case is ranked higher than the second case, while a discordant pair is the reverse in which the first case is ranked lower than the second case.

Tau *b* should be used when there are ties or tied ranks. It can vary from –1 to 1 if the table of ranks is square and if none of the row and column totals are zero. It can be calculated with the following formula:

$$\frac{\text{number of concordant pairs} - \text{number of discordant pairs}}{\sqrt{\text{total number of pairs} - T_1} \times (\text{total number of pairs} - T_2)}$$

where T_1 and T_2 are the numbers of tied ranks for the two variables.

Tau *c* should be used when the table of ranks is rectangular rather than square as the value of tau *c* can come closer to –1 or 1. It can be worked out with the following formula:

$$\frac{(\text{number of concordant pairs} - \text{number of discordant pairs}) \times 2 \times S}{\text{number of cases}^2 \times (S - 1)}$$

where S is the number of columns or rows whichever is the smaller. See also: **correlation**
Siegal and Castellan (1988)

Kolmogorov–Smirnov test for one sample: a non-parametric test for determining whether the distribution of scores on an ordinal variable differs significantly from some theoretical distribution for that variable. For example, we could compare the distribution of the outcome of throwing a die 60 times with the theoretical expectation that it will land with 1 up 10 times, with 2 up 10 times, and so forth, if it is an unbiased die. The largest absolute difference between the cumulative frequency of the observed and the expected frequency of a value is used to determine whether the observed and expected distributions differ significantly.
Siegal and Castellan (1988)

Kolmogorov–Smirnov test for two samples: a non-parametric test which determines whether the distributions of scores on an ordinal variable differ significantly for two unrelated samples. The largest absolute difference between the cumulative frequency of the two samples for a particular score or value is used to determine whether the two distributions differ significantly.
Siegal and Castellan (1988)

Kruskal–Wallis one-way analysis of variance or *H* test: a non-parametric test used to determine whether the mean ranked scores for three or more unrelated samples differ significantly. The scores for all the samples are ranked together. If there is little difference between the sets of scores, their mean ranks should be similar. The statistic for this test is chi-square which can be corrected for the number of ties or tied scores.
Siegal and Castellan (1988)

kurtosis: a mathematically defined term which reflects the characteristics of the tails (extremes) of a frequency distribution. These

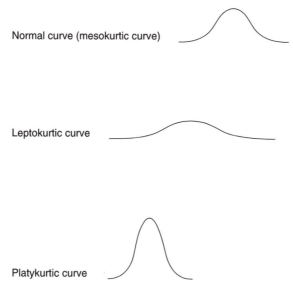

Normal curve (mesokurtic curve)

Leptokurtic curve

Platykurtic curve

Figure K.1   *Main types of kurtosis*

tails may range from the elongated to the relatively stubby (Figure K.1). The benchmark standard is the perfect normal distribution which has zero kurtosis by definition. Such a distribution is described as mesokurtic. In contrast, a shallower distribution with relatively elongated tails is known as a leptokurtic distribution. A steeper distribution with shorter, stubbier tails is described as platykurtic.

The mathematical formula for kurtosis is rarely calculated in many disciplines although discussion of the concept of kurtosis itself is relatively common. See also: **moment; standard error of kurtosis**

L

large-sample formulae: when sample sizes are small to moderate, there are readily available tables giving the critical values of many non-parametric or distribution-free tests of significance. These tables allow quick and easy significance testing especially as many of these statistics are easy to compute by hand. Unfortunately, because of the demands of space and practicality, most of these tables have a fairly low maximum sample size which reduces their usefulness in all circumstances. In circumstances where the tabulated values are insufficiently large, large-sample formulae may be employed which can be used to assess significance. Frequently, but not always, these large-sample formulae give values which approximate that of the z distribution. One disadvantage of the large-sample formulae is the need to rank large numbers of scores in some instances. This is a cumbersome procedure and likely to encourage mistakes when calculating by hand. An alternative approach in these circumstances would be to use the parametric equivalent of the non-parametric test since most of the limitations on the use of parametric tests become unimportant with large-sample sizes.

which either has had its unreliability adjusted for or is based on the variance shared by two or more other measures and thought to represent it (which is similar to adjusting for unreliability). Many theoretical constructs or variables cannot be directly measured. For example, intelligence is a theoretical construct which is measured by one's performance on various tasks which are thought to involve it. However, performance on these tasks may involve variables other than intelligence, such as one's experience or familiarity with those tasks. Consequently, the measures used to assess a theoretical variable may be a partial manifestation of that variable. Hence a distinction is made between a manifest variable and a latent variable. In a path diagram the latent variable may be signified by a circle or ellipse, while a manifest variable is depicted by a square or rectangle. The relationship between a latent variable and a manifest variable is presented by an arrow going from the latent variable to the manifest variable as the latent variable is thought partly to show or manifest itself in the way in which it is measured. See also: **canonical correlation; manifest variable**

latent root: another term for eigenvalue. See also: **eigenvalue, in factor analysis**

latent variable: the term used in structural equation modelling to refer to a variable

Latin Square: a display of rows and columns (i.e. a matrix or array) in which each symbol occurs just once in each column and each row. They are also known as 'magic squares'. An example of a magic square with three different elements is shown in Table L.1.

Table L.I   *A simple Latin Square*

CI	C3	C2
C2	CI	C3
C3	C2	CI

For our purposes, C1, C2 and C3 refer to different conditions of an experiment though this is not a requirement of Latin Squares.

The statistical application of Latin Squares is in correlated or repeated-measures designs. It is obvious from Table L.1 that the three symbols, C1, C2 and C3, are equally frequent and that with three symbols one needs three different orders to cover all possible orders (of the different conditions) effectively. So for a study with three experimental conditions, Table L.1 could be reformulated as Table L.2.

As can be seen, only three participants are required to run the entire study in terms of all of the possible orders of conditions being included. Of course, six participants would allow the basic design to be run twice, and nine participants would allow three complete versions of the design to run.

The advantage of the Latin Square is that it is a fully counterbalanced design so any order effects are cancelled out simply because all possible orders are run and in equal numbers. Unfortunately, this advantage can only be capitalized upon in certain circumstances. These are circumstances in which it is feasible to run individuals in a number of experimental conditions, where the logistics of handling a variety of conditions are not too complicated, where serving in more than one experimental condition does not produce a somewhat unconvincing

or even ludicrous scenario for the participants, and so forth.

It is also fairly obvious that the more conditions there are in an experimental design, the more complex will be the Latin Square. Hence, it is best considered only when the number of conditions is small. The Latin Square design effectively is a repeated-measures ANOVA design. The statistical analysis of such designs can be straightforward so long as it is assumed that the counterbalancing of orders is successful. If this is assumed, then the Latin Square design simplifies to a related analysis of variance comparing each of the conditions involved in the study. See also: **counterbalanced designs; order effect; within-subjects design**

least significant difference (LSD) test: see **Fisher's LSD (Least Significant Difference)** or **protected test**

least squares method in analysis of variance: see **Type II, classic experimental or least squares method in analysis of variance**

leptokurtic: a frequency distribution which has relatively elongated tails (i.e. extremes) compared with the normal distribution and is therefore a rather flat shallow distribution of values. A good example of a leptokurtic frequency distribution is the *t* distribution

Table L.2   *An experimental design based on the Latin Square*

	Participant I	Participant 2	Participant 3
Condition run first	CI	C3	C2
Condition run second	C2	CI	C3
Condition run third	C3	C2	CI

and especially for small numbers of degrees of freedom. Although this distribution is the same as the normal distribution (i.e. z distribution) for very large numbers of degrees of freedom, in general it is flatter and more leptokurtic than the normal distribution. See also: **kurtosis**

levels of treatment: the different conditions or groups that make up an independent variable in a research design and its analysis. A factor or independent variable which has two conditions may be described as having two levels of treatment. It is a term normally applied in the context of research using experimental designs.

Levene's test for equality of related variances: a test of whether the variances of two or more related samples are equal (i.e. homogeneous or similar). This is a requirement for statistics which combine the variances from several samples to give a 'better estimate' of population characteristics. The assumption that these variances do not differ is an assumption of the repeated-measures analysis of variance, for example, which is used to determine whether the means of two or more related samples differ. Of course, the test may be used in any circumstances where one wishes to test whether variances differ. For the Levene test, the absolute difference between the score in a group and the mean score for that group is calculated for all the scores. A single-factor repeated-measures analysis of variance is carried out on these absolute difference scores. If the F ratio for this single factor is significant, this means that two or more of the variances differ significantly from each other. If the assumption that the variances are equal needs to be met, it may be possible to do this by transforming the scores using, for example, their square root or logarithm. This is largely a matter of trial and error until a transformation is found which results in equal variances for the sets of transformed scores. See also: **analysis of variance; heterogeneity**

Levene's test for equality of unrelated variances: one applies this test when dealing with unrelated data from two or more different samples. It tests whether two or more samples of scores have significantly unequal (heterogeneous or dissimilar) variances. Usually this assumption of equality is required in order to combine two or more variance estimates to form a 'better' estimate of the population characteristics. The most common application of the Levene test is in the unrelated analysis of variance where the variances of the different samples should not be significantly different. However, it is equally appropriate to test the hypothesis that two variances differ using this test in more general circumstances. For the Levene test, the absolute difference between the score in a group and the mean score for that group is calculated for all the scores. A single-factor analysis of variance is carried out on these absolute difference scores. If the F ratio for this single factor is significant, this means that two or more of the variances differ significantly from each other. If the assumption that the variances are equal needs to be met, it may be possible to achieve equal variances by transforming all of the scores using, for example, their square root or logarithm. This is normally a matter of trying out a variety of transformations until the desired equality of variances is achieved. There is no guarantee that such a transformation will be found.

likelihood ratio chi-square: a version of chi-square which utilizes natural logarithms. It is different in some respects from the more familiar form which should be known in full as Pearson chi-square (though both were developed by Karl Pearson). It is useful where the components of an analysis are to be separated out since this form of chi-square allows accurate addition and subtraction of components. Because of its reliance on natural logarithms, likelihood ratio chi-square is a little more difficult to compute. Apart from its role in log–linear analysis, there is nothing to be gained by using likelihood ratio chi-square in general. With calculations based on large frequencies, numerically the two differ very little anyway.

The formula for the likelihood ratio chi-square involves the observed and expected frequencies which are common to the regular chi-square test. It also involves natural logarithms, which may be obtained from tables, scientific calculators or statistical software:

$$2 \times \sum \text{natural logarithm of } \frac{\text{observed frequency}}{\text{expected frequency}} \times \text{observed frequency}$$

It is difficult to imagine the circumstances in which this will be calculated by hand. In its commonest application in statistics (log–linear analysis), the computations are too repetitive and complex to calculate without the aid of a computer.

Likert scaling: the name given to the method of constructing measurement scales involving a series of statements to which the respondent is asked to respond on an ordered scale such as

We should throw away the key for convicted sex offenders.

Strongly disagree	Disagree	Neither	Agree	Strongly agree

These response alternatives from strongly disagree to strongly agree are then scored 1 to 5, 1 to 7, or 1 to 9 according to the number of points. The numerical scale is, in fact, arbitrary but seems to work well in practice and it is conventional to score the responses using the above system. Likert scales are extremely familiar and have the big advantage that the questions can simply be summed to obtain a score. (Though it is probably better to transform the scores to standard scores in order to do so.)

The introduction of Likert scaling simplified an earlier type of scale developed by Thurstone. The latter was cumbersome as questions/items had to be developed which covered the whole range of possible attitudes using subtly worded questions/items.

line of best fit: see **regression line**

linear association or **relationship:** see **curvilinear relationship**

LISREL: an abbreviation for *li*near *rel*ationships. It is one of several computer programs for carrying out structural equation modelling. Information about LISREL can be found at the following website:
http://www.ssicentral.com/lisrel/mainlis.htm
  See also: **structural equation modelling**

listwise deletion: a keyword used in some statistical packages such as SPSS to confine an analysis to those cases for which there are no missing values for all the variables listed for that analysis. When this is done where there are some missing values, the number of cases will be the same for all the analyses. Suppose, for example, we want to correlate the three variables of job satisfaction, income and age in a sample of 60 people and that 3 cases have missing data for income and a different set of 4 cases have missing data for age. All 7 cases will be omitted from the analysis. So when using the listwise procedure all the correlations will be based on 53 cases as this number of cases has no missing data on all three variables. An alternative procedure of analysis is to provide correlations for those cases which do not have missing values for those variables. The keyword for this procedure is pairwise deletion in a statistical package such as SPSS. In this case, the correlations will be based on different numbers of cases. The correlation between job satisfaction and income will be based on 57 cases, that between job satisfaction and age on 56 cases and that between income and age on 53 cases. See also: **missing values; pairwise deletion**

loading: see **exploratory factor analysis; factor, in factor analysis**

log likelihood: determines whether the predictor variables included in a model provide a good fit to the data. It is usually multiplied by −2 so that it takes the approximate form of a chi-square distribution. A perfect fit is indicated by 0 while bigger values signify progressively poorer fits. Because the −2 log likelihood will be bigger the larger the sample, the size of the sample is controlled by subtracting the −2 log likelihood value of a model containing the predictors from the −2 log likelihood value of a model not containing any predictors.

The log likelihood is the sum of the probabilities associated with the predicted and actual outcome for each case which can be calculated with the following formula:

(outcome × log of predicted probability) + [(1 − outcome) × log of (1 − predicted probability)]

See also: **logistic regression**

log–linear analysis: conceptually, this may be regarded as an extension of the Pearson chi-square test to cross-tabulation or contingency tables involving three or more variables. It is recommended that the chi-square test be studied in detail prior to attempting the more complex log–linear analysis. Like chi-square, log–linear analysis involves nominal or category (or categorical) data (i.e. frequency counts). However, log–linear analysis can be used for score data if the scores are subdivided into a small number of divisions (e.g. 1–5, 6–10, 11–15, etc.).

Table L.3 contains a three-variable cross-tabulation table for purposes of illustration. This cannot be analysed properly using chi-square because the table has too many dimensions, though researchers in the past commonly would carry out numerous smaller two-variable chi-squares derived from this sort of table. Unfortunately, such an

Table L.3   *A three-variable contingency table*

	Male	Female	Male	Female
	Convicted of crime		Never convicted of crime	
Rural upbringing	29	9	79	65
Urban upbringing	50	17	140	212

approach cannot fully analyse the data no matter how thoroughly applied. There is no simple way of calculating the expected frequencies for three or more variables. In log–linear analysis, the objective is to find the model which best fits the empirical data. The fit of the model to the empirical data is assessed by using chi-square (usually likelihood ratio chi-square). This version of the chi-square formula has the major advantage that the values of chi-square it provides may be added or subtracted directly without introducing error.

Significant values of chi-square mean that the data depart from the expectations of the model. This indicates that the model has a poor fit to the data. A non-significant value of chi-square means that the model and the data fit very well. In log–linear analysis, what this means is that the cross-tabulated frequencies are compared with the expected frequencies based on the selected model (selected combination of main effects and interactions). The closer the actual frequencies are to the expected (modelled) frequencies, the better the model is.

The models created in log–linear analysis are based on the following components:

1   The overall mean frequency (sometimes known as the constant). This would be the equal-frequencies model. Obviously if all of the individual cell means are the same as the overall mean, then we would need to go no further in the analysis since the equal-frequencies model applies.
2   The main effects (i.e. the extent to which the frequencies on any variable depart from equality). A gender main effect would simply mean that there are different

numbers of males and females in the analysis. As such, in much research main effects are of little interest, though in other contexts the main effects are important. For example, if it were found that there was a main effect of sex in a study of an anti-abortion pressure group, this might be a finding of interest as it would imply either more men in the group or more women in the group.

3 Two-way interactions – combinations of two variables (by collapsing the categories or cells for all other variables) which show larger or smaller frequencies which can be explained by the influence of the main effects operating separately.

4 Higher order interactions (what they are depends on the number of variables under consideration). In this example, the highest order interaction would be gender × rural × prison.

5 The saturated model – this is simply the sum of all the above possible components. It is always a perfect fit to the data by definition since it contains all of the components of the table. In log–linear analysis, the strategy is often to start with the saturated model and then remove the lower levels (the interactions and then the main effects) in turn to see whether removing the component actually makes a difference to the fit of the model. For example, if taking away all of the highest order interactions makes no difference to the data's fit to the model, then the interactions can be safely dropped from the model as they are adding nothing to the fit. Generally the strategy is to drop a whole level at a time to see if it makes a difference. So three-way interactions would be eliminated as a whole before going on to see which ones made the difference if a difference was found.

Log–linear analysis involves heuristic methods of calculations which are only possible using computers in practice since they involve numerous approximations towards the answer until the approximation improves only minutely. The difficulty is that the interactions cannot be calculated directly. One aspect of the calculation which can be understood without too much mathematical

knowledge is the expected frequencies for different components of a log–linear model. These are displayed in computer printouts of log–linear analysis.

Interaction in log–linear analysis is often compared with interactions in ANOVA. The key difference that needs to be considered, though, is that the frequencies in the various cells are being predicted by the model (or pattern of independent variables) whereas in ANOVA it is the means within the cells on the dependent variable which are being predicted by the model. So in log–linear analysis, an interaction between sex and type of accommodation (i.e. owned versus rented) simply indicates that, say, there are more males living in rented accommodation than could be accounted for simply on the basis of the proportion of people in rented accommodation and the number of males in the study. See also: **hierarchical** or **sequential entry; iteration; logarithm; natural** or **Napierian logarithm; stepwise entry**

Cramer (2003)

log of the odds: see **logit**

logarithm: to understand logarithms, one needs also to understand what an exponent is, since a logarithm is basically an exponent. Probably the most familiar exponents are numbers like 2^2, 3^2, 4^2, etc. In other words, the squared ^{2} symbol is an exponent as obviously a cube would also be as in 2^3. The squared sign is an instruction to multiply (raise) the first number by itself a number of times: 2^2 means $2 \times 2 = 4$, 2^3 means $2 \times 2 \times 2 = 8$.

The number which is raised by the exponent is called the base. So 2 is the base in 2^2 or 2^3 or 2^4, while 5 is the base in 5^2 or 5^3 or 5^4. The logarithm of any number is given by a simple formula in which the base number is represented by the symbol b, the logarithm may be represented by the symbol e (for exponent), and the number under consideration is given the symbol x:

$$x = b^e$$

So a logarithm of a number is simply the exponent of a given base (which is of one's own choosing such as 10, 2, 5, etc.) which gives that number. One regularly used base for logarithms is 10. So the logarithm for the base 10 is the value of the exponent (e) for 10 which equals our chosen number. Let's suppose that we want the logarithm of the number 100 for the base 10. What we are actually seeking is the exponent of 10 which gives the number 100:

$$10^e = 100$$

In other words, the logarithm for 100 is 2 simply because 10 to the power of 2 (i.e. 10^2 or 10×10) equals 100. Actually the logarithm would look more like other logarithms if we write it out in full as 2.000.

Logarithm tables (especially to the base 10) are readily available although their commonest use has rather declined with the advent of electronic calculators and computers – that was a simple, speedy means of multiplying numbers by adding together two logarithms. However, students will come across them in statistics in two forms:

1   In log–linear analysis, which involves natural logarithms in the computation of the likelihood ratio chi-square. The base in natural logarithms is 2.718 (to three decimal places).
2   In transformations of scores especially when the unmodified scores tend to violate the assumptions of parametric tests. Logarithms are used in this situation since it would radically alter the scale. So, the logarithm to the base 10 for the number 100 is 2.000, the logarithm of 1000 = 3.000 and the logarithm of 10,000 = 4.000. In other words, although 1000 is 10 times as large as the number 100, the logarithmic value of 1000 is 3.000 compared with 2.000 for the logarithm of 100. That is, by using logarithms it is possible to make large scores proportionally much less. So basically by putting scores on a logarithmic scale the extreme scores tend to get compacted to be relatively closer to what were much smaller scores on the untransformed measure. Logarithms

Table L.4   *Logarithms to the base 10*

Number	Logarithm
1	0.00
2	0.30
3	0.48
4	0.60
5	0.70
6	0.78
7	0.85
8	0.90
9	0.95
10	1.00

to any base could be used if they produce a distribution of the data appropriate for the statistical analysis in question. For example, logarithms could be used in some circumstances in order to make a more symmetrical distribution of scores. See also: **Fisher's z transformation; natural or Napierian logarithm; transformations**

logarithmic scale: because the logarithm of numbers increases relatively slowly to the numbers that they represent, logarithms can be used to adjust or modify scores so that they meet the requirements of particular statistical techniques better. Thus, expressed as one form of logarithm (to the base 10), the numbers 1 to 10 can be expressed as logarithms as shown in Table L.4.

In other words, the difference between 1 and 10 on a numerical scale is 9 whereas it is 1.00 on a logarithmic scale.

By using such a logarithmic transformation, it is sometimes possible to make the characteristics of one's data fit better the assumptions of the statistical technique. For example, it may be possible to equate the variances of two sets of scores using the logarithmic transformation. It is not a very common procedure among modern researchers though it is fairly readily implemented on modern computer packages such as SPSS.

logarithmic transformation: see **transformations**

logged odds: see **logit**

Table L.5 *A binary criterion and predictor*

	Cancer	No cancer
Smokers	40	20
Non-smokers	10	30

logistic (and logit) regression: a tech-nique (logit regression is very similar to but not identical with logistic regression) used to determine which predictor variables are most strongly and significantly associated with the probability of a particular category in the cri-terion variable occurring. The criterion vari-able can be a dichotomous or binary variable comprising only two categories or it can be a polychotomous, polytomous or multinomial variable having three or more categories. The term binary or binomial may be used to describe a logistic regression having a binary criterion (dependent variable) and the term multinomial to describe one having a crite-rion with more than two categories. As in multiple regression, the predictors can be entered in a single step, in a hierarchical or sequential fashion or according to some other analytic criterion.

Because events either occur or do not occur, logistic regression assumes that the relationship between the predictors and the criterion is S-shaped or sigmoidal rather than linear. This means that the change in a pre-dictor will have the biggest effect at the mid-point of 0.5 of the probability of a category occurring, which is where the probability of the category occurring is the same as the probability of it not occurring. It will have least effect towards the probability of 0 and 1 of the category occurring. This change is expressed as a logit or the natural logarithm of the odds.

The unstandardized logistic regression coefficient is the change in the logit of the category for every change of 1 unit in the predictor variable. For example, an unstand-ardized logistic regression coefficient of 0.693 means that for every change of 1 unit in the predictor there is a change of 0.693 in the logit of the category. To convert the logit into the estimated odds ratio, we raise or exponenti-ate the value of 2.718 to the power of the logit, which in this case gives an odds ratio of 2.00 ($2.718^{0.693} = 2.00$). Thus, the odds change by 2.00 for every change of 1 unit in the pre-dictor. In other words, we multiply the odds

by 2.00 for every change of 1 unit in the predictor. The operation of raising a constant such as 2.718 to a particular power such as the unstandardized logistic regression coeffi-cient is called exponentiation and may be written as exp (symbol for the unstandard-ized logistic regression coefficient).

It is easiest to demonstrate the meaning of a change in the odds with one predictor con-taining only two categories. Suppose we were interested in determining the associa-tion between smoking and cancer for the data shown in Table L.5 where the criterion also consists of only two categories.

The odds of a smoker having cancer are 2 ($40/20 = 2.00$) while the odds of a non-smoker having cancer are 0.33 ($10/30 = 0.33$). The change in the odds of smokers and non-smokers having cancer is about 6.00 which is the odds ratio ($2.00/0.33 = 6.06$). In other words, smok-ers are six times more likely to get cancer than non-smokers. An odds ratio is a measure of association between two variables. A ratio of 1 means that there is no association between two variables, a ratio of less than 1 a negative or inverse relationship and a ratio of more than 1 a positive or direct relationship.

With a binary predictor and multinomial criterion the change in the odds is expressed in terms of each of the categories and the last category. So, for the data in Table L.6, the odds of being diagnosed as anxious are com-pared with the odds of being diagnosed as normal, while the odds of being diagnosed as depressed are also compared with the odds of being diagnosed as normal. The odds of being diagnosed as anxious rather than as normal for men are 0.40 ($20/50 = 0.40$) and for women are 0.25 ($10/40 = 0.25$). So, the odds ratio is 1.60 ($0.40/0.25 = 1.60$). Men are 1.6 times more likely to be diagnosed as anx-ious than women. The odds of being diag-nosed as depressed rather than as normal for men are 0.20 ($10/50 = 0.20$) and for women

Table L.6 *A multinomial criterion and binary predictor*

	Anxious	Depressed	Normal
Men	20	10	50
Women	10	30	40

are 0.75 (30/40 = 0.75). The odds ratio is about 0.27 (0.20/0.75 = 0.267). It is easier to understand this odds ratio if it had been expressed the other way around. That is, women are about 3.75 times more likely to be diagnosed as depressed than men (0.75/0.20 = 3.75).

The extent to which the predictors in a model provide a good fit to the data can be tested by the log likelihood, which is usually multiplied by −2 so that it takes the form of a chi-square distribution. The difference in the −2 log likelihood between the model with the predictor and without it can be tested for significance with the chi-square test with 1 degree of freedom. The smaller this difference is, the more likely it is that there is no difference between the two models and so the less likely that adding the predictor improves the fit to the data. See also: **hierarchical** or **sequential entry; stepwise entry**

Cramer (2003); Pampel (2000)

logit, logged odds or **log of the odds:** the natural logarithm of the odds. It reflects the probability of an event occurring. It varies from about −9.21, which is the 0.0001 probability that an event will occur, to about 9.21, which is the 0.9999 probability that an event will occur. It also indicates the odds of an event occurring. A negative logit means that the odds are against the event occurring, a positive logit that the odds favour the event occurring and a zero logit that the odds are even. A logit of about −9.21 means that the odds of the event occurring are about 0.0001 (or very low). A logit of 0 means that the odds of the event occurring are 1 or equal. A logit of about 9.21 means that the odds of the event occurring are 9999 (or very high).

Logits are turned to probabilities using a two-stage process. Stage 1 is to convert the logit into odds using whatever tables or calculators one has which relate natural logarithms to their numerical values. Such resources may not be easy to find. Stage 2 is to turn the odds into a probability using the formula below:

$$\text{probability of an event} = \frac{2.718}{1 + 2.718} = \frac{\text{odds}}{1 + \text{odds}}$$

Fortunately, there is rarely any reason to do this in practice as the information is readily available from computer output. See **logistic regression; natural logarithm**

longitudinal design or **study:** tests the same individuals on two or more occasions or waves. One advantage of a panel study is that it enables whether a variable changes from one occasion to another for that group of individuals.

Baltes and Nesselroade (1979)

LSD test: see **Fisher's LSD (Least Significant Difference)** or **protected test**

M

main effect: the influence of a variable acting on its own or independently. It is to be contrasted with an interaction effect which is the conjoint influence of two or more variables which produce greater effects on the data than the main effects would in a summative fashion. See also: **analysis of variance; within-groups variance**

MANCOVA: see **multivariate analysis of covariance**

manifest variable: a term used in structural equation modelling to describe a variable where the measure of that variable represents that variable. For example, an IQ score may be used as a direct measure of the theoretical construct of intelligence. However, a measure, like an IQ score, is often not a perfect representation of the theoretical construct as it may not be totally reliable and may assess other variables as well. For example, an IQ score may also measure knowledge in particular areas. Consequently, a manifest variable is distinguished from a latent variable which may take some account of the unreliability of the manifest variable or which may be based on the variance shared by two or more manifest variables such as separate measures of intelligence or subcomponents of an IQ test. In a path diagram, the manifest variable may be signified by a square or rectangle, while a latent variable is depicted by a circle or ellipse. The relationship between a latent variable and a manifest variable is presented by an arrow going from the latent variable to the manifest variable as the latent variable is thought partly to show or manifest itself in the way in which it is measured.

manipulated variable: a variable which has been deliberately manipulated or varied to determine its effect on one or more other variables. For example, if we are interested in the effects of alcohol on performance, we may manipulate or vary the amount of alcohol consumed by different groups of participants in a between-subjects design or on different occasions in a within-subjects design. If all other factors are held constant apart from the manipulated variable and if we find that there are statistical differences in the measured effects of that manipulated variable, we can be more certain that the different effects were due to the manipulation of that variable.

Mann–Whitney *U* test: a non-parametric test used to determine whether scores from two unrelated samples differ significantly from one another. It tests whether the number of times scores from one sample are ranked higher than scores from the other sample when the scores for both samples have been ranked in a single sample. If the two sets of scores are similar, the number of times this happens should be similar for the two groups. If the samples are 20 or less, the statistical significance of the smaller U value is used. If the samples are greater than 20, the U value is converted into a z value. The value of z has to be 1.96 or more to be statistically significant at the 0.05 two-tailed level or 1.65 or more at the 0.05 one-tailed level.

Howitt and Cramer (2000)

MANOVA: see **multivariate analysis of variance**

margin of error: the range of means (or any other statistic) which are reasonably likely possibilities for the population value. This is normally expressed as the confidence interval.

marginal totals: the total frequency of cases in the rows or columns of a contingency or cross-tabulation table.

matched-samples *t* test: see **t test for related samples**

matching: usually the process of selecting sets (pairs, trios, etc.,) of participants or cases to be similar in essential respects. In research, one of the major problems is the variation between people or cases over which the researcher has no control. Potentially, all sorts of variation between people and cases may affect the outcome of research, for example gender, age, social status, IQ and many other factors. There is the possibility that these factors are unequally distributed between the conditions of the independent variable and so spuriously appear to be influencing scores

on the dependent variable. For example, if one measured examination achievement in two different types of schools, education achievement would be the dependent variable and the different types of schools different values of the independent variable. It is known that girls are more successful educationally. Hence, if there were more girls in one type of school than the other, then we would expect that the type of school with the most girls would tend to appear to be the most educationally successful. This is because of the disproportionate number of girls, not that one type of school is superior educationally, though it might be.

Matching actually only makes a difference to the outcome if one matches on variables which are correlated with the dependent variable. The matching variable also needs to be correlated with the independent variable in the sense that there would have to be a disproportionate number in one condition compared with the other. Sometimes it is known from previous empirical research that there are variables which correlate with both the independent variable and the dependent variable. More commonly, the researcher may simply feel that such matching is important on a number of possibly confounding variables.

The process of matching involves identifying a group of participants about which one has some information. Imagine that it is decided that gender (male versus female) and social class (working-class versus middle-class parents) differences might affect the outcome of your study which consists of two conditions. Matching would entail the following steps:

- Finding from the list two participants who are both male and working class.
- One member of the pair will be in one condition of the independent variable, the other will be in the other condition of the independent variable. If this is an experiment, they will be allocated to the conditions randomly.
- The process would normally be repeated for the other combinations. That is, one selects a pair of two female working-class participants, then a pair of two male

middle-class participants, and then a pair of two female middle-class participants. Then more matched pairs could be selected as necessary.

Of course, matching in this way is time consuming and may not always be practicable or desirable. Because it reduces the uncontrolled variation between groups in a study, it potentially has the advantage of allowing the use of smaller sample sizes. So where there are potentially few appropriate participants available, matching may be a desirable procedure.

In an ideal study, participants in the different conditions ought to be matched in terms of as many characteristics as possible or practicable. One way of achieving this is to use pairs of identical twins since these are alike in a large number of biological, social and psychological respects. They are genetically identical and brought up in similar environments, for example. Another possibility is to use participants as their own control. That is, use the same participants in both (or more) conditions of the study if practicable. If counterbalancing is applied, this will often effectively match on a wide range of variables. The terms correlated subjects design or related subjects design are virtually synonymous with matched subjects designs.

Matching can be positively recommended in circumstances in which there are positive time and economic or other practical advantages to be gained by using relatively small samples. While it can be used to control for the influence of unwanted variables on the data, it can present its own problems. In particular, participants may have to be rejected simply because they do not match others or because the researcher has already found enough of that matched set of individuals. Furthermore, matching has lost some of its usefulness with the advent of increasingly powerful methods of statistical control aided by modern computers. These allow many variables to be controlled for whereas most forms of matching (except twins and own-controls) can cope with only a small number of matching variables before they become unwieldy and unmanageable.

matrix: a rectangle of numbers or symbols that represent numbers. It consists of one or more rows and one or more columns. It is usual to refer to the rows first. So, a 2×3 matrix consists of two rows and three columns. The numbers or symbols in a matrix are called elements. The position of an element is represented by a symbol and two numbers in subscripts. The first number refers to the row and the second to the column in which the element is. So, $a_{2,3}$ refers to the element in the second row of the third column. The position of an element may be referred to more generally by its symbol and the two subscripts, i and j, where i refers to the row and j to the column.

matrix algebra: rules for transforming matrices such as adding or subtracting them. It is used for calculating more complicated statistical procedures such as factor analysis, multiple regression and structural equation modelling. For example, the following two matrices, **A** and **B**, may be added together to form a third matrix, **C**:

$$\mathbf{A} \quad + \quad \mathbf{B} \quad = \quad \mathbf{C}$$
$$\begin{bmatrix} 2 & 4 \\ 3 & 5 \end{bmatrix} + \begin{bmatrix} 1 & 3 \\ 5 & 2 \end{bmatrix} = \begin{bmatrix} 3 & 7 \\ 8 & 7 \end{bmatrix}$$

Mauchly's test of sphericity: like many tests, the analysis of variance makes certain assumptions about the data used. Violations of these assumptions tend to affect the value of the test adversely. One assumption is that the variances of each of the cells should be more or less equal (exactly equal is a practical impossibility). In repeated-measures designs, it is also necessary that the covariances of the differences between each condition are equal. That is, subtract condition A from condition B, condition A from condition C etc., and calculate the covariance of these difference scores until all possibilities are exhausted. The covariances of all of the differences between conditions should be equal. If not, then adjustments need to be made to the analysis such as finding a test which does not rely on these assumptions (e.g. a multivariate analysis of variance is not based on these assumptions and there are non-parametric versions of the related ANOVA). Alternatively, there are adjustments which apply directly to the ANOVA calculation as indicated below.

Put another way, Mauchly's test of sphericity determines whether the variance–covariance matrix in a repeated-measures analysis of variance is spherical or circular, which means that it is a scalar multiple of an identity matrix. An identity or spherical matrix has diagonal elements of 1 and off-diagonal elements of 0. If the assumption of sphericity or circularity is not met, the F ratio is more likely to be statistically significant. There are several tests which adjust this bias by changing the degrees of freedom for the F ratio – that is, making the ANOVA less significant. Examples of such adjustments include the Greenhouse–Geisser correction and the Huynh–Feldt correction.

maximum likelihood estimation, method or **principle:** one criterion for estimating a parameter of a population of values such as the mean value. It is the value that is the most likely given the data from a sample and certain assumptions about the distribution of those values. This method is widely used in structural equation modelling. To give a very simple example of this principle, suppose that we wanted to find out what the probability or likelihood was of a coin turning up heads. We had two hypotheses. The first was that the coin was unbiased and so would turn up heads 0.50 of the time. The second was that the coin was biased towards heads and would turn up heads 0.60 of the time. Suppose that we tossed a coin three times and it landed heads, tails and heads in that order. As the tosses are independent, the joint probability of these three events is the product of their individual probabilities. So the joint probability of these three events for the first hypothesis of the coin being biased is 0.125 $(0.5 \times 0.5 \times 0.5 = 0.125)$. The joint probability of these three events for the

second hypothesis of the coin being biased towards heads is 0.144 $(0.6 \times 0.6 \times 0.4 = 0.144)$. As the probability of the outcome for the biased coin is greater than that for the unbiased coin, the maximum likelihood estimate is 0.60. If we had no hypotheses about the probability of the coin turning up heads, then the maximum likelihood estimate would be the observed probability which is 0.67 $(2/3 = 0.67)$.

Hays (1994)

McNemar test for the significance of changes: a simple means of analysing simple related nominal designs in which participants are classified into one of two categories on two successive occasions. Typically, it is used to assess whether there has been change over time. As such, one measure can be described as the 'before' measure (which is divided into two categories) and the second measure is the 'after' measure. Consider the readership of the two newspapers *The London Globe* and *The London Tribune*. A sample of readers of these newspapers is collected. Imagine that then there is a promotional campaign to sell *The London Tribune*. The question is whether the campaign is effective. One research strategy would be to study the sample again after the campaign. One would expect that some readers of *The London Globe* prior to the campaign will change to reading *The London Tribune* after the campaign. Some readers of *The London Tribune* before the campaign will change to reading *The London Globe* after the campaign. Of course, there will be *Tribune* readers who continue to be *Tribune* readers after the campaign. Similarly, there will be *Globe* readers prior to the campaign who continue to be *Globe* readers after the campaign. If the campaign works, we would expect more readers to shift to the *Tribune* after the campaign than shift to the *Globe* after the campaign (see Table M.1).

In the test, those who stick with the same newspaper are discarded. The locus of interest is in those who switch newspapers – that is, the 6 who were *Globe* readers but read the *Tribune* after the campaign, and the 22 who read the *Tribune* before the campaign but

Table M.I   *Pre-test–post-test design*

		After campaign	
		Tribune	*Globe*
Before campaign	*Tribune*	19	22
	Globe	6	19

switched to the *Globe* after the campaign. If the campaign had *no* effect, we would expect that the switchers would be equally represented for the *Tribune* and the *Globe*. The more unequal the numbers switching to the *Tribune* and the *Globe*, the more likely that the campaign is having an effect. Since we expect half switching in each direction if the null hypothesis is true, then we know the expected frequencies to enter the data into a one-sample chi-square test. The data for the analysis together with the expected frequencies are given in Table M.2.

These observed and expected frequencies may then be entered into the one-sample chi-square formula:

$$\text{chi-square} = \sum \frac{(\text{observed} - \text{expected})^2}{\text{expected}}$$

$$= \frac{(22 - 14)^2}{14} + \frac{(6 - 14)^2}{14}$$

$$= \frac{8^2}{14} + \frac{-8^2}{14} = \frac{64}{14} + \frac{64}{14}$$

$$= 4.571 + 4.571 = 9.14$$

With 1 degree of freedom (always) then this is statistically significant at the 0.01 level. Hence, the changers in newspaper readership are predominantly from the *Tribune* to the *Globe*. This suggests that the campaign is counterproductive as the *Tribune* is losing readers.

mean (M): see **average; mean (M), arithmetic**

mean (M), arithmetic: the sum of scores divided by the number of scores. So the mean of 2 and 4 is the sum of 6 divided by 2 scores which gives a mean of 3.00. The mean is the central point in a set of scores in that the sum of absolute deviations (i.e. ignoring the negative signs) of scores above the mean (4 − 3.00 = 1.00) is equal to the sum of absolute deviations of scores below the mean (2 − 3.00 = − 1.00). The mean is sometimes called the arithmetic mean to distinguish it from other forms of mean such as the harmonic mean or geometric mean. Because it is the most common form of mean it is usually simply called the mean. It is sometimes abbreviated as *M* with or without a bar over it.

mean deviation: the mean of the absolute deviations of the scores from the mean. For example, the mean deviation of the scores of 2 and 6 is the sum of their absolute deviations from their mean of 3.00 which is 2.00 [(4 − 3.00 = 1.00) + (2 − 3.00 = −1.00) = 2.00] divided by the number of absolute deviations which is 2. The mean deviation of these two deviations is 1.00 (2.00/2 = 1.00). The mean deviation is not very widely used in statistics simply because the related concept of standard deviation is far more useful in practice.

Table M.2   *Table M.I recast in terms of changing*

	Frequency of changers	Expected frequency (half of all who change newspapers in either direction)
From the *Tribune* to the *Globe*	22	14
From the *Globe* to the *Tribune*	6	14

mean score: arithmetic mean of a set of scores. See also: **coefficient of variation**

mean square (MS): a measure of the estimated population variance in analysis of variance. It is used to form the F ratio which determines whether two variance estimates differ significantly. The mean square is the sum of squares (or squared deviations) divided by the degrees of freedom. See also: **between-groups variance**

measurement: the act of classification of observations is central to research. There are basically two approaches to measurement. One is categorizing observations such as when plants are categorized as being in a particular species rather than another species. Similar classification processes occur for example when people are classified according to their gender or when people with abnormal behaviour patterns are classified as schizophrenics, manic-depressives, and so forth. Typically this sort of measurement is described as qualitative (identifying the defining characteristics or qualities of something) or nominal (naming the defining characteristics of something) or categorical or category (putting into categories). The second approach is closer to the common-sense meaning of the word measurement. That is, putting a numerical value to an observation. Giving a mass in kilograms or a distance in metres are good examples of such numerical measurements. Many other disciplines measure numerically in this way. This is known as quantitative measurement, which means that individual observations are given a quantitative or numerical value as part of the measurement process. That is, the numerical value indicates the amount of something that an observation possesses.

Not every number assigned to something indicates the quantity of a characteristic it possesses. For example, take the number 763214. If this were the distance in kilometres between city A and city B then it clearly represents the amount of distance. However, if it were a telephone number the exact significance of the numerical value is obscure. For example, the letter sequence GFCBAD could be the equivalent of the number and have no implications of quantity at all.

Quantitative measurements are often subdivided into three types:

1   Ordinal or rank measurement: This is where a series of observations are placed in order of magnitude. In other words, the rank orders 1st, 2nd, 3rd, 4th, 5th, 6th, etc., are applied. This indicates the relative position in terms of magnitude.
2   Interval measurement: This assumes that the numbers applied indicate the size of the difference between observations. So if one observation is scored 5 and another is scored 7, there is a fixed interval of 2 units between them. So something that is 7 centimetres long is 2 centimetres longer than something which is 5 centimetres long, for example.
3   Ratio measurement: This is similar in many ways to interval measurement. The big difference is that in ratio measurement it should be meaningful to say things like X is twice as tall as Y or A is a quarter of the size of B. That is, ratios are meaningful.

This is a common classification but has enormous difficulties for most disciplines beyond the natural sciences such as physics and chemistry. This is because it is not easy to identify just how measurements such as IQ or social educational status relate to the numbers given. IQ is measured on a numerical scale with 100 being the midpoint. The question is whether someone with an IQ of 120 is twice as intelligent as a person with an IQ of 60. There is no clear answer to this and no amount of consideration has ever definitively established that it is.

There is an alternative argument – that is to say, that the numbers are numbers and can be dealt with accordingly irrespective of how precisely those numbers relate to the thing being measured. That is, deal with the numbers just as one would any other numbers – add them, divide them, and so forth.

Both of these extremes have adherents. Why does it matter? The main reason is that different statistical tests assume different things about the data. Some assume that the data can only be ranked, some assume that the scores can be added, and so forth. Without assessing the characteristics of the data, it is not possible to select an appropriate test.

median: the score in the 'middle' of a set of scores when these are ranked from the smallest to the largest. Half of the scores are above it, half below – more or less. Thus, for the following (odd number of) scores, to calculate the median we simply rearrange the scores in order of size and select the score in the centre of the distribution:

19, 17, 23, 29, 12

Rearranged these read

12, 17, 19, 23, 29

Since 19 is the score in the middle (equal distance from the two ends), then 19 is the median.

When there are equal numbers of scores, it becomes necessary to estimate the median as no score is precisely in the middle. Take the following six scores:

19, 17, 23, 29, 12, 14

Rearranged in order these become

12, 14, 17, 19, 23, 29

Quite clearly the median is somewhere between 17 and 19. The simplest estimate of the median is the average of these two scores which is 18.

There are other ways of calculating the median in these circumstances but they appear to be obsolete. Look at the following ordered sequence of scores:

17, 17, 17, 19, 23, 29

The above method gives the median as 18 again. However, it may seem that the median

should be closer to 17 than to 19 in this case. See also: **average**

median test, Mood's: a non-parametric test used to determine whether the number of scores which fall either side of their common median differs for two or more unrelated samples. The chi-square test is used to determine whether the number of scores differs significantly from that expected by chance.

mediating variable: see **intervening variable**

mesokurtic: see **kurtosis**

meta-analysis: involves the consolidation of data and findings from a variety of research studies on a topic. Primarily it involves the combination of the findings of these various studies in order to estimate the general or overall effect of one variable over another. The secondary function, and probably the more illuminating, is to seek patterns in the findings of the various studies in order to understand the characteristics of studies which tend to show strong relationships between the variables in question and those which tend to show weak or no relationship. Meta-analysis does not always work, which may reveal something about the state of research in a particular area. Meta-analysis is a systematic review of studies using relatively simple statistical techniques. It can be contrasted with the more traditional review of the literature in which researchers subjectively attempted to synthesize the research using criteria which were and are difficult to define or identify. Part of the gains of using meta-analysis are to do with systematic definition of a research area and the meticulous preparation of the database of studies.

It is important to be able to define fairly precisely the domain of interest of the meta-analysis. The effectiveness of a particular type of treatment programme or the effects of the amount of delay between witnessing an event and being interviewed by the police on the quality of testimony might be seen as typical examples. An important early stage is defining the domain of interest for the review precisely. While this is clearly a matter for the judgement of the researcher, the criteria selected clarify important aspects of the research area. Generally speaking, the researcher will explore a range of sources of studies in order to generate as full a list of relevant research as possible. Unpublished research is not omitted on the basis of being of poor quality; instead it is sought out because its findings may be out of line with accepted wisdom in a field. For example, non-significant findings may not achieve publication.

The notion of effect size is central to meta-analysis. Effect size is literally what it says – the size of the effect (influence) of the independent variable on the dependent variable. This is expressed in terms which refer to the amount of variance which the two variables share compared with the total variation. It is not expressed in terms of the magnitude of the difference between scores as this will vary widely according to the measures used and the circumstances of the measurement. Pearson's correlation coefficient is one common measure of effect size since the squared correlation is the amount of variation that the two variables have in common. Another common measure is Cohen's d, though this has no obvious advantages over the correlation coefficient and is much less familiar. There is a simple relationship between the two and one can readily be converted to the other (Howitt and Cramer, 2004).

Generally speaking, research reports do not use effect size measures so it is necessary to calculate them (estimate them) from the data of a study (which are often unavailable) or from the reported statistics. There are a number of simple formulae which help do this. For example, if a study reports t tests a conversion is possible since there is a simple relationship of the correlation coefficient between the two variables with the t test. The independent variable has two conditions – the experimental group and the control group – which can be coded 1 and 2 respectively. Once this is done, the point–biserial correlation coefficient may be applied simply by calculating Pearson's correlation coefficient between these 1s and 2s and the scores on the dependent variable. For other statistics there are other procedures which may be applied to the same effect. Recently researchers have shown a greater tendency to provide effect size statistics in their reports. Even if they do not, it is surprisingly easy to provide usable estimates of effect size from very minimal statistical analyses.

Once the effect sizes have been calculated in an appropriate form, these various estimates of effect size can be combined to indicate an overall effect size. This is slightly more complex than a simple average of the effect size but conceptually is best regarded as this. The size of the study is normally taken into account. One formula for the average effect size is simply to convert each of the effect sizes into the Fisher z transformation of Pearson's correlation. The average of these values is easily calculated. This average Fisher z transformation value is reconverted back to a correlation coefficient. The table of this transformation is readily available in a number of texts. See also: **correlations, averaging; effect size**

Howitt and Cramer (2004); Hunter and Schmidt (2004)

Minitab: this software was originally written in 1972 at Penn State University to teach students introductory statistics. It is one of several widely used statistical packages for manipulating and analysing data. Information about Minitab can be found at the following website:
http://www.minitab.com/

missing values or **data:** are the result of participants in the research failing to provide the researcher with data on each variable in the analysis. If it is reasonable to assume that these are merely random omissions, the analysis is straightforward in general. Unfortunately, the case for this assumption is not strong. Missing values may occur for any number of reasons: the participant has inadvertently failed to answer a particular question, the interviewer has not noted down the participant's answer, part of the data is unreadable, and so forth. These leave the possibility that the data are not available for non-random reasons – for example, the question is unclear so the participant doesn't answer, the interviewer finds a particular question boring etc., and has a tendency to overlook it. Quite clearly the researcher should anticipate these difficulties to some extent and allow the reasons for the lack of an answer to a question to be recorded. For example, the interviewer records that the participant could not answer, would not answer, and so forth. Generally speaking, the fewer the missing values the fewer difficulties that arise as a consequence. It is difficult to give figures for acceptable numbers of missing values and it is somewhat dependent on the circumstances of the research. For example, in a survey of voting intentions missing information about the participants' political affiliation may significantly influence predictions.

Computer programs for the analysis of statistical data often include a missing values option. A missing value is a particular value of a variable which indicates missing information. For example, for a variable like age a missing value code of 999 could be specified to indicate that the participant's age is not known. The computer may then be instructed to ignore totally that participant – essentially delete them from the analysis of the data. This is often called listwise deletion of missing values since the individual is deleted from the list of participants for all intents and purposes. The alternative is to select step wise deletion of missing values. This amounts to an instruction to the computer to omit that participant from those analyses of the data involving the variable for which they supplied no information. Thus, the participant would be omitted from the calculation of the mean age of the sample (because they are coded 999 on that variable) but included in the analysis of the variable gender

(because information about their gender is available). Some statistical packages (SPSS) allow the user to stipulate the value that should be inserted for a missing score. One approach is to use the average of scores on that variable.

Another approach to calculating actual values for missing values is to examine the correlates in the data of missing data and use these correlates to estimate what the score would have been had the score not been missing. See also: **listwise deletion; sample size**

mixed analysis of variance or **ANOVA:** an analysis of variance which contains at least one between-subjects factor and one within-subjects or repeated-measures factor.

mixed design: a research design which contains both within-subjects and between-subjects elements. For example, Table M.3 summarizes research in which a group of men and a group of women are studied before and after taking a course on counselling. The dependent variable is a measure of empathy.

The within-subjects aspect of this design is that the same group of individuals have been measured twice on empathy – once before the course and once after. The between-subjects aspect of the design is the comparison between men and women – with different groups of participants. See also: **analysis of variance**

mode: one of the common measures of the typical value in the data for a variable. The mode is simply the value of the most frequently occurring score or category in one's data. It is *not* a frequency but a value. So if in the data there are 12 electricians, 30 nurses and 4 clerks the modal occupation is nurses. If there were seven 5s, nine 6s, fourteen 7s, three 8s and two 9s, the mode of the scores is

Table M.3 *An example of a mixed design*

	Before course	After course
Men	Mean = 21.2	Mean = 28.3
Women	Mean = 24.3	Mean = 25.2

7. The mode (unlike mean and median) can be applied to category (categorical or nominal) data as well as score data. See also: **average; bimodal; frequency; multimodal**

model: a simplified representation of something. In statistics, a model is a way of accounting for the data in question. Typically, then, a statistical model is a mathematical description of how several variables explain the data in question. A good model fits (explains) the data as closely as possible without becoming so complicated that it begins to obscure understanding.

moderating or **moderator effect** or **variable, moderated relationship:** where the relationship between two variables differs for the values of one or more other variables. It represents an interaction between the variables. For example, the relationship between gender and depression may differ according to marital status. Married women may be more depressed than married men while never married women may be less depressed than never married men. In this case, the relationship between gender and depression is moderated by marital status. Marital status is the moderating variable. See also: **multiple regression**

moment: the mean or expected value of the power of the deviation of each value in a distribution from some given value, which is usually the mean. For example, the first moment about the arithmetic mean is 0:

$$m_1 = \frac{\text{sum of (each value } - \text{ mean value)}^1}{\text{number of values}} = 0$$

If we raise the deviation of each value to the power of 1, we have the mean deviation which is 0.

The second moment about the arithmetic mean is the variance:

$$m_2 = \frac{\text{sum of (each value } - \text{ mean value)}^2}{\text{number of values}} = \text{variance}$$

The third moment about the arithmetic mean is skewness:

$$m_3 = \frac{\text{sum of (each value } - \text{ mean value)}^3}{\text{number of values}} = \text{skewness}$$

The fourth moment about the arithmetic mean is kurtosis:

$$m_4 = \frac{\text{sum of (each value } - \text{ mean value)}^4}{\text{number of values}} = \text{kurtosis}$$

Monte Carlo methods: means of calculating, among other things, the probability of outcomes based on a random process. So any statistical test which is based on calculating the probability of a variety of outcomes consequent of randomly allocating a set of scores is a Monte Carlo method. See **bootstrapping**

multicollinearity: see **collinearity**

multimodal: a distribution of scores having more than two modes. See **bimodal**

multiple coefficient of determination or **R²:** the square of the multiple correlation. It is commonly used in multiple regression to represent the proportion of variance in a criterion or dependent variable that is shared with or explained by two or more predictor or independent variables.

multiple comparison tests or **procedures:** are used to determine which or which combinations of three or more means differ significantly from each other. If there are good grounds for predicting which means differ from each other, an a priori or planned test is used. *Post hoc*, a posteriori or unplanned tests are used to find out which other means differ significantly from each other. A number of a priori and *post hoc* tests have been developed. Particularly with respect to the *post hoc* tests, there is controversy surrounding which test should be used. See **a priori comparison or tests; Bonferroni test; Bryant–Paulson simultaneous test procedure; Duncan's new multiple range test; Dunn's test; Dunn–Sidak multiple comparison test; Dunnett's C test; Dunnett's T3 test; Dunnett's test; familywise error rate; Fisher's LSD (Least Significant Difference)** or **protected test; Gabriel's simultaneous test procedure; Games–Howell multiple comparison procedure; Hochberg GT2 test; Newman–Keuls method, procedure** or **test; *post hoc*, a posteriori** or **unplanned tests; Ryan** or **Ryan–Einot–Gabriel–Welsch F (REGWF) multiple comparison test; Ryan** or **Ryan–Einot–Gabriel–Welsch Q (REGWQ) multiple comparison test; Scheffé test; studentized range statistic q; Tamhane's T2 multiple comparison test; trend analysis in analysis of variance; Tukey$_a$** or **HSD (Honestly Significant Difference) test; Tukey$_b$** or **WSD (Wholly Significant Difference) test; Tukey–Kramer test; Waller–Duncan t test**

multiple correlation or **R:** a term used in multiple regression. In multiple regression a criterion (or dependent) variable is predicted using a multiplicity of predictor variables. For example, in order to predict IQ, the predictor variables might be social class, educational achievement and gender. For every individual, using these predictors, it is possible to make a prediction of the most likely value of their IQ based on these predictors. Quite simply, the multiple correlation is the correlation between the actual IQ scores of the individuals in the sample and the scores predicted for them by applying the multiple regression equation with these three predictors.

As with all correlations, the larger the numerical value, the greater the correlation. See also: **canonical correlation; F ratio; multiple regression**

multiple regression: a method designed to analyse the linear relationship between a quantitative criterion or dependent variable and two or more (i.e. multiple) predictors or independent variables. The predictors may be qualitative or quantitative. If the predictors are qualitative, they are turned into a set of dichotomous variables known as dummy variables which is always one less than the number of categories making up the qualitative variable.

There are two main general uses to this test. One use is to determine the strength and the direction of the linear association between the criterion and a predictor controlling for the association of the predictors with each other and the criterion. The strength of the association is expressed in terms of the size of either the standardized or the unstandardized partial regression coefficient which is symbolized by the small Greek letter β or its capital equivalent B (both called beta) although which letter is used to signify which coefficient is not consistent. The direction of the association is indicated by the sign of the regression coefficient as it is with correlation coefficients. No sign means that the association is positive with higher scores on the predictor being associated with higher scores on the criterion. A negative sign shows that the association is negative with higher scores on the predictor being associated with lower scores on the criterion. The term partial is often omitted when referring to partial regression coefficients. The standardized regression coefficient is standardized so that it can vary from -1.00 to 1.00 whereas the unstandardized coefficient can be greater than ±1.00. One advantage of the standardized coefficient is that it enables the size of the association between the criterion and the predictors to be compared on the same scale as this scale has been standardized to ±1.00. Unstandardized coefficients enable the value of the criterion to be predicted if we know the values of the predictors.

Another use of multiple regression is to determine how much of the variance in the criterion is accounted for by particular predictors. This is usually expressed in terms of the change in the squared multiple correlation (R^2) where it corresponds to the proportion of variance explained. This proportion can be re-expressed as a percentage by multiplying the proportion by 100.

Multiple regression also determines whether the size of the regression coefficients and of the variance explained is greater than that expected by chance, in other words whether it is statistically significant. Statistical significance depends on the size of the sample. The bigger the sample, the more likely that small values will be statistically significant.

Multiple regression can be used to conduct simple path analysis and to determine whether there is an interaction between two or more predictors and the criterion and whether a predictor acts as a moderating variable on the relationship between a predictor and the criterion. It is employed to carry out analysis of variance where the number of cases in each cell is not equal or proportionate.

There are three main ways in which predictors can be entered into a multiple regression. One way is to enter all the predictors of interest at the same time in a single step. This is sometimes referred to as standard multiple regression. The size of the standardized partial regression coefficients indicates the size of the unique association between the criterion and a predictor controlling for the association of all the other predictors that are related to the criterion. This method is useful for ascertaining which variables are most strongly related to the criterion taking into account their association with the other predictors.

A second method is to use some statistical criteria for determining the entry of predictors one at a time. One widely used method is often referred to as stepwise multiple regression in which the predictor with the most significant F ratio is considered for entry. This is the predictor which has the highest correlation with the criterion. If the probability of this F ratio is higher than a particular criterion, which is usually the 0.05 level, the analysis

stops. If the probability meets this criterion, the predictor is entered into the first step of the multiple regression.

The next predictor that is considered for entry into the multiple regression is the predictor whose F ratio has the next smallest probability value. If this probability value meets the criterion, the predictor is entered into the second step of the multiple regression. This is the predictor that has the highest squared semi-partial or part correlation with the criterion taking into account the first predictor. The F ratio for the first predictor in the second step of the multiple regression is then examined to see if it meets the criterion for removal. If the probability level is the criterion, this criterion may be set at a higher level (say, the 0.10 level) than the criterion for entry. If this predictor does not meet this criterion, it is removed from the regression equation. If it meets the criterion it is retained. The procedure stops when no more predictors are entered into or removed from the regression equation. In many analyses, predictors are generally entered in terms of the proportion of the variance they account for in the criterion, starting off with those that explain the greatest proportion of the variance and ending with those that explain the least. Where a predictor acts as a suppressor variable on the relationship between another predictor and the criterion, this may not happen.

When interpreting the results of a multiple regression which uses statistical criteria for entering predictors, it is important to remember that if two predictors are related to one another and to the criterion, only one of the predictors may be entered into the multiple regression, although both may be related to a very similar degree to the criterion. Consequently, it is important to check the extent to which this may be occurring when looking at the results of such an analysis.

A third method of multiple regression is called hierarchical or sequential multiple regression in which the order and the number of predictors entered into each step of the multiple regression are determined by the researcher. For example, we may wish to group or to block predictors together in terms of similar characteristics such as socio-demographic variables (e.g. age, gender, socio-economic status), personality variables (e.g. extroversion, neuroticism) and attitudinal variables and to enter these blocks in a particular order such as the order presented here. In this case, the proportion of variance explained by the second block of personality variables is that which has not already been explained by the first block of socio-demographic variables. In effect, when we are using this method we are controlling or partialling out the blocks of variables that have been previously entered.

Hierarchical multiple regression is used to determine whether the relationship between a predictor and a criterion is moderated by another predictor called a moderator or moderating variable. The predictor and the moderator are entered in the first step and the interaction which is the product of the predictor and the moderator is entered into the second step. If the interaction accounts for a significant proportion of the variance in the criterion, the relationship between the predictor and the criterion is moderated by the other variable. The nature of this moderated relationship can be examined by using the moderator variable to divide the sample into two groups and to examine the relationship between the predictor and the criterion in these two groups.

The particular step of a statistical or hierarchical method of multiple regression is, in effect, a standard multiple regression of the predictors in that step. In other words, the partial regression coefficients represent the association between each predictor and the criterion controlling their association with all the other predictors on that step. The regression coefficient of a predictor is likely to vary when other predictors are entered or removed.

Multiple regression, like simple regression and Pearson's product moment correlation, is based on the assumption that the values of the variables are normally distributed and that the relationship between a predictor and the criterion is homoscedastic in that the variance of one variable is similar for all values of the other variable. Homoscedasticity is the opposite of heteroscedasticity where the variance of one variable is not the same for all values of the other variable. See also: **dummy**

coding; hierarchical or **sequential entry; logistic regression; multiple coefficient of determination; multiple regression: predictor variable; standardized partial regression coefficient; stepwise entry; unstandardized partial regression coefficient**
Cramer (2003), Pedhazur (1982)

multiplication rule: a basic principle of probability theory. It really concerns what happens in a sequence of random events such as throwing dice. What is the probability of throwing a 6 on two successive throws? Since there are six possible outcomes (1, 2, 3, 4, 5 and 6 spots) for the first throw then the probability of obtaining 6 is $1/6 = 0.167$. Once we have thrown a 6, then the probability of the next throw being a 6 is governed by the same probability. The multiplication rule is basically that the likelihood of getting the two 6s in a row is $0.167 \times 0.167 = 0.028$. Put another way, there is one chance in six of getting 6 spots on the first toss and a one chance in six of getting another 6 spots on the second toss. That is, 1 divided by 6×6 or 1 divided by $36 = 0.028$.

multiply: increasing a number by a number of times. So 3×2 is 3 increased two times – that is, $3 + 3 = 6$. See also: **negative values**

multistage sampling: a method of sampling which proceeds in two or more stages. This term is often used with cluster sampling in which an attempt is made to reduce the geographical area covered. For example, if we were to sample people in a city, the first stage might be to select the electoral wards in that city. The next step might be to select streets in those wards. The third stage might be to select households in those streets. The fourth and final stage might be to select people in those households. This would be a four-stage cluster sample.

multivariate analysis: an analysis involving three or more variables at the same time.

multivariate analysis of covariance or **MANCOVA:** an analysis of covariance (ANCOVA) which is carried out on two or more dependent variables at the same time and where the dependent variables are related to each other. One advantage of this method is that the dependent variables analysed together may be significant whereas the dependent variables analysed separately may not be significant. When the combined or multivariate effect of the dependent variables is significant, it is useful to know which of the single or univariate effects of the dependent variables are significant.

multivariate analysis of variance or **MANOVA:** an analysis of variance (ANOVA) which is conducted on two or more dependent variables simultaneously and where the dependent variables are inter-related. One advantage of this procedure is that the dependent variables analysed together may be significant whereas the dependent variables analysed on their own may not be significant. When the combined or multi-variate effect of the dependent variables is significant, it is usual to determine which of the single or univariate effects are also significant. See also: **analysis of variance; Hotelling's trace criterion; multivariate normality; Roy's gcr; Wilks's lambda**

multivariate normality: the assumption that each variable and all linear combinations of the variables in an analysis are normally distributed. As there are potentially a very large number of linear combinations, this assumption is not easy to test. When the data are grouped as in multivariate analysis of variance, the sampling distribution of the means of the dependent variables in each of the cells has to be normally distributed as well as the variables' linear combinations. With relatively large sample sizes, the central limit theorem states that the sampling distribution of means will be normally distributed. If there is multivariate normality, the sampling distribution of means will be normally distributed. When the data are ungrouped as in discriminant function analysis and structural equation modelling, if there is multi-variate normality each variable will be normally distributed and the relationship of pairs of variables will be linear and homoscedastic.

Tabachnick and Fidell (2001)

N

natural or **Napierian logarithm:** of a particular number (such as 2) this is the exponential or power of the base number of 2.718 which gives rise to that particular number. For example, the natural logarithm of 2 is 0.69 as the base number of 2.718 raised to the power of 0.69 is 2.00. As the base number is a constant, it is sometimes symbolized as e (after Euler's number). The natural logarithm may be abbreviated as log e or ln. Natural logarithms are used in statistical tests such as log–linear analysis. They may be calculated from tables, scientific electronic calculators or statistical software such as SPSS. Few researchers ever have to use them personally. See also: **correlations, averaging; Fisher's z transformation; logarithm; logit; odds**

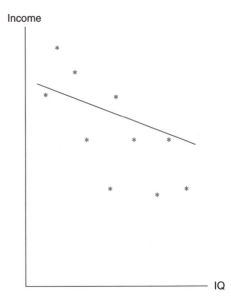

Figure N.1   *A negative correlation between two variables*

negative: a value less than zero. See also: **absolute deviation**

negative correlation: an inverted relationship between two variables (Figure N.1). Thus, as the scores on variable *A* increase the scores on variable *B* decrease. This means that people with high scores on variable *A* will tend to get the lower scores on variable *B*. Those with lower scores on variable *A* tend to get higher scores on variable *B*. Sometimes confusion can arise if the researcher is not clear what a high score on each variable indicates. This is especially so when variables have not been clearly named or where they consist of a list of questions which vary in terms of what agreement and disagreement imply.

negative values: a value less than zero. Negative values are fairly common in statistical calculations simply because differences between scores or values above or below the mean are used. For this reason, students are likely to use negative values in calculations than when collecting their data. Little data in the social science disciplines have negative values in the form that they are collected. Negative values are like being in debt – they are amounts you owe other people. Positive values are like having money to spend. The basic mathematical operations that involve positive and negative signs and which are at all common in statistical calculations are as follows.

Adding

If one adds two positive numbers one ends up with a positive outcome:

$$5 + 2 = 7$$

If one adds two negative numbers, one ends up with a negative number (you owe money to two people not just one):

$$-4 + -7 = -11$$

If one adds a negative number to a positive number then one ends up with either a positive or negative number depending on circumstances. For example, if you have 5 euros in your pocket and you owe 2 euros to someone else, you would have 3 euros when you paid that person back:

$$5 + -2 = 3$$

but if you owed someone 7 euros and only paid them back 5 euros you would still owe 2 euros:

$$5 + -7 = -2$$

Subtracting

Taking away minus numbers is effectively the same as adding them. So, $5[-]3 = 2$. Hence, $5 - -3 = 8$ since the formula tells us to remove -3 from 5. The implication of this is that the 5 was obtained by giving away 3 to another person. If that person gives us that 3 back (minuses the minus 3) then we get 8. Another example:

$$-8 - -3 = -5$$

Multiplying

A negative number multiplied by a positive number gives a negative number:

$$-4 \times 3 \text{ means } -4 + -4 + -4 = -12$$

A negative number multiplied by a positive number yields a positive number:

$$-4 \times -3 = 12$$

negatively skewed: see **skewness**

nested model: a model which is similar to the one it has been derived from except that one or more of the parameters of the original model have been removed or restricted to zero. It is a simplification of the original model. Because the original model has more parameters (i.e. it has more features to explain the data) it might be expected to provide a better fit to the data. The statistical fit of a nested model may be compared with that of the original model. If the statistical fit of the nested model to the data is significantly poorer than that of the original model, the original model gives a better fit to the data. That is, the extra feature of the original model is of value. If, however, there is no significant difference in the fit of the two models, the nested model provides a simpler and more parsimonious model for the data. In that sense, it would be the preferred model since the removed or restricted features of the model seem not to contribute anything to the power of the model to explain the data. Nested models are often compared in structural equation modelling. See **structural equation modelling**

Newman–Keuls method, procedure or **test:** a *post hoc* or multiple comparison test which is used to determine whether three or more means differ significantly in an analysis of variance. It may be used regardless of whether the analysis of variance is significant. It assumes equal variance and is approximate for unequal group sizes. It is a stepwise or sequential test which is similar to

Table N.1 *Individual scores and mean scores for four unrelated groups*

	Group 1	Group 2	Group 3	Group 4
	6	10	10	0
	2	15	12	2
	10	17	14	4
Sum	18	42	36	6
Mean	6	14	12	2

Table N.2 *Newman–Keuls test*

Group	Means	4 2	1 6	3 12	2 14	W	r
4	2	–	4	10*	12*	7.97	4
1	6		–	6*	8*	7.11	3
3	12			–	2	5.74	2
2	14				–		

Duncan's new multiple range test in that the means are first ordered in size. However, it differs in the significance level used. For the Newman–Keuls test the significance level is the same no matter how many comparisons there are, while for Duncan's test the significance level becomes more lenient the more comparisons there are. Consequently, differences are less likely to be significant for this test.

The use of this test will be illustrated with the data in Table N.1 which shows the individual and mean scores for four unrelated groups. The means for the four groups are 6, 14, 12 and 2 respectively. See also: **Duncan's new multiple range test; Ryan F and Q tests; Scheffé test; trend analysis in analysis of variance**

A one-way analysis of variance indicates that there is an effect which is significant at less than the 0.01 level.

To conduct a Newman–Keuls test the groups are first ordered according to the size of their means, starting with the smallest and ending with the largest as shown in the second row and column of Table N.2. Group 4 is listed first followed by groups 1, 3 and 2.

The absolute differences between the means of the four groups are then entered into the table. So the absolute difference between groups 4 and 1 is 4 ($2 - 6 = -4$), groups 4 and 3 is 10 ($2 - 12 = -10$), and so on.

The value that this difference has to exceed is symbolized as W. It is based on the number of means that separate the two means being compared. This number is symbolized by r and includes the two means being compared. So the minimum number that r can be is 2. The maximum number it can be is the number of groups which in this case is 4. As r

becomes smaller, so does W. In other words, the more means that separate the two means being compared, the bigger the difference between those means has to be in order to be statistically significant.

The formula for calculating this critical difference is the value of the studentized range multiplied by the square root of the error mean square divided by the number of cases in each group:

$$W = \text{studentized range} \times \sqrt{\text{error mean square/group } n}$$

The error mean square is obtained from the analysis of variance and is 9.25. The number of cases in each group is 3. So the value of the studentized range needs to be multiplied by 1.76 [$\sqrt{(9.25/3)} = \sqrt{3.083} = 1.76$]. This value is the same for all the comparisons.

The value of the studentized range varies according to the value of r (and the degrees of freedom for the error mean square but this will be the same for all the comparisons being made). This value can be obtained from a table which is available in some statistics texts such as the source below. The degrees of freedom for the error mean square for this example are 8. This is the number of groups subtracted from the number of cases ($12 - 4 = 8$). For these degrees of freedom and the 0.05 significance level, the value of the studentized range is 3.26 when r is 2, 4.04 when r is 3, and 4.53 when r is 4.

Consequently, the value that W has to be is 7.97 when r is 4 ($4.53 \times 1.76 = 7.97$), 7.11 when r is 3 ($4.04 \times 1.76 = 7.11$) and 5.74 when r is 2 ($3.26 \times 1.76 = 5.74$). These values have been inserted in Table N.2.

We now start with the third row of Table N.2 and the biggest difference between the four groups which is 12. As 12 is bigger than the value of W when r is 4 (7.97), the difference in the means between groups 4 and 2 is statistically significant. That this difference is significant is indicated by an asterisk in Table N.2. If this difference were not statistically significant, the analysis would stop here.

As it is significant, we proceed to the next biggest difference in this row which is 10. As r is 3 for this comparison, we need to compare this difference with the value of W when r is 3 (7.11) which is in the next row. As 10 is bigger than a W of 7.11, the difference between groups 2 and 3 is also significant. If this difference had not been significant, we would ignore all comparisons to the left of this comparison in this row and those below and move to the biggest difference in the next row.

As this difference is significant, we examine the last difference in this row which is 4. As r is 2 for this comparison, we need to compare this difference with the value of W when r is 2 (5.74) which is in the next row. As 4 is smaller than a W of 5.74, this difference is not significant.

We now follow the same procedure with the next row. The biggest difference is 8. As r is 3 for this comparison, we compare this difference with the value of W when r is 3, which is 7.11. As 8 is larger than a W of 7.11, the difference in the means between groups 1 and 2 is statistically significant. The next biggest difference is 6 which is bigger than a W of 5.74 when r is 2.

In the last row the difference of 2 is not bigger than a W of 5.74 when r is 2. Consequently, this difference is not statistically significant.

We could arrange these means into two homogeneous subsets where the means in a subset would not differ significantly from each other but where means in one subset would differ significantly from those in the other. We could indicate these two subsets by underlining the means which did not differ as follows:

<u>2 6</u>   <u>12 14</u>

Kirk (1995)

nominal data: see **nominal level of measurement; score nominal level of measurement, scale** or **variable:** a measure where numbers are used simply to name or nominate

the different categories but do not represent any order or difference in quantity. For example, we may use numbers to refer to the country of birth of an individual. The numbers that we assign to a country are arbitrary and have no other meaning than labels. For example, we may assign 1 to the United States and 2 to the United Kingdom but we could assign any two numbers to label these two countries. The only statistical operation we can carry out on nominal variables is a frequency analysis where we compare the frequency of cases in different categories.

non-directional or **direction-less hypothesis:** see **hypothesis**

non-parametric tests: any of a large number of inferential techniques in statistics which do not involve assessing the characteristics of the population from characteristics of the sample. These involve ranking procedures often, or may involve re-randomization and other procedures. They do not involve the use of standard error estimates characteristic of parametric statistics.

The argument for using non-parametric statistics is largely in terms of the inapplicability of parametric statistics to much data. Parametric statistics assume a normal distribution which is bell shaped. Data that do not meet this criterion may not be effectively analysed by some statistics. For example, the distribution may be markedly asymmetrical which violates the assumptions made when developing the parametric test. The parametric test may then be inappropriate. On the other hand the non-parametric test may equally be inappropriate for such data. Furthermore, violations of the assumptions of the test may matter little except in the most extreme cases. The other traditional argument for using non-parametric tests is that they use ordinal (rankable) data and do not require interval or ratio levels of measurement. This is an area of debate as some statisticians argue that it is the properties of the numbers which are important and not some abstract scale of measurement which is deemed to underlie the numbers. Both arguments have their adherents. The general impression is that modern researchers err towards using parametric analyses as often as possible, resorting to non-parametric tests only when the distribution of scores is exceptionally skewed. This allows them to use some of the most powerful statistical techniques.

Once non-parametric tests had ease of calculation on their side. This no longer applies with the ready availability of statistical computer packages. See also: **distribution-free tests; Kruskal–Wallis one-way analysis of variance; Mann–Whitney U-test; median test, Mood's; ranking tests; skewness**

non-random sample: see **convenience sample; quota sampling**

non-reciprocal relationship: see **unidirectional relationship**

non-recursive relationship: see **bidirectional relationship**

normal curve or **distribution:** a bell-shaped curve or distribution, like that shown in Figure N.2. It is a theoretical distribution which shows the frequency or probability of all the possible values that a continuous variable can take. The horizontal axis of the distribution represents all possible values of the variable while the vertical axis represents the frequency or probability of those values. The distribution can be described in terms of its mean and its standard deviation or variance. The exact form of the distribution will depend on the values of the mean and its standard deviation. Its shape will become flatter, the bigger the variance is. The tails of the distribution never touch the horizontal

Figure N.2 *The normal distribution curve*

axis, indicating that these extreme values may occur but are very unlikely to do so. Most of the scores will fall within three standard deviations of the mean. About 68.26% of the scores will fall within one standard deviation of the mean, 95.44% within two standard deviations and 99.70% within three standard deviations.

If the distribution of a variable approximates normality, we can determine what proportion or percentage of scores lies between any two values of that variable or what the probability is of obtaining a score between those two values by converting the original scores into standard scores and determining their z values. See also: **Gaussian distribution; parametric tests**

null hypothesis: in statistical inferences the null hypothesis is actually the hypothesis which is tested. It is often presented as being the nullification of the researcher's hypothesis but really is the claim that the independent variable has no influence on the dependent variable or that there is no correlation between the two variables. The null hypothesis assumes that the samples come from the same population or that the two variables come from a population where there is zero correlation between the two variables. Thus, the simplest ways of writing the null hypothesis are 'There is no relationship between variable A and variable B', or 'The independent variable has no influence on the dependent variable.' Unfortunately, by presenting the adequacy of the null hypothesis as being in competition with the adequacy of the alternative hypothesis, the impression is created that the disconfirmation of the null hypothesis means that the hypothesis as presented by the researcher is true. This is misleading since it merely suggests that the basic stumbling block to the hypothesis can be dismissed – that is, that chance variations are responsible for any correlations or differences that are obtained. See also: **confidence interval; hypothesis testing; sign test; significant**

number of cases: see **count**

numerator: the number at the top of a fraction such as $\frac{4}{7}$. The numerator in this case is 4. The denominator is the bottom half of the fraction and so equals 7. See also: **denominator**

numerical scores: see **score**

O

oblique factor: see **oblique rotation**

oblique rotation: a form of rotating factors (see **orthogonal rotation**) in factor analysis. In oblique rotation, the factors are allowed to correlate with each other; hence the axes can cease to be at right angles. There are various methods of orthogonal rotation of which Promax is a typical and well-known example. One important consequence of oblique rotation is that since the factors may correlate, it is possible to calculate a correlation matrix of the correlations of the oblique factors one with each other. This secondary correlation matrix can then itself be factor analysed yielding what are known as second-order factors or higher order factors. See also: **axis; exploratory factor analysis**

odds: the ratio of the probability of an event occurring to the probability of it not occurring. It can also be expressed as the ratio of the frequency of an event occurring to the frequency of other events occurring. Suppose, for example, that six out of nine students pass an exam. The probability of a student passing the exam is about 0.67 (6/9 = 0.667). The probability of a student failing the exam is about 0.33 (3/9 = 0.33 or 1 − 0.67 = 0.33). Consequently, the odds of a student passing the exam are about 2 (0.667/0.333 = 2.00). This is the same as the number of students

Table O.1 *Mental illness and family background*

	No mental illness in family	Mental illness in family
Person suffers mental illness	30	41
Person does not suffer mental illness	180	27

passing the exam divided by the number of students failing it (6/3 = 2). See also: **logit**

odds ratio: an indicator of relative probabilities when outcomes are dependent (conditional) on another factor. For example, what is the probability of mental illness in a person who comes from a family in which at least one member has been in a mental hospital compared with one in which no members have been in a mental hospital? The imaginary data in Table O.1 might be considered. See also: **logistic regression**

The probability of a person suffering mental illness if there is no mental illness in the family is 30/(30 + 180) = 0.143. The probability of a person suffering mental illness if there is mental illness in the family is 41/68 = 0.603.

The odds ratio for suffering mental illness is obtained simply by dividing the larger probability by the smaller probability. In our example, the odds ratio is $0.603/0.143 = 4.2$. In other words, one is over four times more likely to suffer mental illness if there is mental illness in one's family than if there is not.

The odds ratio is a fairly illuminating way of presenting relative probabilities. It is a feature of logistic regression.

omnibus test: a test to determine whether three or more means differ significantly from one another without being able to specify in advance of collecting the data which of those means differ significantly. It is the F ratio in an analysis of variance which determines whether the between-groups variance is significantly greater than the within-groups or error variance. If there are good grounds for predicting which means differ from each other, an a priori or planned test should be carried out to see whether these differences are found. If differences are not expected, *post hoc* or unplanned tests should be conducted to find out which means or combination of means differ from each other.

one-sample t test: see **t test for one sample**

one-tailed level or **test of statistical significance:** see **chi-square; significant**

one-way relationship: see **uni-directional relationship**

operationalization: a procedure for measuring or manipulating a variable. There is often more than one way of measuring or manipulating a variable. For example, the variable of anxiety may be assessed through self-report, ratings by observers, physiological indices, projective methods, behavioural

tests, and so on. It may also be manipulated in various ways such as subjecting people to frightening experiences or asking them to imagine being in frightening situations. While it is very difficult to provide conceptual definitions of variables (e.g. just what is intelligence?), it is more practical to describe the steps by which a variable is measured or manipulated in a particular study.

order effect: the order in which a participant etc. is required to undertake two or more tasks or treatments may affect how they respond. For example, participants may become less interested the more tasks they carry out or they may become more experienced in what they have to do. When requiring participants to conduct more than one task, it may be important to determine whether the order in which they carry out the tasks has any effect on their performance. If the number of tasks is very small, it is possible to have each task carried out in all possible orders. For example, with three tasks, A, B and C, there are six different orders: ABC, ACB, BAC, BCA, CAB and CBA. This is known as counterbalancing and it assumes that by varying the order in such a systematic fashion, order effects are systematically cancelled out. If there are a large number of tasks, it may be useful to select a few of these either at random or on some theoretical basis to determine if order effects exist. Assessing order effects essentially requires that comparisons are made according to the order of carrying out the tasks, not according to type of task.

ordinal level of measurement, scale or **variable:** this is data which are collected in the form of scores. Its distinguishing feature is that these scores only allow the data to be put into ranks (rank order). Rank order is based on ordinal numbers which refer to the 1st, 2nd, 3rd, 4th, 5th etc., scores. These represent the smallest score to the largest one but it is not known how much the 3rd and 5th scores actually differ from each other in any meaningful sense. The ordinal scale of measurement is the basis for many non-parametric tests of significance. Researchers rarely actually collect data that are in the form of ranks. Ordinal measurement refers to the issue of the nature of the measurement scale that underlies the scores. Some statisticians argue that the scores collected in the social sciences and some other disciplines are incapable of telling us anything other than the relative order of individuals. In practice, one can worry too much about such conceptual matters. What is of importance is to be aware that non-parametric tests, some of which are based on ranked data, can be very useful when one's data are inadequate for other forms of statistical tests. See also: **chi-square; Kendall's rank correlation; Kolmogorov–Smirnov test for one sample; measurement; partial gamma; score**

ordinary least squares (OLS) regression: see **multiple regression**

ordinate: the vertical or y axis on a graph. It usually represents the quantity of the dependent variable. See also: **y-axis**

orthogonal: indicates that right angles are involved. Essentially it means in statistics that two variables (or variants of variables such as factors) are unrelated to each other. As such, this means that they can be represented in physical space as two lines (axes) at 90° to each other. See **orthogonal rotation**

orthogonal factors: see **orthogonal rotation**

orthogonal rotation: the process by which axes for pairs of variables which are uncorrelated (at right angles) are displaced around a centre point from their original position while

retaining the right angle between them. This occurs in factor analysis when the set of factors emerging out of the mathematical calculations is considered unsatisfactory for some reason. It is somewhat controversial, but it should be recognized that the first set of factors to emerge in factor analysis is intended to maximize the amount of variation extracted (or explained). However, there is no reason why this should be the best outcome in terms of interpretation of the factors. So many researchers rotate the first axes or factors. Originally rotation was carried out graphically by simply plotting the axes and factors on graph paper, taking pairs of factors at a time. These axes are moved around their intersection (i.e. the axes are spun around). Only the axes move. Hence, the rotated factors have different loadings on the variables than did the original factors. There are various ways of carrying out rotation and various criteria for doing so. The net outcome is that a new set of factors (and new factor loadings) are calculated. Seem Figure O.1 (a) and (b) which illustrate an unrotated factor solution for two factors and the consequence of rotation respectively. The clearest consequence is the change in factor loadings. Varimax is probably the best known orthogonal rotation method. See also: **exploratory factor analysis; orthogonal rotation; varimax rotation, in factor analysis**

outliers: cases which are unusually extreme and which would have an undue and misleading influence on the interpretation of data in a naïve analysis of the data. They are generally a relatively minor problem in a non-parametric analysis (because the scores are 'compacted' by turning them into ranks). In parametric analyses they can be much more problematic. They are particularly important in bivariate analyses because of the extra weight placed on extreme values in calculating covariance. Figure O.2(a) shows a scattergram for a poor or near zero correlation between two variables – variable A and variable B. Any attempt to fit a best fitting straight line is difficult because there is no apparent trend in the data as the correlation is zero. Figure O.2(b) shows the same data but another

(a) Unrotated

(b) Rotated

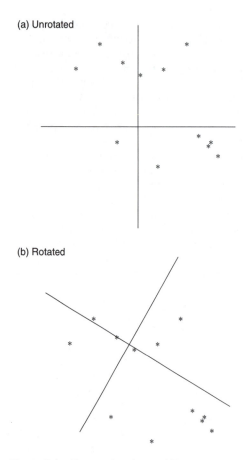

Figure O.1   *Unrotated and rotated factors*

running the parametric analysis (using Pearson's correlation coefficient) in parallel with a non-parametric analysis (e.g. using Spearman's correlation coefficient – a ranking test). If both analyses produce the same broad findings and conclusions then there is no problem created by outliers. If the non-parametric analysis yields substantially different findings and conclusions to the parametric analysis then the influence of outliers should be suspected. An alternative procedure is to delete the suspected outliers to see whether this makes a difference. If the complete data produce significant findings and the partial analysis produces very different non-significant (or very much less significant) findings then the influence of outliers is likely. See also: **transformations**

over-identified model: a term used in structural equation modelling to describe a model for which there is more information than necessary to identify or estimate the parameters of the model. See also: **identification**

case has been included. This shows the characteristics of an outlier – it is high on the two variables (though equally an outlier may have low scores on the two variables). A mechanical application of statistical techniques (correlation and best fitting straight line) would lead to an apparent correlation between variables *A* and *B* and a line of best fit as shown in Figure O.2(b). However, we know that the correlation and significance are the result of the outlier since without the outlier there is no such trend. So a correct interpretation of the data has to resist the temptation to interpret the data in Figure O.2(b) as reflecting a positive trend. Unfortunately, unless a researcher examines the scattergram, there is no automatic check for outliers. Some authors (e.g. Howitt and Cramer, 2004) recommend

(a) Without outlier

(b) With outlier

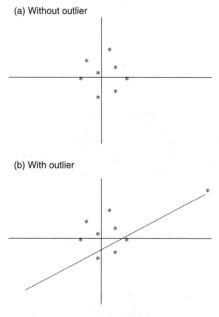

Figure O.2   *The effects of outliers*

P

paired-samples _t_ test: see _t_ test for related samples

pairing: see **matching**

pairwise deletion: a keyword used in some statistical packages such as SPSS to restrict an analysis to those cases for which there are no missing values on the variable or variables for that analysis. When this is done where there are some missing values, the number of cases may not be the same for all the analyses. Suppose, for example, we want to correlate the three variables of job satisfaction, income and age in a sample of 60 people and that three cases have missing data for income and a different set of four cases have missing data for age. The correlation between job satisfaction and income will be based on 57 cases, that between job satisfaction and age on 56 cases and that between income and age on 53 cases. An alternative procedure of analysis is to provide correlations for those cases which do not have missing values on any of those variables in which the number of cases will be the same for all the analyses. The keyword for this procedure is listwise deletion in a statistical package such as SPSS. Using this procedure with this example, all the correlations will be based on 53 cases. See also: **listwise deletion**

panel design or **study:** see **cohort analysis; longitudinal design** or **study**

parameter: a numerical characteristic of a population or a model. For example, the mean and standard deviation are two parameters of a population. The regression coefficient in a model is a parameter. The term statistic is used for the equivalent characteristics of samples rather than populations.

parametric statistics: see **parametric tests; ratio level of measurement**

parametric tests: tests of significance which assume that the distribution of the population values has a particular shape which is usually a normal distribution. For example, the _t_ test, which is based on estimating the variance of the population, assumes that the population values are normally distributed.

part correlation: see **multiple correlation; semi-partial correlation coefficient**

partial correlation: the correlation between two variables (a predictor and criterion or independent and dependent variable) adjusted for a third (control) variable. Partialling is a way of controlling for the effects of other variables. It is used as a simple form of causal modelling. For example, it is believed that adult criminality is determined by adolescent delinquency. Imagine the correlation between the two measures is 0.5. This appears to support the model. However, it is possible that a better explanation of the relationship is that both of these are the consequences of another (or third variable). People who live their lives in families that are prone to crime may themselves be encouraged in their criminal ways both as adolescents and as adults. What would be the correlation between adult and adolescent criminality if family criminality could be controlled (i.e. variation in family criminality eliminated)? There are a number of ways of doing this.

One simple way is to separate family criminality into different levels (high and low will do for illustration). If family criminality is not involved then there should be a correlation of 0.5 between adolescent delinquency and adult criminality for the high-criminality families and a similar correlation size for the low-criminality families. If the two correlations become zero or near zero, this is evidence that criminality in the family is responsible for the correlation between adolescent delinquency and adult criminality.

A more common method to achieve more or less the same end is the use of partial correlation. This can be used to control for a number of control variables (five or six is probably the practical limit). This is complex without a computer package but simple enough if we only wish to control for a single variable at a time. The formula is

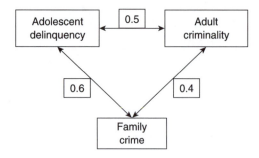

Figure P.1   *Correlations between three variables*

In our example we know that adult criminality (variable x) correlates with adolescent delinquency ($r = 0.5$). Imaging that adult criminality correlates 0.4 with family criminality and adolescent delinquency correlates 0.6 with family criminality. This could be presented in a diagram such as Figure P.1. There are double arrows between the various points because it is not known what, if anything, is the cause of what. Some points can be eliminated logically. For example, adult crime could not cause adolescent delinquency because a cause must precede an effect.

Entering these values into the above formula:

$$r_{xy.c} = \frac{0.5 - (0.6 \times 0.4)}{\sqrt{1 - 0.6^2}\sqrt{1 - 0.4^2}}$$

$$= \frac{0.5 - 0.24}{\sqrt{1 - 0.36}\sqrt{1 - 0.16}}$$

$$= \frac{0.26}{\sqrt{0.64}\sqrt{0.84}}$$

$$= \frac{0.26}{0.800 \times 0.917}$$

$$= \frac{0.26}{0.734}$$

$$= 0.35$$

As can be seen, the correlation has become smaller as a consequence of partialling (i.e. controlling for family crime). Nevertheless the remaining correlation of 0.35 still indicates a relationship between adolescent delinquency

Correlation between x and y with variable c controlled

Correlation between x and y

Correlations of variables x and y with the third variable c

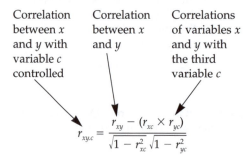

$$r_{xy.c} = \frac{r_{xy} - (r_{xc} \times r_{yc})}{\sqrt{1 - r_{xc}^2}\sqrt{1 - r_{yc}^2}}$$

Table P.1   *Some possible changes as a result of partialling and their implications*

Initial correlation between x and y	Correlation between x and y partialling for c	Description	Conclusion
$r_{xy} = 0.5$	$r_{xy.c} = 0.5$ (no change)	There is no significant change following partialling	Partialling makes no difference so c is neither the cause of nor an intervening variable in the relationship between x and y
$r_{xy} = 0.5$	$r_{xy.c} = 0.0$	Correlation declines significantly or becomes 0	c could be an antecedent* (cause) of the relationship between x and y; or it could be an intervening variable in the relationship
$r_{xy} = 0.0$	$r_{xy.c} = 0.5$	Correlation changes from a low value to a high value after partialling	c is a suppressor variable in the relationship between x and y, i.e. it hides the relationship which is revealed when the effects of c are removed

*For c to be an antecedent or cause of the relationship between x and y, one needs to ask questions about the temporal order and logical connection between the two. For example, the number of children a person has cannot be a cause of that person's parents' occupation. The time sequence is wrong in this instance.

and adult crime. Consequently the net effect of controlling for the third variable in this example leaves a smaller relationship but one which still needs explaining. Table P.1 gives some examples of the possible outcomes of controlling for third variables.

Partial correlation is a common technique in statistics and is a component of some important advanced techniques in addition. Because of the complexity of the calculation (i.e. the large number of steps) it is recommended that computer packages are used when it is intended to control for more than two variables. Zero-order partial correlation is another name for the correlation coefficient between two variables, first-order partial correlation occurs when one variable is controlled for, second-order partial correlation involves controlling for two variables, and so forth. The higher order partial correlations are denoted by extending the notation to include more control variables. Consequently $r_{xy.cde}$ means the partial correlation between variables x and y controlling (partialling out) for variables c, d and e.

Partial correlation is a useful technique. However, many of its functions are possibly better handled using, for example, multiple regression. This allows for more subtlety in generating models and incorporating control variables. See also: **Kendall's partial rank correlation coefficient; multiple regression**

partial gamma: a measure of partial association between two ordinal variables controlling for the influence of a third ordinal variable. It is the number of concordant pairs minus the number of discordant pairs for the two variables summed across the different levels of the third variable divided by the number of concordant and discordant pairs summed across the different levels of the third variable. A concordant pair is one in which the first case is ranked higher than the second case, while a discordant pair is the reverse, in which the first case is ranked lower than the second case.

Cramer (1998); Siegal and Castellan (1988)

participant: the modern term for subject. The term participant more accurately reflects the active role of the participant in the research process. The term subject implies subjugation and obedience. Unfortunately, many terms in statistics use the term subject (e.g. related-subjects, between-subjects, etc.) which makes it difficult to replace the term subject.

partitioning: another word for dividing something into parts. It is often used in analysis of variance where the total sum of squares is partitioned or divided into its component parts or sources such as the between- or within-groups sum of squares.

partitioning chi-square: denotes the process by which a large cross-tabulation/contingency table is broken down into smaller tables. This helps the researcher to assess just exactly where differences are occurring. Large contingency tables such as 2 × 3 or 4 × 2 are difficult to analyse since differences may occur in just sections of the table. Other parts of the table may show no trends at all. Table P.2 gives a 3 × 3 contingency table. It can probably be seen that sample 1 and sample 3 are virtually indistinguishable. In both cases apples are favourites with bananas second. Sample 2 seems very different. Bananas are by far the favourite in sample 2 with apples hardly selected by anyone. Through all of the samples, grapes show similar rates of choice. So it would not really be correct to suggest that all of the samples differ from each other (even if chi-square applied to these data were significant) since differences occur in only parts of the table.

One solution to identifying precisely where in the table a difference occurs is to partition the contingency table into a number of smaller tables. Each of these smaller tables is then interpretable since it will produce either significant or non-significant results. Table P.3 shows one smaller table that the data could be partitioned into. Here we have a 2 × 2 table that is not ambiguous as to interpretation since sample 1 and sample 2 are different in respect of what fruits they like.

Table P.2   *Data on favourite fruits in three samples*

Favourite fruit	Sample 1	Sample 2	Sample 3
Apple	35	4	32
Banana	22	54	23
Grape	12	16	13

Table P.3   *A small table taken from Table P.2 to illustrate one partition of the data*

Favourite fruit	Sample 1	Sample 2
Apple	35	4
Banana	22	54

Such partitioning does only what common sense tells us to do when examining something as complex as Table P.2. We simply look at a smaller part of the whole. A 2 × 2 table is the smallest unit for analysing two variables at a time. The chi-square based on this 2 × 2 table gives its significance level.

The main difficulties in employing partitioning lie in the quantity of partitioned tables that may be produced and the consequent question of what the correct significance level should be for each one. One solution is to use the Bonferroni inequality, which gives the maximum number of outcomes that would be expected by chance with the increased testing rate. In effect this means taking the exact significance levels of the 2 × 2 chi-squares and multiplying by the number of times the original contingency table was partitioned.

Partitioning may help reduce erroneous interpretations of large chi-square or contingency tables. Typical among the errors is the assumption that significant values of chi-square for large tables indicate that that all groups or samples are different from each other. The differences may only occur in parts of the data.

path analysis: an analysis in which three or more variables are ordered by the researcher in terms of their presumed causal relationships.

The causal relationship between the variables is more readily understood when presented in terms of a path diagram, in which arrows are used to indicate the direction and existence of a relationship between variables. Variables may be ordered in more than one way. Each arrangement of variables is called a model. The size and sign of these relationships are estimated. The simplest way of estimating these relationships is with correlation and multiple regression. However, these methods do not take account of the fact that the reliability of the measurement of the variables may differ. The relationship for a measure with lower reliability will be less strong than for one with higher reliability. Consequently, the relationships for less reliable measures may be underestimated. Structural equation modelling takes account of measurement error and so is a more appropriate method for estimating these relationships although it is more complicated. It also provides an index of the extent to which the relationships assumed to hold fit the data. A variable where no account is taken of its reliability is known as a manifest variable and may be represented by a square or rectangle in a path diagram. A variable where its reliability is taken into consideration is known as a latent variable and may be represented by a circle or ellipse. See also: **endogenous variable; exogenous variable; structural equation modelling**

Cramer (2003)

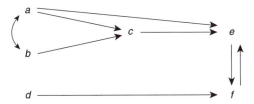

Figure P.2   *An example of a path diagram*

mediated through c. There is a direct and an indirect relationship between a and c. The indirect relationship is also mediated through c. A reciprocal or bi-directional relationship between two variables is indicated by two arrows between them, such as those between e and f indicating that e influences f and f influences e. A curved line with an arrow at either end, such as that between a and b, shows that two variables are related to one another but there is no causal relationship between them. Although not shown here, a variable enclosed in a square or rectangle is a manifest variable and one enclosed in a circle or ellipse is a latent variable. See also: **manifest variable; path analysis**

Cramer (2003)

Pearson chi-square: see **chi-square; likelihood ratio chi-square**

path diagram: shows the presumed causal relationships between three or more variables. An example of a path diagram in presented in Figure P.2. The variables are usually ordered from left to right in terms of their causal sequence, a uni-directional causal relationship being indicated by a straight, single right-pointing arrow. So variables to the left of other variables are assumed to influence variables to their right. For example, variables a and b influence variable c which in turn influences variable e. There is no causal relationship between variable b and variable e or between variable b and variable f because there is no arrow between them. There is an indirect relationship between b and e which is

Pearson's correlation coefficient: see **correlation; eta; outliers; phi coefficient; point–biserial correlation coefficient; T_2 test; z test**

Pearson's partial correlation: see **partial correlation**

Pearson's product moment correlation coefficient: see **correlation**

percentage: the proportion or fraction of something expressed as being out of 100 – literally 'for every hundred'. So another way of saying 65% is to say sixty-five out of every hundred or $\frac{65}{100}$. This may be also expressed as 65 per cent. The way of calculating percentages is the fraction × 100. Thus, if a sample has 25 females out of a total of 60 cases, then this expressed as a percentage is $\frac{25}{60}$ × 100 = 0.425 × 100 = 42.5%.

percentage probability: probabilities are normally expressed as being out of one event, – for example one toss of a coin or die. Thus, the probability of tossing a head with one flip of a coin is 0.5 since there are two equally likely outcomes – head or tail. Percentage probabilities are merely probabilities expressed out of 100 events. Thus, to calculate a percentage probability, one merely takes the probability and multiplies it by 100. So the percentage probability of a head on tossing a coin is 0.5 × 100 = 50%. See also: **probability**

percentiles: if a set of scores is put in order from the smallest to the largest, the 10 percentile is the score which cuts off the bottom 10% of scores (the smallest scores). Similarly, the 30th percentile is the score which cuts off the bottom 30% of scores. The 100th percentile is, of course, the highest score by this reasoning. The 50th percentile is also known as the median. Percentiles are therefore a way of expressing a score in terms of its relative standing to other scores. For example, in itself a score of 15 means little. Being told that a score of 15 is at the 85th percentile suggests that it is a high score and that most scores are lower.

There are a number of different ways of estimating what the percentile should be when there is no score that is actually the percentile. These different methods may give slightly different values. The following method has the advantage of simplicity. We will refer to the following list of 15 scores in the estimation:

1, 3, 4, 4, 6, 7, 8, 9, ⑭ 15, 16, 16, 17, 19, 22

1   Order the scores from smallest to largest (this has already been done for the list above).
2   Count the number of scores (N). This is 15.
3   To find the percentile (p) calculate p × (N + 1). If we want the 60th percentile, the value of p is 0.6 (i.e. the numerical value of the percentile required divided by 100).
4   So with 15 scores, the calculation gives us 0.6 × (15 + 1) = 0.6 × 16 = 9.6.
5   The estimate of the 60th percentile is found by splitting the 9.6 into an integer (9) and a fraction (0.6).
6   We use the integer value to find the score corresponding to the integer (the Ith score). In this case the integer is 9 and so we look at the 9th score in the ordered sequence of scores. This is the score of 14.
7   We then find the numerical difference between the 9th score and the next higher score (the score at position I + 1) in the list of scores. The value of this score is 15. So the difference we calculate is the difference between 14 and 15 in this case. Thus, the difference is 1.
8   We then multiply this difference by the 0.6 that we obtained in step 5 above. This gives us 1 × 0.6 = 0.6.
9   We then add this to the value of the 9th score (i.e. 14 + 0.6) to give us the estimated value of the percentile. So, this estimated value is 14.6.
10 Quite clearly the 60th percentile had to lie somewhere between the scores of 14 and 15. However, this estimate places it at 14.6 rather than 14.5 which would be the value obtained from simply splitting (averaging) the scores.

Percentiles are a helpful means of presenting an individual's score though they have limited utility and show only a part of the total picture. More information is conveyed by a frequency distribution, for example. Percentiles are a popular way of presenting normative data on tests and measurements which are designed to present information about individuals compared with the general

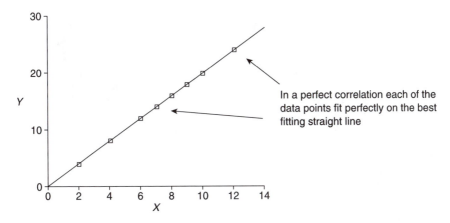

Figure P.3   *Illustrating a perfect correlation coefficient*

population or some other group. Quartiles and deciles are related concepts. See also: **box plot**

perfect correlation: a correlation coefficient of 1.00 or −1.00 in which all the points of the scattergram for the two variables lie exactly on the best fitting straight line through the points. If a perfect correlation is obtained in a computer analysis, it is probably worthwhile checking the corresponding scattergram (and the other descriptive statistics pertinent to the correlation) as it may be suspiciously high and the result of, say, some sort of coding error. A perfect correlation coefficient is an unrealistically high ideal in most disciplines given the general limited adequacy of measurement techniques. Hence if one occurs in real data then there is good reason to explore why this should be the case. Figure P.3 gives the scattergram for a perfect positive correlation – the slope would be downwards from the left to the right for a perfect negative correlation.

permutation: a sequence of events in probability theory. For example, if the sequence of events were the toss of a coin, then one permutation of events might be T, T, T, T, T, H, H,

H. This is a distinct permutation from the series T, H, T, T, H, T, H, T despite the fact that both series contain exactly three heads and five tails each. (If we ignore sequence, then the different possibilities are known as combinations.) Permutations of outcomes such as taking a name from a hat containing initially six names can be calculated by multiplying the possibilities at each selection. So if we take out a name three times the number of different combinations is $6 \times 5 \times 4 = 120$. This is because for the first selection there are six different names to choose from, then at the second selection there are five different names (we have already taken one name out) and at the third selection there are four different names. Had we replaced the name into the hat then the permutations would be $6 \times 6 \times 6$. See also: **combination**

Permutations are rarely considered in routine statistical analyses since they have more to do with mathematical probability theory than with descriptive and inferential statistics which form the basis of statistical analysis in the social sciences. See also: **combination; sampling with replacement**

phi coefficient: a variant of Pearson's correlation applied to two variables each of which takes one of two values which may be coded

1 or 2 (or any other pair of values for that matter). As such, its most common applications are in correlating two items on a questionnaire where the answers are coded yes or no (or as some other binary alternatives), and in circumstances in which a 2×2 chi-square would alternatively be employed. While there is a distinct formula for the phi coefficient, it is simply a special case of Pearson's correlation with no advantage in an era of computer statistical packages. In cases where it needs to be computed by hand, simply applying Pearson's correlation formula to the variables coded as above gives exactly the same value. Its advantage was that it made the calculation of the phi coefficient a little more speedy, which saved considerable time working by hand on large questionnaires, for example. See also: **correlation; Cramer's V; dummy coding**

pictogram: essentially a form of bar chart in which the rectangular bars are replaced by a pictorial representation appropriate to the measures being summarized. For example, the frequencies of males and females in a sample could be represented by male and female figures of heights which correspond to the frequencies. This is illustrated in Figure P.4. Alternatively, the figures could be piled above each other to give an equivalent, but different, representation.

Sometimes a pictogram is used to replace a bar chart, though attempts to do this are likely to be less successful. A frequent difficulty with pictograms lies in their lack of correspondence to the bars in a bar chart except in terms of their height. Classically, in a bar chart the area of a bar actually relates directly to the number of cases. Hence, typically the bars are each of the same width. This correspondence is lost with any other shape. This can be seen in Figure P.4 where the male figure is not just taller than the female figure, but wider too. The net effect is that the male figure is not about twice the height of the female, but four times the area. Hence, unless the reader concentrates solely on height in relation to the frequency scale a misleading impression may be created. Nevertheless, a pictogram is visually appealing, communicates

Figure P.4 *Pictogram indicating relative frequencies of males and females*

the nature of the information fairly well, and appeals to non-statistically minded audiences. See also: **bar chart**

pie chart: a common way of presenting frequencies of categories of a variable. The complete data for the variable are represented by a circle and the frequencies of the subcategories of the variable are given as if they were slices of the total pie (circle). Figure P.5 illustrates the approach although there are many variations on the theme. The size of the slice is determined by the proportion of the total that the category represents. For example, if 130 university students are classified as science, engineering or arts students and 60 of the students are arts students, they would be represented by a slice which was $\frac{60}{130}$ of the total circle. Since a circle encompasses 360°, the angle for this particular slice would be $\frac{60}{130} \times 360° = 0.462 \times 360° = 166°$.

Pie diagrams are best reserved, in general, for audio-visual presentations when their visual impact is maximized. They are much less appropriate in research reports and the like where they take up rather a lot of space for the information that they communicate. Pie diagrams are most effective when there are few slices. Very small categories may be combined as 'others' to facilitate the clarity of the presentation. See also: **bar chart; frequency distribution**

Pillai's criterion: a test used in multivariate statistical procedures such as canonical

Pie-diagrams may also include the frequency
in each slice or percentage frequencies. This
diagram is clear because of the small number
of slices. Slices may be 'exploded' out for
emphasis

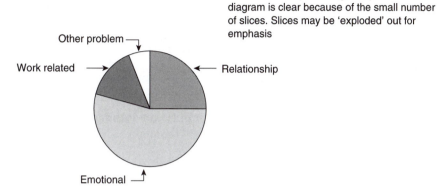

Figure P.5 *Types of cases taken on by psychological counsellors*

correlation, discriminant function analysis
and multivariate analysis of variance to determine whether the means of the groups differ
on a discriminant function or characteristic
root. This test is said to be more robust than
Wilks's lambda, Hotelling's trace criterion and
Roy's *gcr* criterion when the assumption of the
homogeneity of the variance–covariance
matrix is violated. This assumption is more
likely to be violated with small and unequal
sample sizes. See also: **Wilks's lambda**
  Tabachnick and Fidell (2001)

planned comparison or **test:** see **analysis
of variance**

platykurtic: see **kurtosis**

point–biserial correlation coefficient: a
variant of Pearson's correlation applied in
circumstances where one variable has two
alternative discrete values (which may be
coded 1 and 2 or any other two different
numerical values) and the other variable has
a (more or less) continuous distribution of
scores. This is illustrated in Table P.4. The discrete variable may be a nominal variable so
long as there are only two categories. Hence a

Table P.4 *Illustrating how a binary nominal
variable may be recoded as a score
variable to enable a correlation
coefficient to be calculated*

Gender (discrete variable)	Recode gender 1 for female, 2 for male	Linguistic aptitude (continuous variable)
Female	1	49
Female	1	17
Male	2	15
Male	2	21
Male	2	19
Female	1	63
Female	1	70
Male	2	29

variable such as gender (male and female) is
suitable to use as the discrete variable. See
also: **dummy coding**
  Pearson's correlation (which is also known
as the point–biserial correlation) between the
numbers in the second and third columns =
−0.70. The minus is purely arbitrary and the
Table P.4 of consequence of the arbitrary value
for females being lower than that for males, but
the females typically have the higher scores on
linguistic aptitude. See also: **correlation**

point estimates: a single figure estimate
rather than a range. See also: **confidence
interval**

pooled variances: combined or averaged variances. Variances are pooled to provide a better population estimate in the *t* test for unrelated samples where the variances are equal but the number of cases is unequal in the two groups. The formula for pooling variances is as follows where the size of the sample is indicated by *n* and the two samples are referred to by the two subscripts 1 and 2:

$$\sqrt{\frac{[\text{variance}_1 \times (n_1 - 1)] + [\text{variance}_2 \times (n_2 - 1)]}{n_1 + n_2 - 2} \times \left(\frac{1}{n_1} + \frac{1}{n_2}\right)}$$

See also: **variance**

population: a deceptively simple concept which actually means two quite distinct things in research and statistics respectively. Hence, it can cause a great deal of confusion. In research, population means much the same as in everyday language – a population is all of a particular type of individual. This may be limited by geographical location or one or more other characteristics. So populations would include all children attending schools in London, or all gay people in the country, and so forth. The nature of a population changes according to the nature and purpose of the research.

In statistics, this sort of concept of population would be somewhat cumbersome. Consequently, the term is applied to a variable rather than an identifiable group of individuals or cases. So a population in statistics really refers to a population of scores on a particular variable. This could be the IQs of the geographical grouping which is the population of the British Isles in everyday terms. But it can be much more abstract than that. Variables often do not exist separate from the process of measuring them, so populations in statistics can be difficult to define. That is, until a researcher invents, say, an attitude scale and gives it to a sample, the variable which the scale measures simply does not exist. Each time a researcher tries to measure something new with a sample of people, a new population is created. Nevertheless, despite the intangible nature of some populations in

statistics, the concept of population is essential since it describes the wider set from which the research's sample is regarded as being drawn. See also: **convenience sample; estimated standard deviation; parameter; sample; significant**

population standard deviation: see **standard deviation**

population variance: see **variance** or **population variance**

positivism: a major aspect of the philosophy of science. It has as its basic principle that knowledge should be obtained from observation as a means of assessing the value of our notions about the nature of things. It then is very different from non-scientific thought such as theism, which holds that knowledge resides in religion and religious teachings, and metaphysics, which holds that knowledge emerges from philosophical thought about issues. It has its origins as a formal philosophy of science in the work of August Comte in the nineteenth century. Some researchers virtually equate statistical analysis with positivism though there is little in statistics itself (rather than the way it has been applied) which justifies this. Possibly the major difficulty that positivism has presented is that it has historically been associated with the idea of universalism, which is the view that the object of science is to develop universal laws of nature which apply anywhere – such that the principles of gravity should apply throughout the universe. Unfortunately, universalism when applied to *human* nature does not work very well. Human beings operate in the context of a cultural system such that cultural factors need to be taken into account when studying society and human activity. To some extent, then, social science needs to be culturally specific: in other words, not universal. Classic examples of universalism are abundant in psychology, for example, when the researcher seeks to discover 'the laws of human behaviour'. Laboratory experiments encourage such an enterprise since they divorce the participants from the context in which they usually operate. In a nutshell, the subject statistics does not equate to positivism although it has traditionally been a common feature of positivistic research.

Owusu-Bempah and Howitt (2000)

post hoc, a posteriori or **unplanned tests** or **multiple comparison tests:** statistical tests applied after the data have been collected without any prior consideration of what comparisons are essential to the research questions. They are comparisons done after the facts (data) have been collected and where overall the analysis of variance has indicated that the null hypothesis that there is no difference between the means is not sustainable (i.e. where the F ratio is statistically significant). The point is that statistical significance merely means that some but not necessarily all of the treatment means are unequal. The question is which ones are unequal? The *post hoc* tests allow comparisons between pairs of treatment means in order to indicate which of the pairs of means are statistically significantly different from each other.

The risk is, of course, simply dredging through the data in order to find significant findings without making any allowance for the fact that the more significance tests one does the more likely one is to obtain significance due to chance rather than 'true' effects. Hence, to do repeated t tests, for example between all possible pairs of means, is frowned upon. One can employ the Bonferroni correction, which basically says that if one does three t tests, for example using a 5% significance level, this is in the worst instance like really testing at the 15% level of significance. That is, the 15% level of significance is extremely conservative and is the highest value it could be.

So all *post hoc* tests make some correction for the number of comparisons involved. These adjustments tend to be rather large and are described as being conservative (i.e. tending to support the null hypothesis of no difference). There is a variety of *post hoc* tests which is rather bewildering. A lack of consensus about where and when to apply the different measures is another limitation. Some have limitations such as being inapplicable where the groups are of different size (e.g. Tukey's HSD test) and others are regarded as being too biased towards detecting no differences (e.g. the Scheffé test). A reasonable recommendation, given that few will calculate the values of *post hoc* tests without the use of a computer, is to do a range of *post hoc* tests. Where they all indicate the same conclusions then clearly there is no problem. If they indicate very different conclusions for a particular set of data, then the reasons and importance of this have to be assessed. However, in this way the problem has been identified as existing. See also: **analysis of variance; Bonferroni test; Duncan's new multiple range test; Fisher's LSD test; Gabriel's simultaneous test procedure; Games–Howell multiple comparison procedure; Hochberg *GT2* Test; multiple comparison tests; Newman–Keuls method; Ryan *F* and *Q* tests; Scheffé test; Tamhane's *T2* multiple comparison test; Tukey$_a$ and Tukey$_b$ tests; Tukey–Kramer test; Waller–Duncan t test**

post-test: the measurement made immediately after the experimental treatment or the control for the experimental treatment has been made. See **pre-test**

power: the number of times that a quantity or number is multiplied by itself. It is usually written as an exponent, which is a number or symbol placed above and to the right of that quantity. For example, the exponent 2 in the expression 3^2 indicates that the quantity 3 is raised or multiplied to the second power or the power of 2, which is 3×3. The exponent 3 in the expression 3^3 indicates that the quantity 3 is raised to the third power or the power of 3, which is $3 \times 3 \times 3$. See **exponent**

power of a test: the probability of a statistical test of finding a relationship between two variables when there is such a relationship. The maximum power a test can have is 1 and the minimum 0 with 0.80 indicating an acceptable level of power. The power of a test is generally greater for one- than two-tailed hypotheses, parametric than non-parametric tests, lower (e.g. 0.05) than higher (e.g. 0.001) significance levels and larger samples.

predictive validity: the extent to which a variable predicts or is related to another variable which is measured subsequently. It may be distinguished from concurrent validity in which the two variables are measured at the same or similar time.

predictor variable: often used to refer to the variables in a multiple regression which are employed to predict the values of the criterion or criterion variable. This criterion variable may be measured at the same time as some or all of the predictor variables or it may be measured subsequently to them. This term is also used more generally to refer to variables that are employed to predict a variable which is measured subsequently. See also: **log likelihood; logistic regression; regression equation**

pre-test: a measurement stage preceding the administration of the experimental treatment. It provides a baseline measurement against which change due to the experimental treatment can be assessed. Without a pre-test, it is not possible to know whether scores have increased, stayed the same or reduced. It also shows whether the means of the groups are similar prior to the subsequent measurement. If the pre-test means differ significantly and if the pre-test is correlated with the post-test, these pre-test differences need to be taken into account when examining the post-test differences. The recommended statistical test for doing this is analysis of covariance.

Experimental treatment or merely passage of time

Figure P.6   *The pre-test design*

Research designs involving pre-tests are not without their problems. For one thing, the pre-test may sensitize the participants and affect the degree of influence of the experimental treatment (Figure P.6). For example, if the study is about changing attitudes, forewarning participants by giving them a pre-test measure of their attitudes may make them realize that their susceptibility to influence is being assessed. Consequently, they may try their hardest not to change their attitude under the experimental treatment. Hence, sometimes a pre-test design also includes additional groups which are not pre-tested to see whether the pre-test may have had an influence. See also: **baseline; quasi-experiments**

pre-test–post-test design: involves a pre-test and a post-test. See **pre-test**

principal axis factoring: a form of factor analysis in which only the variance shared between the variables is analysed. Variance which is unique to a variable or is error is not analysed. The shared variance or communality can vary from a minimum of 0 to a maximum of 1. It is generally less than 1.

principal components analysis: a form of factor analysis in which all the variance of the variables is analysed. The communality of each variable is 1.

probability: the mathematical chance or likelihood that a particular outcome will occur. It is expressed in terms of the ratio of a particular outcome to all possible outcomes. Thus, the probability of a coin landing heads is 1 divided by 2 (the possible outcomes are heads or tails). Probability is expressed per event so will vary between 0 and 1. Probabilities are largely expressed as decimals such as 0.5 or 0.67. Sometimes probabilities are expressed as percentage probabilities, which is simply the probability (which is out of a single event) being re-expressed out of 100 events (i.e. the percentage probability is the probability $\times$ 100).

The commonest use of probabilities is in significance testing. While it is useful to know the basic ideas of probability, many researchers carry out thorough and appropriate analyses of their data without using other than a few very basic notions about probability. Hence, the complexities of mathematical probability theory are of little bearing on the practice of statistical analysis of psychological and social science data.

probability level: see **significant**

probability sampling: a form of sampling in which each case or element in the population has a known probability of being included in the sample. In the simplest situation of simple random sampling each case has the same probability of being sampled. In stratified random sampling each case may not have the same probability of being included as the population is divided into different strata or groups which may not

have the same probability of being chosen. Probability sampling may be distinguished from non-probability sampling in which the probability of a case being selected is unknown. Non-probability sampling is often euphemistically described as convenience sampling.

probability theory: see **Bayesian inference; Bayes's theorem; odds; percentage probability; probability**

proband: see **subject**

proportion: the frequency of cases in a category divided by the total number of cases. It varies from a minimum of 0 to a maximum of 1. For example, if there are 8 men and 12 women in a sample, the proportion of men is 0.40 (8/20 = 0.40). A proportion may be converted into a percentage by multiplying the proportion by 100. A proportion of 0.40 represents 40% (0.40 $\times$ 100 = 40).

prospective design or **study:** see **cohort analysis; longitudinal design or study**

pseudo-random number or **tables:** see **random number tables**

Q

Q analysis, methodology or technique: the usual strategy in factor analysis is to look for patterns in the data supplied by the participants. For example, a questionnaire may be factor analysed to see what groupings of questions tend to be responded to similarly. An alternative to this involves looking for patterns in the participants. That is, to form the factors on the basis of which people show similar patterns in their replies to the questions compared with others in the sample. In its simplest form, this involves producing a correlation matrix in which the different participants are the variables and their answers to the questions are the equivalent of different cases in normal factor analysis. In other words, the data are entered such that the rows become the columns and the columns become the rows compared with normal factor analysis. This will then generate a correlation matrix of correlations between people rather than one of correlations between variables. The factors are then interpreted in terms of the individuals who load highly on a factor (rather than variables which load highly on a factor).

It is possible to carry out Q analysis on any data which have been analysed using factor analysis by simply using the facility of computer packages such as SPSS to transpose the data matrix (spreadsheet). This option essentially moves the matrix through 90° so that the rows become the columns and vice versa. The transposed matrix can then be factor analysed yielding Q factors. See also: **exploratory factor analysis**

qualitative research: generally research where there is little or no attempt to summarize the data and/or describe the relationships found using numbers. It is difficult to discuss qualitative research briefly since it varies enormously in its style, scope, methods and theoretical underpinnings. Some researchers regard it as a prelude to quantitative research in which the researchers familiarize themselves with the matter of their research with the intention of developing much more structured ways of collecting data. Other researchers regard qualitative methods as a means of correcting what they see as the fundamental errors in quantification. Qualitative research is largely concerned with the development of coding categories to describe fully the data in question. In grounded theory, for example, the researcher employs data analysis methods which essentially require numerous revisions of codings of textual data in order to force a close fit between the data and the analytic scheme being developed.

In terms of statistical analysis, in many ways the distinction between qualitative and quantitative data analysis is misleading. Research which analyses data in terms of coding categories is potentially amenable to the use of statistical techniques for nominal (category or categorical) data. This form of data has sometimes been referred to as qualitative data in the statistical literature. In this sense, qualitative researchers may not always be right to reject statistics as part of the analysis of their data.

There are lessons for quantitative researchers to learn from qualitative research. Perhaps the most important of these is the importance of closely matching the analysis to the detail of the data. It is interesting to note that exploratory data analysis stresses this sort of detailed fit in quantitative data analysis.

qualitative variables: see **categorical (category) variable; frequency distribution**

quantitative measurement: see **measurement**

quantitative research: generally research where there is some attempt to summarize the data and/or describe the relationships found using numbers. Statistical analysis is certain to accompany such data collection.

quantitative variables: see **categorical variable; frequency distribution**

quartile deviation or **semi-interquartile range:** a measure of dispersion (spread of data) which is sometimes used instead of the interquartile range. It is the interquartile range divided by 2.

quartiles: scores which cut off the bottom 25%, 50% and 75% of scores in a sequence of scores ordered from the smallest to the largest. They are known as the first, second and third quartiles. They refer to specific values of scores. The second quartile is also known as the median. They are calculated in the same way as the 25th percentile, the 50th percentile and the 75th percentile would be (see **percentiles**). The interquartile range is the range of scores from the 25th percentile to

the 75th percentile or the 1st quartile (lower quartile) to the 3rd quartile (upper quartile). See also: **interquartile range; percentile**

quasi-experiments: research designs which may be regarded as close to proper or true experiments. In many areas of research, it is not possible to allocate participants randomly to experimental and control conditions in order to study the influence of the independent variable. That is, true experiments are not practical or feasible or the researcher may be unsympathetic to the use of invasive experimental techniques when studying real-world phenomena. Quasi-experiments are a number of research designs which by various means attempt to improve the researcher's ability to identify causal influences compared with a correlational study. There may be ethical difficulties in random assignment (e.g. in a study of the effects of medical treatment, to withhold treatment from a control group may result in deaths or other serious consequences for the control group). There may be practical difficulties. For example, in a study of the effects of management style in different organizations, companies may be unwilling to take the financial risk associated with changing their management style in accordance with the desires of researchers. Some random allocations are also simply impossible – people cannot be assigned to different genders randomly. Laboratory-based research is the most amenable in general to randomized experiments, whereas field-based disciplines may find such designs inappropriate.

Quasi-experiments attempt to emulate the strengths of randomized experiments by the following means:

1   By obtaining pre-test (baseline) measurements on the dependent variable, it is possible to adjust statistically for pre-test differences between the groups in the study. In other words, there are experimental and control groups but participants could not be randomly assigned so are allocated to the groups on some other

basis. Sometimes the research will employ pre-existing groups such as when, say, students at two different types of school are compared by school type.

2   By observing the effects of interventions over a series of temporal points (time series), it is possible to assess whether change occurs following the intervention. For example, if a researcher was studying the effects of the introduction of incentives on office morale, the morale of office workers could be assessed monthly for a year. At some stage (perhaps at random), the management would introduce the incentive scheme. Later it could be removed. And perhaps later still reintroduced. One would expect that if the incentive scheme was effective, morale would increase when it is introduced, decrease when it is taken away, and increase on its reintroduction.

Variations are possible and, for example, the time-series feature may be combined with a control time series which does not have the intervention. Since quasi-experimental design is a term which covers a large proportion of research designs which are not experiments, it is a major aspect of research design. Of course, there is a lot of research which does not set out to address issues of causality.

questionnaire: a list of written questions or statements which is given to a person to complete (self-completion questionnaire) or may be read to the participant by a researcher or interviewer who records their response. Questionnaires vary greatly in their degree of structure. Perhaps the majority of questionnaires structure the replies by supplying a range of alternative responses from which the participant chooses.

quota sampling: a non-random sample of a population which has been divided into various categories of respondent (e.g. males and female, employed and unemployed). The purpose of quota sampling is to ensure that certain categories of person are included in sufficient proportions in the data. For each of the categories a certain number or quota of cases are specified and obtained. This ensures that there is sufficient cases in each of these categories. (Random sampling, in theory, may result in inadequate samples for some purposes. Random sampling from a population containing equal numbers of males and females may result in a sample with few males.) For example, we may want to have a certain number of gay and lesbian people in the sample. Samples obtained in this way are normally not random samples and are obtained through a range of practical means. Consequently, we do not know how representative these cases are of their categories.

R

R analysis, methodology or **technique:** *R* equates to regular factor analysis in which the correlations between variables are factored and the factors account for clusters of variables measuring similar things. This is different from the *Q* technique in which the objective is to identify groups of cases which are highly similar to each other. In other words, *R* analysis groups variables, *Q* analysis groups cases.

random allocation: see **randomization**

random assignment: see **quasi-experiments; randomization**

random effects model: a term used in experimental design and the analysis of variance to denote the selection of levels of the experimental treatment at random. It requires selection from the full possible range of levels. It is relatively uncommon to find it employed in practice but it is of conceptual importance. The difficulties include that the full range of treatments may not be known (especially if the independent variable is essentially nominal categories rather than particular values of a score). More generally, researchers tend to use a fixed effects model in which the researcher selects which levels

of treatment to use on the basis of some reasoned decisions (which do not involve random selection). The type of model has a bearing on ANOVA calculations in particular. Generally speaking, the random effects model is rarely employed in branches of many social science disciplines simply because of the practical and conceptual difficulties of identifying different levels of the independent variable from which to sample randomly. See also: **fixed effects; levels of treatment**

random number tables: sometimes known as pseudo-random number tables. These were particularly useful in the past when researchers did not have ready access to computers capable of generating random sequences. As the name implies, these are tables of random sequences of the digits 0, 1, 2, 3, 4, 5, 6, 7, 8 and 9. Typically they consist of many pages of numbers. Usually the sequences are listed in columns with, say, every six digits separated from the next by a space. For example,

901832	143912	861543	672315	531250
167321	784321	422649	216975	356217
636298	157823	916421	436126	752318
264843	652365	132863	254731	534174

To use the table, typically the researcher would choose a starting point (with eyes shut using a pin, for example) and a pre-specified interval. So if the starting point selected was the 8 underlined above and numbers in the range 01 to 90 were needed for selection, then the first number would be 84. Assume that the interval selected was seven digits. The researcher would then ignore the next seven digits (4321 422) and so the next chosen number would be 64 and the one after that 35. If a selection were repeated by chance, then the researcher would simply ignore the repetition and proceed to the next number instead. So long as the rules applied by the researcher are clear and consistently applied then these tables are adequate. The user should not be tempted to depart from the procedure chosen during the course of selection in any circumstances otherwise the randomness of the process is compromised. The tables are sometimes known as pseudo-random numbers partly because they were generated using mathematical formulae that give the appearance of randomness but at some level actually show complex patterns. True random numbers would show no patterns at all no matter how hard they are sought. For practical purposes, the problem of pseudo-randomness does not undermine the usefulness of random number tables for the purposes of most researchers in the social sciences since the patterns identified are very broad. See also: **randomization**

random sampling: see **simple random sampling**

random sampling with replacement: see **sampling with replacement**

random selection: see **randomization**

random variable: one meaning of this term is a variable whose values have not been chosen. For example, age is a random variable if we simply select people regardless of what age they are. The opposite of a random variable is a fixed variable for which particular values have been chosen. For example, we may select people of particular ages or who lie within particular age ranges. Another meaning of the term is that it is a variable with a specified probability distribution.

randomization: also known as random allocation or assignment. It is used in experiments as a means of 'fairly' allocating participants to the various conditions of the study. Random allocation methods are those in which every participant or case has an equal likelihood of being placed in any of the various conditions. For example, if there are two different conditions in a study (an experimental condition and a control condition), then randomization could simply be achieved by the toss of a coin for each participant. Heads could indicate the experimental condition, tails the control condition. Other methods would include drawing slips from a container, the toss of dice, random number tables and computer-generated random number tables. For example, if there were four conditions in a study, the different conditions could be designated A, B, C and D, equal numbers of identical slips of paper labelled A, B, C or D placed in a container, and the slips drawn out one by one to indicate the particular condition of the study for a particular participant.

Randomization can also be used to decide the order of the conditions in which a particular individual will take part in repeated-measures designs in which the individual serves in more than one condition.

Randomization (random allocation) needs to be carefully distinguished from random selection. Random selection is the process of selecting samples from a population of potential participants. Random allocation is the process of allocating individuals to the conditions of an experiment. Few experiments in the social sciences employ random selection whereas the vast majority use random allocation. Failure to select participants randomly from the population affects the external validity of the research since it becomes impossible to specify exactly what the population in question is and, hence, who the findings of the research apply to. The failure to use randomization (random allocation) affects the internal validity of the study – that is, it is impossible to know with any degree of certainty why the different experimental conditions produced different outcomes (or even why they produced the same outcome). This is because randomization (random allocation) results in each condition having participants who are similar to each other on all variables other than the experimental manipulation. Because each participant is equally likely to be allocated to any of the conditions, it is not possible to have systematic biases favouring a particular condition in the long run. In other words, randomization helps maximize the probability that the obtained differences between the different experimental conditions are due to the factors which the researcher systematically varied (i.e. the experimental manipulation).

Randomization can proceed in blocks. The difficulty with, for example, random allocation by the toss of a coin is that it is perfectly possible that very few individuals are allocated to the control condition or that there is a long run of individuals assigned to the control condition before any get assigned to the experimental condition. A block is merely a subset of individuals in the study who are treated as a unit in order to reduce the possible biases which simple randomization cannot prevent. For example, if one has a study with an experimental condition (A) and a control condition (B), then one could operate with blocks of two participants. These are allocated at the same time – one at random to the experimental group and the other consequently to the control group. In this way, long runs are impossible as would be unequal numbers in the experimental and control groups. There is a difficulty with this approach – that is, it does nothing to prevent the possibility that the first person of the two is more often allocated to the experimental condition than the control condition. This is possible in random sampling in the short term. This matters if the list of participants is structured in some way – for example, if the participants consisted of the head of a household followed by their spouse on the list, which

could result in more employed people being in the experimental condition. Consequently, the researcher might consider using a system in which runs are eliminated by running participants in fours with the first two assigned randomly to AB and the next two to BA.

Failure to understand the importance of and careful procedures required for randomization can lead to bad practices. For example, it is not unknown for researchers to speak of randomization when they really mean a fairly haphazard allocation system. A researcher who allocates to the experimental and control conditions alternate participants is not randomly allocating. Furthermore, ideally the randomization should be conducted by a disinterested party since it is possible that the randomization procedure is ignored or disregarded for seemingly good reasons which nevertheless bias the outcome. For example, a researcher may be tempted to put an individual in the control condition if they believe that the participant may be stressed or distressed by the experimental procedure.

Randomization may be compromised in other ways. In particular, the different conditions of an experiment may produce differential rates of refusal or drop-out. A study of the effects of psychotherapy may have a treated group and a non-treated group. The non-treated group may have more drop-outs simply because members of this group are arrested more by the police and are lost to the researchers due to imprisonment. This, of course, potentially might effect the outcome of the research. For this reason, it is important to keep notes on rates of refusal and attrition (loss from the study).

Finally, some statistical tests are based on randomized allocations of scores to conditions. That is, the statistic is based on the pattern of outcomes that emerge in the long run if one takes the actual data but then randomly allocates the data back to the various conditions such as the experimental and control group. In other words, the probability of the outcome obtained in the research is assessed against the distribution of outcomes which would apply if the distribution of scores were random. Terms like resampling, bootstrapping and permutation methods describe different means of achieving statistical tests based on randomization. See also: **control group**

randomized block design: see **matching**

range: the size of the difference between the largest and the smallest score in a set of scores. Thus, if the highest value obtained is 18 and the lowest value is 11 then the range is $18 - 11 = 7$. There is also the interquartile range which is the range of the middle 50% of scores.

One common misunderstanding is to present the range as the largest value to the smallest value. This is not the range – the *difference* numerically between the extreme values constitutes the range. See also: **dispersion, measure of**

rank measurement: see **measurement**

rank order: see **ordinal level of measurement**

ranking tests: a term often used to denote non-parametric statistical tests in general but more appropriate for those techniques in which scores or differences are converted into ranks prior to the application of the statistical formulae. It should really refer to tests where ranking is carried out. For example, there are versions of the *t* test which utilize ranks whereas the *t* test is usually regarded as operating directly with scores. See **distribution-free tests**

ratio: a measure which shows the relative size of two numbers. It can be expressed as two numbers separated by a colon, as one number divided by another or as the result of that division. For example, the ratio of 12 to 8 can be expressed as 12:8, 12/8 or 1.5. See also: **score**

ratio level of measurement, scale or **variable:** a measure in which the adjacent intervals between the points of the scale are of equal extent and where the measure has an absolute zero point. For example, the measure or scale of age in years has adjacent intervals of equal extent. The extent of the interval between age 7 and 8 is the same as that between age 8 and 9, namely 1 year. It also has an absolute zero point in that the lowest possible age is 0. It is called a ratio measure because ages can be expressed as ratios. Age 10 is twice as old as age 5 ($10:5 = 2:1$). It is frequently suggested that ratio and interval levels of measurement, unlike ordinal ones, should be analysed with parametric statistics. See also: **measurement**

reciprocal relationship: see **bi-directional relationship**

recursive relationship: see **uni-directional relationship**

refusal rates: participation in research is essentially a voluntary action for virtually all studies actively involving people. Participants may refuse to take part in the research study at all or refuse to take part in aspects of the research (e.g. they may be happy to answer any question but the one to do with their age). Researchers should keep a record of the persons approached and as much information as possible about their characteristics. Rates of refusal should be presented and any comparisons possible between participants and refusers identified. Some forms of research have notoriously high refusal rates such as telephone surveys and questionnaires sent out by post. Response rates as low as 15% or 20% would not be unusual.

Refusal rates are a problem because of the (unknown) likelihood that they are different for different groupings of the sample. Research is particularly vulnerable to refusal rates if its purpose is to obtain estimates of population parameters from a sample. For example, if intentions to vote are being assessed then refusals may bias the estimate in one direction or another. High refusal rates are less problematic when one is not trying to obtain precise population estimates. Experiments, for example, may be less affected than some other forms of research such as surveys.

Refusal rates are an issue in interpreting the outcomes of any research and should be presented when reporting findings. See also: **attrition; missing values**

regression: see **heteroscedasticity; intercept; multiple regression; regression equation; simple** or **bivariate regression standard error of the regression coefficient; stepwise entry; variance of estimate**

regression coefficient: see **standardized** or **unstandardized partial regression coefficient** or **weight**

regression equation: expresses the linear relationship between a criterion or dependent variable (symbolized as Y) and one or more predictor or independent variables (symbolized as X if there is one predictor and as X_1, X_2 to X_k where there is more than one predictor).

Y can express either the actual value of the criterion or its predicted value. If Y is the predicted value, the regression equation takes the following form:

$$Y = a + \beta_1 X_1 + \beta_2 X_2 + \cdots + \beta_k X_k$$

If Y is the actual value, the regression equation includes an error term (or residual) which is symbolized as e. This is the difference between the predicted and actual value:

$$Y = a + \beta_1 X_1 + \beta_2 X_2 + \cdots + \beta_k X_k + e$$

X represents the actual values of a case. If we substitute these values in the regression equation together with the other values, we can work out the value of Y. β is the regression coefficient if there is one predictor and the partial regression coefficient if there is more than one predictor. It can represent either the standardized or the unstandardized regression coefficient. The regression coefficient is the amount of change that takes place in Y for a specified amount of change in X. To calculate this change for a particular case we multiply the actual value of that predictor for that case by the regression coefficient for that predictor. a is the intercept, which is the value of Y when the value of the predictor or predictors is zero.

regression line: a straight line drawn through the points on a scatter diagram of the values of the criterion and predictor variables so that it best describes the linear relationship between these variables. If these values are standardized scores the regression line is the same as the correlation line. This line is sometimes called the line of best fit in that this straight line comes closest to all the points in the scattergram.

This line can be drawn from the values of the regression equation which in its simplest form is

predicted value = intercept + (regression coefficient × predictor value)

The vertical axis of the scatter diagram is used to represent the values of the criterion and the horizontal axis the values of the predictor. The intercept is the point on the vertical axis which is the predicted value of the criterion when the value of the predictor is 0. This predicted value will be 0 when the standardized regression coefficient is used. To draw a straight line we need only two points. The intercept provides one point. The other point is provided by working out the predicted value for one of the other values of the predictor.

related designs: also known as related samples designs, correlated designs and correlated samples designs. This is a crucial concept in planning research and its associated statistical analysis. A related design is one in which there is a relationship between two variables. The commonest form of this design is where two measures are taken on a single sample at two different points in time. This is essentially a test–retest design in which changes over time are being assessed. There are obvious advantages to this design in that it involves fewer participants. However, its big advantage is that it potentially helps the researcher to gain some control over measurement error. All measures can be regarded as consisting of a component which reflects the variable in question and another component which is measurement error. For example, when asked a simple question like age, there will be some error in the replies as some people will round up, some round down, some will have forgotten their precise age, some might tell a lie, and so forth. In other words, their answers will not be always their true age because of the difficulties of measurement error.

The common circumstances in which related designs are used are:

- ones in which individuals serve as their own controls;
- where change over time in a sample is assessed;
- where twins are used as members of pairs one of which serves in the experimental condition and the other serves in the control condition;
- where participants are matched according to characteristics which might be related to the dependent variable.

See also: **counterbalanced designs; matching**

related t test: see **analysis of variance; t test for related samples**

relationship: see **causal relationship; correlation; curvilinear relationship; unidirectional relationship**

reliability: a rather abstract concept since it is dependent on the concept of 'true' score. It is the ratio of the variation of the 'true' scores when measuring a variable to the total variation on that measure. In statistical theory, the 'true' score cannot be assessed with absolute precision because of factors, known as 'error', which give the score as measured. In other words, a score is made up of a true score plus an error score. Error is the result of any number of factors which can affect a score – chance fluctuations due to factors such as time of day, mood, ambient noise, and so forth. The influence of error factors is variable from time of measurement to time of measurement. They are unpredictable and inconsistent. As a consequence, the correlation between two measures will be less than perfect.

More concretely, reliability is assessed in a number of different ways such as test–retest reliability, split–half reliability, alpha reliability and interjudge (coder, rater) reliability. Since these are distinctive and different techniques for assessing reliability, they should not be confused with the concept itself. In other words, they will provide different estimates of the reliability of a measure.

Reliability is not really an invariant characteristic of a measure since it is dependent on the sample in question and the circumstances of the measurement as well as the particular means of assessing reliability employed.

Not all good measures need to be reliable in every sense of the term. So variables which are inherently stable and change from occasion to occasion do not need good test–retest reliability to be good measures. Mood is a good example of such an unstable variable. See also: **attenuation, correcting correlations for; Spearman–Brown formula**

repeated-measures analysis of variance or ANOVA: an analysis of variance which is based on the same or similar (matched) cases and where cases are tested more than once on one or more factors. For example, each case or a matched case may take part in each of three different conditions.

repeated-measures design: see **analysis of variance; carryover** or **asymmetrical transfer effect; randomization; within-groups variance; within-subjects design**

representative sample: a sample which is representative of the population from which it is drawn. For example, if 55% of the population is female, then a similar percentage of the sample should be female. Some form of random sampling should be used to ensure that the cases are representative of those in the population.

resampling techniques: involve the use of the scores obtained in the study to produce a 'sampling' distribution of the possible outcomes of the study based on that data. Take the simple example of a study comparing two groups (A and B) on the variable C. The data might look as in Table R.1.

If the null hypothesis were true (that there is no difference between group A and group B), then the distribution of scores between group A and group B is just haphazard. If this is so, then what we can do is to collect together the scores for group A and group B and then randomly allocate each score to either group A or group B. This will produce two samples which can be compared. Repeating the process will produce increasing numbers of pairs of samples each of which are easily compared. So, based on the data above, it is possible to produce a sampling difference between all of the possible combinations of scores in the table. This, in effect, is like any other sampling distribution

Table R.1 *Possible data for resampling*

Group A	Group B
4	6
2	9
5	7
3	6
2	3
1	8
4	9
3	6
2	7
4	

except that it is rigidly limited by the scores in the data. They are the same scores but resampling assigns them to group A and group B differently.

There are a number of statistical techniques which employ such procedures. Their major difficulty is that they require computer software capable of generating the random sampling distribution. See also: **bootstrapping**

residual: the difference between the actual value of a criterion or dependent variable and its predicted value. Larger differences or residuals imply that the predictions are less accurate. The concept is commonly used to indicate the disparity between the data and the statistical model for that data. It has the big advantage of simplicity. Careful scrutiny of the residuals will help a researcher identify where the model or statistic is especially poor at predicting the data.

The variance of the residual (scores) is quite simply the residual variance.

response rate: the proportion or percentage of cases who take part in a study or in different stages of a study. People or organizations may not be contactable or may not agree to participate in a study when approached to do so. If the sample is supposed to be a representative one or if it is to be tested on more than one occasion, a low response rate will increase the chances of the sample being less representative.

response sets: see **acquiescence** or **yea-saying response set** or **style**

robust: a robust test means that a significant relationship will be found to be statistically significant when there is such a relationship even when the assumptions underlying the test about the distribution of the data are not met.

rotation of factors: see **exploratory factor analysis; simple solution; varimax rotation, in factor analysis**

rounding decimal places: the process by which long strings of decimals are shortened. To avoid systematic biases in reporting findings (albeit very small ones in most terms), there are rules in terms of how decimals are shortened. These involve checking the decimal place after the final decimal place to be reported. If that 'extra' decimal place has a numerical value between 0 and 4 then we simply report the shortened number by deleting the extra decimals. Thus

17.632 = 17.63 (to two decimal places)
103.790 = 103.79 (to two decimal places)
12.5731 = 12.573 (to three decimal places)

However, if the 'additional' decimal place is between 5 and 9 then the last figure reported in the decimal is increased by 1. For example,

17.639 is reported as 17.64 (to two decimal places)
103.797 is reported as 103.80 (to two decimal places)
12.5738 is reported as 12.574 (to three decimal places)

In general it is bad practice *not* to adopt this scheme. While much of the time it will not matter much, failure to do so leaves the researcher open to criticism – for example, when reporting exact significance levels at the margins of being statistical significance.

rounding errors: many fractions of numbers cannot be handled with absolute precision in decimal form. No matter the number of decimal places, the figure will be slightly imprecise. Rounding errors occur when a calculation produces a slightly inaccurate value simply because of the use of too few decimal places, though some calculations are especially prone to such problems. Rounding errors can be seen, for example, when calculating percentages of cases. By rounding each percentage properly using the appropriate rules, sometimes the sum of the percentages will differ from 100%. Some researchers will draw attention to the fact that their frequencies do not sum to 100% because of rounding errors.

Rounding errors occasionally occur in computer statistical packages giving what might be regarded as a slightly incorrect outcome. Mostly users will be unaware of these and rarely is it of material importance.

Roy's gcr or **greatest characteristic root criterion:** a test used in multivariate statistical procedures such as canonical correlation, discriminant function analysis and multivariate analysis of variance to determine whether the means of the groups differ on a discriminant function or characteristic root. As the name implies, it only measures differences on the greatest or the first canonical root or discriminant function. See also: **Wilks's lambda**
   Tabachnick and Fidell (2001)

r to z transformation: see **Fisher's z transformation**

run: an uninterrupted series of one or more identical events in a sequence of events which is followed and preceded by different events or no events. For example, the following sequence of heads (H) and tails (T), HHTHH, contains a run of two heads, followed by a run of one tail and a run of two heads. The total number of runs in the sequence of events indicates whether the sequence of events is likely to be random. A run would indicate non-randomness. For example, the following sequence of heads and tails, HHH-HTTTT, consists of two runs and suggests that each event is grouped together and not random.

Ryan or Ryan–Einot–Gabriel–Welsch F (REGWF) multiple comparison test: a *post hoc* or multiple comparison test which is used to determine whether three or more means differ significantly in an analysis of variance. It may be used regardless of whether the analysis of variance is significant. It assumes equal variance and is approximate for unequal group sizes. It is a stepwise or sequential test which is a modification of the Newman–Keuls method, procedure or test. It is based on the F distribution rather than the Q or studentized range distribution. This test is generally less powerful than the Newman–Keuls method in that differences are less likely to be statistically significant.

Toothaker (1991)

Ryan or Ryan–Einot–Gabriel–Welsch Q (REGWQ) multiple comparison test: This is like the Ryan or Ryan–Einot–Gabriel–Welsch F (REGWF) multiple comparison test except that it is based on the Q rather than the F distribution.

Toothaker (1991)

S

sample: a set of cases drawn or selected from a larger set or population of cases, usually with the aim of estimating characteristics of the larger set or population. For example, we may be interested in finding out what the relationship is between childhood sexual abuse and subsequent psychiatric disorder. Because it would not be possible or practical to investigate this relationship in the population, we take a sample of the population and study this relationship in the sample. From this sample we can determine to what extent this relationship is likely to be found in the population from which the sample was drawn. There are various ways of sampling a population. See also: **convenience sample**

sample size: the number of cases or individuals in the sample studied. Usually represented by the symbol N. Sometimes because of missing data the sample size for parts of the statistical analysis is reduced. In computer analysis, care is needed to check on final sample sizes because of this. In inferential statistics, sample size is important as the test distribution often varies with sample size (or the degrees of freedom which are sometimes based on an adjustment to sample size).

sample size (minimum): the minimum size of sample needed to run a study is a complex matter to assess. Nevertheless it is a frequently asked question. It depends on a range of factors. The most important is the researcher's expectations of the likely size of the trend in the data. The greater the trend the smaller the appropriate sample size. Experienced researchers in a particular field are likely to be able to estimate an appropriate sample size based on experience and convention in the particular field of study. In terms of estimating the minimum sample size to use, the most practical advice is to use a sample size which has proven effective in other research using similar measures, samples and methods to the proposed study.

Other researchers may have an idea of the minimum effect or relationship that would be of practical or theoretical interest to them. If one requires a fairly large effect to make the outcome of the research of value, one could use a commensurately smaller sample size.

Small sample sizes with a large trend in the data are adequate to establish statistical significance. Unfortunately, small sample sizes lack intuitive credibility in the minds of other researchers, the public and research users and are best avoided unless the scarcity of appropriate participants for the study in question makes it impracticable to obtain a larger sample. Sample sizes should never be so small that statistical significance is not properly testable. These minimal sample sizes can be estimated by examining tables of significance for particular statistical techniques.

Very large samples, apart from the obvious time and cost disadvantages, have an obvious drawback. That is, very minimal trends in the data may prove to be statistically significant with very large samples. For example, with a sample size of 1000 a Pearson correlation coefficient of 0.062 is significant at the 5% level of significance. It only explains (accounts for) four-thousandths of the variation. Such a small correlation is virtually negligible or negligible for most purposes. The equally difficult issue of what size of correlation is worthy of the researcher's attention becomes more central in these circumstances.

The first concern of the researcher should be to maximize the effectiveness of the measures and procedures used. Poor measures (ones which are internally unreliable) of a variable will need larger sample sizes to produce statistically significant findings, all other things being equal. The maximum value of correlations, for example, between two unreliable measures (as all measures are to a degree in practice) will be limited by the reliabilities of the two measures involved. This can be corrected for if a measure of the reliability of each measure is available. Care in the wording and piloting of questionnaires is appropriate in an attempt to improve reliability of the measures. Poor, unstandardized, procedures for the conduct of the study will increase the uncontrolled variability of responses in the study. Hence, in some fields of research rigorous and meticulous procedures are adopted for running experiments and other types of study.

The following are recommended in the absence of previous research. Carry out small pilot study using the procedures and materials to be implemented in the full study. Assess, for the size of effect found, what the minimum sample size is that would be required for significance. For example, for a given t value or F value, look up in tables what N or df would be required for significance and plan the final study size based on these. While one could extend the sample size if findings are near significance, often the analysis of findings proceeds after the study is terminated and restarting is difficult. Furthermore, it is essentially a non-random process to collect more data in the hope that eventually statistical significance is obtained.

In summary, the question of appropriate sample size is a difficult one for a number of reasons which are not conventionally discussed in statistics textbooks. These include:

1 the purpose of the research
2 the costs of poor statistical decisions
3 the next stage in the research process – is this a pilot study, for example?

sample standard deviation: see **estimated standard deviation**

sample variance: see **variance estimate**

sampling: see **cluster sample; convenience sample** or **sampling; multistage sampling; probability sampling; quota sampling; representative sample; simple random sampling; snowball sampling; stratified random sample; systematic sample**

sampling distribution: the characteristics of the distribution of the means (etc.,) of numerous samples drawn at random from a population. A sampling distribution is obtained by taking repeated random samples of a particular size from a population. Some characteristic of the sample (usually its mean but any other characteristic could be chosen) can then be studied. The distribution of the means of samples, for example, could then be plotted on, say, a histogram. This distribution in the histogram illustrates the sampling distribution of the mean. Different sample sizes will produce different distributions (see **standard error of the mean**). Different population distributions will also produce different sampling distributions. The concept of sampling distribution is largely of theoretical importance in terms of the needs of practitioners in the social sciences. It is most usually associated with testing the null hypothesis.

sampling error: the variability of samples from the characteristics of the population from which they came. For example, the means of samples will tend to vary from the mean of the population from which they are taken. This variability from the population mean is known as the sampling error. It might be better termed sampling variability or sampling uncertainty since it is not a mistake in the usual sense but a feature of random sampling from a population.

sampling frame: in surveys, the sampling frame is the list of cases from which the sample is selected. Easily obtained sampling frames would include telephone directories and lists of electors. These have obvious problems in terms of non-representativeness – for example, telephone directories only list people with telephones who are responsible for paying the bill. It is extremely expensive to draw up a sampling frame where none is available – hence the willingness of researchers to use less than optimum sources. See **quota sampling; sampling with replacement; simple random sampling; stratified random sample**

sampling with replacement: means that once something has been selected randomly, it is replaced into the population and, consequently, may be selected at random again. Curiously, although virtually all statistical calculations are based on sampling with replacement, the practice is *not* to replace into the population. The reasons for this are obvious. There is little point in giving a person a questionnaire to fill in twice or three times simply because they have been selected two or three times at random. Hence, we do not replace.

While this is obviously theoretically unsatisfactory, in practice it does not matter too much since with fairly large sampling frames the chances of being selected twice or more times are too small to make any noticeable difference to the outcome of a study.

SAS: an abbreviation for *Statistical Analysis System*. It is one of several widely used statistical packages for manipulating and analysing data. Information about SAS can be found at the following website:
http://www.sas.com/products/index.html

scale: generally a measure of a variable which consists of one or more items where the score for that scale reflects increasing quantities of that variable. For example, an anxiety scale may consist of a number of questions or statements which are designed to indicate how anxious the respondent is. Higher scores on this scale may indicate higher levels of anxiety than lower scores.

scatter diagram, scattergram or **scatterplot:** a graph or diagram which plots the position of cases in terms of their values on two quantitative variables and which shows the way the two variables are related to one another as shown in Figure S.1. The vertical or Y axis represents the values of one variable which in a regression analysis is the criterion or dependent variable. The horizontal or X axis represents the values of the other variable which in a regression analysis is the predictor or independent variable. Each point on the diagram indicates the two values on those variables that are shown by one or more cases. For example, the point towards the bottom left-hand corner in Figure S.1 represents an X value of 1 and a Y value of 2.

The pattern of the scatter of the points indicates the strength and the direction of the relationship between the two variables. Values on the two axes are normally arranged so that values increase upwards on the vertical scale and rightwards on the horizontal scale as shown in the figure. The closer the points are to a line that can be drawn through them, the stronger the relationship is. In the case of a linear relationship between the two variables, the line is a straight one which is called a regression or correlation line depending on what the statistic is. In the case of a curvilinear

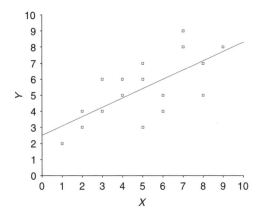

Y axis labeled from 0 to 10, X axis labeled from 0 to 10.

Figure S.1   *An example of a scatter diagram*

relationship the line is a curved one. If there does not appear to be a clear linear or curvilinear relationship between the two variables, there is no relationship between the variables. A straight line sloping from lower left to upper right, as illustrated in the figure, indicates a positive or direct linear relationship between the two variables. A straight line running from upper left to lower right indicates a negative or inverse linear relationship between the two variables. See also: **correlation; perfect correlation**

Scheffé test: a *post hoc* or multiple comparison test which is used to determine whether three or more means differ significantly in an analysis of variance. Equal variances are assumed but it is suitable for unequal group sizes. Generally, it is regarded as one of the most conservative *post hoc* tests. The test can compare any contrast between means and not just comparisons between pairs of means. It is based on the F statistic which is weighted according to the number of groups minus one. For example, the 0.05 critical value of F is about 4.07 for a one-way analysis of variance comprising four groups with three cases in each group. For the Scheffé test this critical value is increased to 12.21 [4.07 × (4 − 1) = 12.21]. In other words, a comparison has to have an F value of 12.21 or greater to be statistically significant at the 0.05 level.

The following formula is used to calculate the F value for the comparison:

$$F = \frac{[(\text{group 1 weight} \times \text{group 1 mean}) + (\text{group 2 weight} \times \text{group 2 mean}) + \cdots]^2}{\text{error mean square} \times \left(\frac{\text{group 1 weight}^2}{\text{group 1 } n} + \frac{\text{group 2 weight}^2}{\text{group 2 } n} + \cdots\right)}$$

The numerator of the formula represents the comparison. If we take the case where there are four groups and we wanted to compare the mean of groups 1 and 2, the weights for this comparison could be

$$1 \quad -1 \quad 0 \quad 0$$

Suppose the means for the four groups are 6, 14, 12 and 2 respectively as shown in the example for the entry under the Newman–Keuls method. As multiplying a number by 0 gives 0, the comparison reduces to subtracting the group 2 mean from the group 1 mean and squaring the difference. This gives a value of 8.

$$[(1 \times 6) + (-1 \times 14) + (0 \times 12) + (0 \times 2)]^2 =$$
$$[6 + (-14) + 0 + 0]^2 = (-8)^2 = 64$$

The denominator represents the weighted error mean square. The error mean square for this example is 9.25. As dividing 0 by a number gives 0, we are weighting the error mean square by groups 1 and 2.

$$9.25 \times \left(\frac{1^2}{3} + \frac{-1^2}{3} + \frac{0^2}{3} + \frac{0^2}{3}\right) = 9.25 \times \left(\frac{1}{3} + \frac{1}{3} + \frac{0}{3} + \frac{0}{3}\right)$$

$$= 9.25 \times \left(\frac{1 + 1 + 0 + 0}{3}\right)$$

$$= 9.25 \times \left(\frac{2}{3}\right)$$

$$= 9.25 \times 0.67 = 6.20$$

The F value for this comparison is the squared difference of 64 divided by the weighted error mean square of 6.20, which gives 10.32 (64/6.20 = 10.32). As this F value is smaller than the critical value of 12.21, these two means do not differ significantly. See also: **analysis of variance**
   Kirk (1995)

score: a numerical value which indicates the quantity or relative quantity of a variable/

construct. In other words, it is normally the data collected from an individual case on a particular variable or measure. Scores include ratio, interval and ordinal measurement. The alternative to scores is nominal data (or categorical or category or qualitative data).

In statistics, there is a conceptual distinction drawn between two components – the 'true' score and the 'error' score. A score = 'true' score + 'error' score. These two components can, at best, only be estimated. The true score is really what the score would be if it were possible to eliminate all forms of measurement error. If one were measuring the weight of an individual, measurement error would include inconsistencies because of inconsistencies of the scales, operator recording errors, variations in weight according to the time of day the measure was taken, and other factors.

Error scores and true scores will not correlate by definition. If they did correlate, then the two would be partially indistinguishable. The greater the proportion of true score in a score the better in terms of the measure's ability to measure something substantial.

Often the 'true' score is estimated by using the 'average' of several different measures of a variable just as one might take the average of several measures of length as the best measure of the length of something. Thus, in some research designs (related designs) the measurement error is reduced simply because the measure has been taken more than once. The term measurement error is a little misleading since it really applies to aspects of the measurement which the researcher does not understand or over which the researcher has no control.

It is also important to note that measurement error is uncorrelated with the score and the true score. As such, consistent biases in measurement (e.g. a tape measure which consistently overestimates) is not reflecting measurement error in the statistical sense. These errors would correlate highly with the correct measures as measured by an accurate rule. See also: **categorical (category) variable; error**

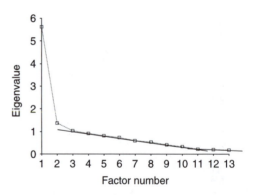

Figure S.2 *An example of a scree test*

rotation in a factor analysis. The eigenvalue or the amount of variance accounted for by each factor is plotted against the number of the factor on a graph like that shown in Figure S.2. The vertical axis represents the eigenvalue while the horizontal axis shows the number of the factors in the order they are extracted, which is in terms of decreasing size of their eigenvalue. So, the first factor has the greatest eigenvalue, the second factor the next largest eigenvalue, and so on. Scree is a geological term to describe the debris that accumulates at the bottom of a slope and that obscures it. The factors to be retained are those represented by the slope while the factors to be discarded are those represented by the scree. In other words, the factors to be kept are the number of the factor just before the scree begins. In Figure S.2 the scree appears to begin at the factor number 3 so the first two of the 13 factors should be retained. The point at which the scree begins may be determined by drawing a straight line through or very close to the points represented by the scree as shown in Figure S.2. The factors above the first line represent the number of factors to be retained. See also: **exploratory factor analysis**

Cattell (1966)

scree test, Cattell's: one test for determining the number of factors to be retained for

second-order factors: factors obtained in factor analysis from factor analysing the results of an oblique factor rotation which allows the factors to correlate. The correlation matrix of the factors can then be factor analysed to give new factors which are factors of factors. Hence, they are termed second-order factors. Care should be taken to recognize the difference as some researchers and theorists report second-order factors that seem materially different from the factors of other researchers. That is, because they are a different order of factor analysis. See also: **exploratory factor analysis; oblique rotation; orthogonal rotation**

second-order interactions: an interaction between three independent variables or factors (e.g. $A \times B \times C$). Where there are three independent variables, there will also be three first-order interactions which are interactions between the independent variables taken two at a time ($A \times B, A \times C$ and $B \times A$). Obviously, there cannot be an interaction for a single variable.

semi-interquartile range: see **quartile deviation**

semi-partial correlation coefficient: similar to the partial correlation coefficient. However, the effect of the third variable is only removed from the dependent variable. The independent variable would not be adjusted. Normally, the influence of the third variable is removed from both the independent and the dependent variable in partial correlation. Semi-partial correlation coefficients are rarely presented in reports of statistical analyses but they are an important component of multiple regression analyses.

What is the point of semi-partial correlation? Imagine we find that there is a relationship between intelligence and income of 0.50. Intelligence is our independent variable and income our dependent variable for the present purpose. We then find out that social class is correlated with income at a level 0.30.

In other words, some of the variation in income is due to social class. If we remove the variation due to social class from the variable income, we have left income without the influence of social class. So the correlation of intelligence with income adjusted for social class is the semi-partial correlation. But there is also a correlation of social class with our independent variable intelligence – say that this is the higher the intelligence, the higher the social class. Partial correlation would take off this shared variation between intelligence and social class from the intelligence scores. By not doing this, semi-partial correlation leaves the variation of intelligence associated with social class still in the intelligence scores. Hence, we end up with a semi-partial correlation in which intelligence is exactly the variable it was when we measured it and unadjusted any way. However, income has been adjusted for social class and is different from the original measure of income.

The computation of the partial correlation coefficient in part involves adjusting the correlation coefficient by taking away the variation due to the correlation of each of the variables with the control variable. For every first-order partial correlation there are *two* semi-partial correlations depending on which of the variables x or y is being regarded as the dependent or criterion variable.

This is the partial correlation coefficient:

$$r_{xy.c} = \frac{r_{xy} - (r_{xc} \times r_{yc})}{\sqrt{1 - r_{xc}^2}\,\sqrt{1 - r_{yc}^2}}$$

The following are the two semi-partial correlation coefficients:

$$r_{x(c.y)} = \frac{r_{xy} - (r_{xc} \times r_{yc})}{\sqrt{1 - r_{xc}^2}}$$

$$r_{x(y.c)} = \frac{r_{xy} - (r_{xc} \times r_{yc})}{\sqrt{1 - r_{yc}^2}}$$

Table S.1 *llustrating data for the sign test plus calculating the sign of the difference*

Condition A	Condition B	Difference	Sign of difference
18	22	−4	−
12	15	−3	−
15	18	−3	−
29	29	0	0 (zero differences are dropped from analysis)
22	24	−2	−
11	10	+1	+
18	26	−8	−
19	27	−8	−
21	24	−3	−
24	27	−3	−

The difference between the formulae for partial and semi-partial correlation is obvious – the bottom of the semi-partial correlation formula is shorter. This is because no adjustment is being made for the variance shared between the control and predictor variables in semi-partial correlation. This in effect means that the semi-partial correlation coefficient is the correlation between the predictor and criterion variables with the correlation of each with the control variable removed. The amount of variation in the criterion variable is adjusted for by its correlation with the control variable. Since this adjustment is only applied to the criterion variable, the adjustment is smaller than for the partial correlation in virtually all cases. Thus, the partial correlation is almost invariably larger than (or possibly equal to) the semi-partial correlation. See also: **multiple regression**

sequential method in analysis of variance: see **Type I, hierarchical** or **sequential method in analysis of variance**

sequential multiple regression: see **multiple regression**

Sidak multiple comparison test: see **Dunn–Sidak multiple comparison test**

sign test: a very simple test for differences in related data. It is called a sign test because the difference between each matched pair of scores is converted simply into the sign of the difference (zero differences are ignored). The smaller of the numbers of signs (i.e. the smaller of the number of pluses or the number of minuses) is identified. The probability is then assessed from tables or calculated using the binomial expansion. Statistical packages also do the calculation.

Despite its simplicity, generally the loss of information from the scores (the size of the differences being ignored) makes it a poor choice in anything other than the most exceptional circumstances.

The calculation of the sign test is usually presented in terms of a related design as in Table S.1. In addition, the difference between the two related conditions is presented in the third column and the sign of the difference is given in the final column.

We then count the number of positive signs in the final column (1) and the number of negative signs (8). The smaller of these is then used to check in a table of significance. From such a table we can see that our value for the sign test is statistically significant at the 5% level with a two-tailed test. That is, there is a significant difference between conditions A and B.

The basic rationale of the test is that if the null hypothesis is true then the differences between the conditions should be positive and negative in equal numbers. The greater the disparity from this equal distribution of pluses and minuses the less likely is the null hypothesis to be true; hence, the hypothesis is more supported.

significance level or **testing:** see **significant**

significance testing: see **probability; significant**

significant: implies that it is not plausible that the research findings are due to chance. Hence, the null hypothesis (of no correlation or no difference) is rejected in favour of the (alternative) hypothesis. Significance testing is only a small part of assessing the implications of a particular study. Failure to reach significance may result in the researcher re-examining the methods employed especially where the sample appears of a sufficient size. Furthermore, where the hypothesis under test is deemed important for some theoretical or applied reason the researcher may be more highly motivated to re-examine the research methods employed. If significance is obtained, then the researcher may feel in a position to examine the implications and alternatives to the hypothesis more fully.

The level at which the null hypothesis is rejected is usually set as 5 or fewer times out of 100. This means that such a difference or relationship is likely to occur by chance 5 or fewer times out of 100. This level is generally described as the proportion 0.05 and sometimes as the percentage 5%. The 0.05 probability level was historically an arbitrary choice but has been acceptable as a reasonable choice in most circumstances. If there is a reason to vary this level, it is acceptable to do so. So in circumstances where there might be very serious adverse consequences if the wrong decision were made about the hypothesis, then the significance level could be made more stringent at, say, 1%. For a pilot study involving small numbers, it might be reasonable to set significance at the 10% level since we know that whatever tentative conclusions we draw they will be subjected to a further test.

Traditionally the critical values of a statistical test were presented in tables for specific probability levels such as 0.05, 0.01 and 0.001. Using these tables, it is possible to determine whether the critical value of the statistical test was equal to or lower than one of these less frequent probability levels and to report this probability level if this was the case, for example as 0.01 rather than 0.05. Nowadays, most statistical analyses are carried out using statistical packages which give exact probability levels such as 0.314 or 0.026. It is common to convert these exact probability levels into the traditional ones and to report the latter. Findings which have a probability of greater than 0.05 are often simply described as being non-significant, which is abbreviated as *ns*. However, it could be argued that it is more informative to present the exact significance levels rather than the traditional cut-off points.

Significance levels should also be described in terms of whether they concern only one tail of the direction of the results or the two tails. If there are strong grounds for predicting the direction of the results, the one-tailed significance level should be used. If the result was not predicted or if there were no strong grounds for predicting the result, the two-tailed level should be used. The significance level of 0.05 in a two-tailed level of significance is shared equally between the two tails of the distribution of the results. So the probability of finding a result in one direction (say, a positive difference or correlation) is 0.025 (which is half the 0.05 level) while the probability of finding a difference in the other direction (say, a negative difference or correlation) is also 0.025. In a one-tailed test, the 0.05 level is confined to the predicted tail. Consequently, the probability of a particular result being significant is half as likely for a two-tailed than a one-tailed test of significance. See also: **confidence interval; hypothesis testing; probability**

significantly different: see **confidence interval; significant**

simple or **bivariate regression:** describes the size and direction of a linear association between one quantitative criterion or dependent variable and one quantitative predictor or independent variable. The direction of the association is indicated by the sign of the regression coefficient in the same way as with a correlation coefficient. The lack of a sign denotes a positive association in which higher scores on the predictor are associated with higher scores on the criterion. A negative sign shows a negative or inverse association in which higher scores on the predictor go with lower scores on the criterion.

The size of the linear association can be expressed in terms of a standardized or an unstandardized regression coefficient. The standard regression coefficient is the same as a correlation coefficient. It can vary from -1.00 to 1.00. The unstandardized regression coefficient can be bigger than this as it is based on the original rather than the standardized scores of the predictor. The unstandardized regression coefficient is used to predict the scores of the criterion. The bigger the coefficient, the stronger the association between the criterion and the predictor. Strength of the association is more difficult to gauge from the unstandardized regression coefficient as it depends on the scale used by the predictor. For the same-sized association, a scale made up of more points will produce a bigger unstandardized regression coefficient than a scale comprised of fewer points. These two regression coefficients are signified by the small Greek letter β or its capital equivalent B (both called beta) although which letter is used to represent which coefficient is not consistent.

These two coefficients can be calculated from each other if the standard deviation of the criterion and the predictor are known. A standardized regression coefficient can be converted into its unstandardized coefficient by multiplying the standardized regression coefficient by the standard deviation (SD) of the criterion and dividing it by the standard deviation of the predictor:

$$\begin{array}{l}\text{unstandardized} \\ \text{regression} \\ \text{coefficient}\end{array} = \begin{array}{l}\text{standardized} \\ \text{regression} \\ \text{coefficient}\end{array} \times \dfrac{\text{criterion SD}}{\text{predictor SD}}$$

An unstandardized regression coefficient can be converted into its standardized coefficient by multiplying the unstandardized regression coefficient by the standard deviation of the predictor and dividing it by the standard deviation of the criterion:

$$\begin{array}{l}\text{standardized} \\ \text{regression} \\ \text{coefficient}\end{array} = \begin{array}{l}\text{unstandardized} \\ \text{regression} \\ \text{coefficient}\end{array} \times \dfrac{\text{predictor SD}}{\text{criterion SD}}$$

The statistical significance of these two coefficients is the same and can be expressed as a t value. One formula for calculating the t value for the standardized regression coefficient is

$$t = \sqrt{\begin{array}{l}\text{standardized} \\ \text{regression} \\ \text{coefficient}\end{array} \times \dfrac{\text{number of cases} - 2}{1 - \begin{array}{l}\text{squared standardized} \\ \text{regression coefficient}\end{array}}}$$

A formula for working out the t value for the unstandardized regression coefficient is

$$t = \dfrac{\text{unstandardized regression coefficient}}{\begin{array}{c}\text{standard error of the unstandardized} \\ \text{regression coefficient}\end{array}}$$

simple random sampling: in random sampling every case in the population has an equal likelihood of being selected. Suppose, for example, that we want a sample of 100 people from a population of 1000 people. First, we draw up a sampling frame in which every member of the population is listed and numbered from 1 to 1000. We then need to select 100 people from this list at random. Random number tables could be used to do this. Alternatively, slips for the 1000 different numbers could be put into a big hat and 100 slips taken out to indicate the final sample. See also: **probability sampling; systematic sample**

simple solution: a term used in factor analysis to indicate the end point of rotation of factors. The initial factors in factor analysis are the product of a purely mathematical process which usually has the maximization of the amount of variance accounted for by each of the factors in turn. What this means in practice is that the factors should have as many variables as possible with reasonably high factor loadings. Unfortunately, such a mathematically based procedure does not always lead to factors which are readily inter-pretable. A simple solution is a set of criteria proposed by the psychologist L.L. Thurstone to facilitate the interpretation of the factors. The factors are rotated to a simple structure which has the key feature that the factor load-ings should ideally be either large or small in numerical value and *not* of a middle value. In this way, the researcher has factors which can be defined more readily by the large loadings and small loadings without there being a con-fusing array of middle-size loadings which obscure meaning. See also: **exploratory factor analysis; oblique rotation; orthogonal rotation**

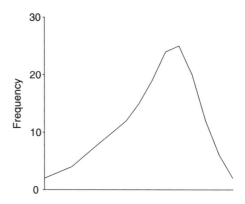

Figure S.3   *Illustrating negative skewness*

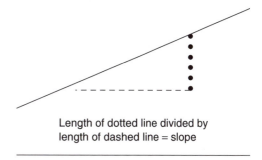

Length of dotted line divided by
length of dashed line = slope

Figure S.4   *The slope of a scattergram*

single-sample t test: see **t test for one sample**

skewed: see **skewness**

skewness: the degree of asymmetry in a fre-quency distribution. A perfectly symmetrical frequency distribution has no skewness. The tail of the distribution may be longer either to the left or to the right. If the tail is longer to the left then this distribution is negatively skewed (Figure S.3): if it is longer to the right then it is positively skewed. If the distribu-tion of a variable is strongly skewed, it may be more appropriate to use a non-parametric test of statistical significance. A statistical for-mula is available for describing skewness and it is offered as an option in some statistical packages. See also: **moment; standard error of skewness; transformations**

slope: the slope of a scattergram or regression analysis indicates the 'angle' or orientation of the best fitting straight line through the set of points. It is not really correct to describe it as an angle since it is merely the number of units that the line rises up the vertical axis of the scattergram for every unit of movement along the horizontal axis. So if the slope is 2.0 this means that for every 1 unit along the horizontal axis, the slope rises 2 units up the vertical axis (see Figure S.4).

The slope of the regression line only par-tially defines the position of the line. In addi-tion one needs a constant or intercept point which is the position at which the regression line cuts the vertical or y axis. See also: **multiple regression; regression line**

Somers' d: a measure of association between two ordinal variables which takes account of ties or tied pairs of scores. It provides an asymmetric as well as a symmetric measure. The formula for the asymmetric measure for the first variable is

$$\frac{C - D}{C + D + T_1}$$

where C is the number of concordant pairs, D the number of discordant pairs and T_1 the number of tied pairs for the first variable. A concordant pair is one in which the first case is ranked higher than the second case, a discordant pair is where the first case is ranked lower than the second case and a tied pair is where they have the same rank. The formula for the asymmetric measure for the second variable is the same as the first except that T is the number of tied ranks for the second variable. The formula for the symmetric measure is

$$\frac{C - D}{(C + D + T_1 + C + D + T_2)/2}$$

See also: **correlation**
  Siegal and Castellan (1988)

small expected frequencies: a term used in chi-square especially to denote expected frequencies of under five. If too many cells (greater than about 20%) have expected frequencies of this size, then chi-square ceases to be an effective test of significance. See **chi-square**

snowball sampling: a method of obtaining a sample in which the researcher asks a participant if they know of other people who might be willing to take part in the study who are then approached and asked the same question. In other words, the sample consists of people who have been proposed by other people in the sample. This technique is particularly useful when trying to obtain people with a particular characteristic or experience which may be unusual and who are likely to know one another. For example, we may use this technique to obtain a sample of divorced individuals.

Spearman's rank order correlation or **rho (ρ):** see **correlation**

Spearman–Brown formula: indicates the increase in the reliability of a test following lengthening by adding more items. The formula is

$$r_{kk} = \frac{k(r_{11})}{[1 + (k - 1)r_{11}]}$$

where r_{kk} is the reliability of the test lengthened by a factor of k, k is the increase in length and r_{11} is the original reliability.

  Thus, if the reliability of the original test is 0.6 and it is proposed to double the length of the test, the reliability is likely to be

$$r_{kk} = \frac{2(0.6)}{[1 + (2 - 1)0.6]}$$

$$= \frac{1.2}{1 + 0.6} = \frac{1.2}{1.6} = 0.75$$

Thus, having doubled the length of the test, the reliability increases from 0.6 to 0.75. Whether this increase is worth the costs of lengthening the scale so much depends on a range of factors such as the deterrent effect this would have on participants.

specific variance: the variance of a variable that is not shared with other variables and does not represent random error. The variance of a variable may be thought of as made up of three components:

1 common variance – that is, variance that it shares with another identified variable;
2 error variance – that is, variance which has not been identified in terms of its nature or source;
3 specific variance – that is, variance on a variable which only is measured by that variable and no other.

These notions are largely conceptual rather than practical and obviously what is error variance in one circumstance is common variance in another. Their big advantage is when understanding the components of a correlation matrix and the perfect self-correlations of 1.000 found in the diagonals of correlation matrices.

split-half reliability: a measure of the internal consistency of a scale to measure a variable. It consists of scoring one half of the items on the scale and then scoring separately the other half of the items. The correlation coefficient between the two separate halves is essentially the split-half reliability, though typically a statistical adjustment is made for the fact that the scale has been effectively halved. Split-half reliability is sometimes assessed as odd–even reliability in which the scores based on the odd-numbered items are correlated with the scores based on the even-numbered items.

Split-half reliability is a measure of the internal consistency of the items of a scale rather than a measure of consistency over time (test–retest reliability). See also: **alpha reliability, Cronbach's; internal consistency; reliability**

SPSS: an abbreviation for *Statistical Package for the Social Sciences*. It is one of several widely used statistical packages for manipulating and analysing data. Information about SPSS can be found at the following website: http://www.spss.com/

spurious relationship: a relationship between two variables which is no longer apparent when one or more variables are statistically controlled and do not appear to be acting as intervening or mediating variables. For example, there may be a positive relationship between the size of the police force and amount of crime in that there may be a bigger police force where there is more crime. This relationship, however, may be due entirely to size of population in that areas with more people are likely to have both more police and more crime. If this is the case the relationship between the size of the police force and the amount of crime would be a spurious one.

square root: of a number is another number which when squared gives the first number. Thus, the square root number of 9 is 3 since 3 multiplied by itself equals 9. The sign $\sqrt{}$ is an instruction to find the square root of what follows. It is sometimes written as $\sqrt[2]{}$ and as the exponent 1/2. Square roots are not easy to calculate by hand but are a regular feature of even the most basic hand-held calculators.

squared or **squaring:** multiplying a number by itself. It is normally written as 2^2 or 3^2 or 3.2^2 indicating 2 squared, 3 squared and 3.2 squared respectively. This is simply another way of writing 2×2, 3×3 and 3.2×3.2. Another way of saying the same thing is to say two to the power of two, three to the power of two, and three point two to the power of two. It is very commonly used in statistics.

squared Euclidean distance: a widely used measure of proximity in a cluster analysis. It is simply the sum of the squared differences between the scores on two variables for the cases in a sample. See also: **cluster analysis**

stacked or **component bar chart:** see **compound bar chart**

standard deviation (SD): quite a difficult concept to understand because of its non-intuitive nature. Possibly the easiest while still accurate way to regard it is as the average amount by which scores in a set of scores differ from the mean of that set of scores. In other words, it is similar to the average deviation from the mean. There are a couple of problems. The first is that we are speaking of the average absolute deviation from the mean (otherwise, the average deviation would always be zero). Second, the way in which the average is calculated is not the common way of calculating the average.

The formula for the calculation of the standard deviation is, of course, the clearest definition of what the concept is. The formula for standard deviation is

$$\text{standard deviation} = \sqrt{\frac{\sum(\text{score} - \text{mean})^2}{\text{sample size}}}$$

$$= \sqrt{\frac{\sum(X - \bar{X})}{N}}$$

The formula would indicate the mean deviation apart from the square sign and the square root sign. This is a clue to the fact that standard deviation is merely the average deviation from the mean but calculated in an unusual way.

There is no obvious sense in which the standard deviation is standard since its value depends on the values of the observations on which it is calculated. Consequently, the size of standard deviation varies markedly from sample to sample.

Standard deviation has a variety of uses in statistical analyses. It is important in the calculation of standard scores (or z scores). It is also appropriate as a measure of variation of scores although variance is a closely related and equally acceptable way of doing the same.

When the standard deviation of a sample is being used to estimate the standard deviation of the population, the sum of squared deviations is divided by the number of cases minus one: $(N - 1)$. The estimated standard deviation rather than the standard deviation is used in tests of statistical inference. See also:

bias; coefficient of variation; dispersion, measure of; estimated standard deviation

standard error of the difference in means: an index of the degree to which the difference between two sample means will differ from that between other samples. The bigger this standard error is, the more likely it is that this difference will vary across samples. The smaller the samples, the bigger is the standard error likely to be. The standard error is used to determine whether two means are significantly different from one another and to provide an estimate of the probability that the difference will fall within specified limits of this difference.

The way that the standard error is calculated depends on whether the scores from the two samples are related or unrelated and, if they are unrelated, whether the variances of the scores for the two samples differ from each other. Unrelated samples consist of different cases or participants while related samples consist of the same cases on two occasions or similar or matched cases such as wife and husband.

One formula for the standard error for related means is

$$\sqrt{\frac{\text{sum of (mean deviation} - \text{deviation})^2}{\text{number of scores}}}$$

The deviation or difference between pairs of related scores is subtracted from the mean difference for all pairs of scores. These differences are squared and added together to form the deviation variance. The deviation variance is divided by the number of scores. The square root of this result is the standard error.

A formula for the standard error for unrelated means with different or unequal variances is:

$$\sqrt{\frac{\text{variance of one sample}}{\text{size of one sample}} + \frac{\text{variance of other sample}}{\text{size of other sample}}}$$

The formula for the standard error for unrelated means with similar or equal variances is more complicated. Consequently, the terms in the formula are abbreviated so that the size of the sample is indicated by n and the two samples are referred to by the two subscripts 1 and 2:

$$\sqrt{\frac{[\text{variance}_1 \times (n_1 - 1)] + [\text{variance}_2 \times (n_2 - 1)]}{n_1 + n_2 - 2}} \times \left(\frac{1}{n_1} + \frac{1}{n_2}\right)$$

To determine whether the two means differ significantly, a t test is carried out in which the two means are subtracted from each other and divided by the appropriate standard error. The statistical significance of this t value is looked up against the appropriate degrees of freedom. For the related t test this is the number of cases minus one. For the unrelated t test with unequal variances it is the number of cases in both samples minus two. For the unrelated t test the formula is more complicated and can be found in the reference below.

The calculation of the estimated probability of the confidence interval for this difference is the same as that described in the standard error of the mean. See also: **sampling distribution**

Cramer (1998)

standard error of kurtosis: an index of the extent to which the kurtosis of a distribution of scores varies from sample to sample. The bigger it is, the more likely it is to differ from one sample to another. It is likely to be bigger for smaller samples. The standard error is used to determine whether the kurtosis of a distribution of scores differs significantly from that of a normal curve or distribution.

One formula for this standard error is as follows, where N represents the number of cases in the sample:

$$\sqrt{\frac{\text{variance of skewness} \times 4 \times (N^2 - 1)}{(N - 3) \times (N + 5)}}$$

To ascertain whether the kurtosis of a distribution of scores differs significantly from that for a normal curve, divide the measure of kurtosis by its standard error. This value is a z score, the significance of which can be looked up in a table of the standard normal distribution. A z value of 1.96 or more is statistically significant at the 95% or 0.05 two-tailed level.

Cramer (1998)

standard error of the estimate: a measure of the extent to which the estimate in a simple or multiple regression varies from sample to sample. The bigger the standard error, the more the estimate varies from one sample to another. The standard error of the estimate is a measure of how accurate the observed score of the criterion is from the score predicted by one or more predictor variables. The bigger the difference between the observed and the predicted scores, the bigger the standard error is and the less accurate the estimate is.

The standard error of the estimate is the square root of the variance of estimate. One formula for the standard error is as follows:

$$\sqrt{\frac{\text{sum of squared differences between the criterion's predicted and observed scores}}{\text{number of cases} - \text{number of predictors} - 1}}$$

standard error of the mean: a measure of the extent to which the mean of a population is likely to differ from sample to sample. The bigger the standard error of the mean, the more likely the mean is to vary from one sample to another. The standard error of the mean takes account of the size of the sample as the smaller the sample, the more likely it is that the sample mean will differ from the population mean. One formula for the standard error is

$$\sqrt{\frac{\text{variance of sample means}}{\text{number of cases in the sample}}}$$

The standard error is the standard deviation of the variance of sample means of a particular size. As we do not know what is the variance of the means of samples of that size, we assume that it is the same as the variance of that sample. In other words, the standard error is the standard deviation of the variance of a sample taking into account the size of that sample. Consequently, one formula for the standard error is

$$\sqrt{\frac{\text{variance of sample}}{\text{number of cases in the sample}}}$$

The standard error of the mean is used to determine whether the sample mean differs significantly from the population mean. The sample mean is subtracted from the population mean and this difference is divided by the standard error of the mean. This test is known as a one-sample t test.

$$t = \frac{\text{population mean} - \text{sample mean}}{\text{standard error of the mean}}$$

The standard error is also used to provide an estimate of the probability of the difference between the population and the sample mean falling within a specified interval of values called the confidence interval of the difference. Suppose, for example, that the difference between the population and the sample mean is 1.20, the standard error of the mean is 0.20 and the size of the sample is 50. To work out the 95% probability that this difference will fall within certain limits of a difference of 1.20, we look up the critical value of the 95% or 0.05 two-tailed level of t for 48 degrees of freedom $(50 - 2 = 48)$, which is 2.011. We multiply this t value by the standard error of the mean to give the interval that this difference can fall on either side of the difference. This interval is 0.4022 $(2.011 \times 0.20 = 0.4022)$. To find the lower limit or boundary of the 95% confidence interval of the difference we subtract 0.4022 from 1.20 which gives about 0.80 $(1.20 - 0.4022 = 0.7978)$. To work out the upper limit we add 0.4022 to 1.20 which gives about 1.60 $(1.20 + 0.4022 = 1.6022)$. In other words, there is a 95% probability that the difference will fall between 0.80 and 1.60. If the standard error was bigger than 0.20, the confidence interval would be bigger.

standard error of the regression coefficient: a measure of the extent to which the unstandardized regression coefficient in simple and multiple regression is likely to vary from one sample to another. The larger the standard error, the more likely it is to differ from sample to sample.

The standard error can be used to give an estimate of a particular probability of the regression coefficient falling within certain limits of the coefficient. Suppose, for example, that the unstandardized regression coefficient is 0.50, its standard error is 0.10 and the size of the sample is 100. We can calculate, say, the 95% probability of that coefficient varying within certain limits of 0.50. To do this we look up the two-tailed 5% or 0.05 probability level of the t value for the appropriate degrees of freedom. These are the number of cases minus the number of predictors minus one. So if there is one predictor the degrees of freedom are 98 $(100 - 1 - 1 = 98)$. The 95% two-tailed t value for 98 degrees of freedom is about 1.984. We multiply this t value by the standard error to give the interval that the coefficient can fall on one side of the regression coefficient. This interval is 0.1984 $(1.984 \times 0.10 = 0.1984)$. To find the lower limit or boundary of the 95% confidence interval for the regression coefficient we subtract 0.1984 from 0.50 which gives about 0.30 $(0.50 - 0.1984 = 0.3016)$. To work out the upper limit we add 0.1984 to 0.50 which gives about 0.70 $(0.50 + 0.1984 = 0.6984)$. For this example, there is a 95% probability that the unstandardized regression coefficient will fall between 0.30 and 0.70. If the standard error was bigger than 0.10, the confidence interval would be bigger. For example, a standard error of 0.20 for the same example would give an interval of 0.3968 $(1.984 \times 0.20 = 0.3968)$, resulting in a lower limit of about 0.10 $(0.50 - 0.3968 = 0.1032)$ and an upper limit of about 0.90 $(0.50 + 0.3968 = 0.8968)$.

The standard error is also used to determine the statistical significance of the regression coefficient. The t test for the regression coefficient is the unstandardized regression coefficient divided by its standard error:

$$t = \frac{\text{unstandardized regression coefficient}}{\text{standard error of the unstandardized regression coefficient}}$$

For this example with a standard error of 0.10, the t value is 10.00 ($0.50/0.10 = 10.00$). As this value of 10.00 is greater than the two-tailed 0.05 critical value of t, which is about 1.984, we would conclude that the regression coefficient is statistically significant at less than the 0.05 two-tailed level.

One formula for the standard error is as follows:

$$\sqrt{\frac{\text{variance of estimate}}{\text{sum of squares of the predictor} \times (1 - R^2)}}$$

where R^2 is the squared multiple correlation between the predictor and the other predictors.
  Pedhazur (1982)

standard error of skewness: a measure of the extent to which the skewness of a distribution of scores is likely to vary from one sample to another. The bigger the standard error, the more likely it is that it will differ from one sample to another. The smaller the sample, the bigger the standard error is likely to be. It is used to determine whether the skewness of a distribution of scores is significantly different from that of a normal curve or distribution.

One formula for the standard error of skewness is

$$\sqrt{\frac{6 \times N \times (N - 1)}{(N - 2) \times (N + 1) \times (N + 3)}}$$

where N represents the number of cases in the sample.

To determine whether skewness differs significantly from the normal distribution, divide the measure of skewness by its standard error. This value is a z score, the significance of which can be looked up in a table of the standard normal distribution. A z value of 1.96 or more is statistically significant at the 95% or 0.05 two-tailed level.
  Cramer (1998)

standard normal or **z distribution:** a normal distribution with a mean of 0 and a standard deviation of 1. It is a normal distribution of standard scores. See also: **standardized score; z score**

standardized partial regression coefficient or **weight:** the statistic in a multiple regression which describes the strength and the direction of the linear association between a predictor and a criterion. It provides a measure of the unique association between that predictor and criterion, controlling for or partialling out any association between that predictor, the other predictors in that step of the multiple regression and the criterion. It is standardized so that its values vary from −1.00 to 1.00. A higher value, ignoring its sign, means that the predictor has a stronger association with the criterion and so has a greater weight in predicting it. Because all the predictors have been standardized in this way, it is possible to compare the relative strengths of their association or the weights with the criterion. The direction of the association is indicated by the sign of the coefficient in the same way as it is with a correlation coefficient. No sign means that the association is positive with high scores on the predictor being associated with high scores on the criterion. A negative sign indicates that the association is negative with high scores on the predictor being associated with low scores on the criterion. A coefficient of 0.50 means that for every standard deviation increase in the value of the predictor there is a standard deviation increase of 0.50 in the criterion.

The unstandardized partial regression coefficient is expressed in the unstandardized scores of the original variables and can be greater than ±1.00. A predictor which is measured in units with larger values is more likely to have a bigger unstandardized partial regression coefficient than a predictor measured in units of smaller values, making it difficult to compare the relative weights of predictors when they are not measured in terms of the same scale or metric.

A standardized partial regression coefficient can be converted into its unstandardized coefficient by multiplying the standardized partial regression coefficient by the standard deviation (SD) of the criterion and dividing it by the standard deviation of the predictor:

$$\begin{array}{c}\text{unstandardized} \\ \text{partial} \\ \text{regression} \\ \text{coefficient}\end{array} = \begin{array}{c}\text{standardized} \\ \text{partial} \\ \text{regression} \\ \text{coefficient}\end{array} \times \dfrac{\text{criterion SD}}{\text{predictor SD}}$$

The statistical significance of the standardized and the unstandardized partial coefficients is the same value and can be expressed in terms of either a t or an F value. The t test for the partial regression coefficient is the unstandardized partial regression coefficient divided by its standard error:

$$t = \frac{\text{unstandardized regression coefficient}}{\begin{array}{c}\text{standard error of the unstandardized} \\ \text{regression coefficient}\end{array}}$$

standardized regression coefficient or weight: see **correlation; regression equation; standardized partial regression coefficient or weight**

standardized, standard or z score: a score which has been transformed to the standard scale in statistics. Just as measures of length can be standardized into metres, such as when an imperial measure is turned into a metric measure (i.e. 1 inch becomes 25.4 millimetres), so can scores be converted to the standard measuring scale of statistics. Here the analogy with physical scales breaks down as in statistics scores are standardized by converting into new 'standardized' scores with a mean of 0 and a standard deviation of 1. For any set of scores such as

5, 9, 14, 17 and 20

it is a relatively easy matter to convert them to a sample of scores with a mean of 0. All that is necessary is that the mean of the sample of scores is calculated and then this mean subtracted from each of the scores. The mean of the above five scores is $65/5 = 13.0$. Subtract 13.0 from each of the above scores:

$$5 - 13.0, 9 - 13.0, 14 - 13.0, 17 - 13.0 \text{ and } 20 - 13.0$$

This gives the following set of scores in which the mean score is 0.0:

$$-8, -4, 1, 4 \text{ and } 7$$

By doing this, only the mean has been adjusted. The next step would be to ensure that the standard deviation of the scores equals 1.0. The standard deviation of the above scores as they stand can be calculated with the usual formula and is 5.404. If we divide each of the adjusted scores (deviations from the mean) by the standard deviation of 5.404 we get the following set of scores:

$$-1.480, -0.740, -0.185, -0.740 \text{ and } 1.295$$

If we then calculate the standard deviation of these new scores, we find that the new standard deviation is 1.0. Hence, we have transformed a set of scores into a new set of scores with a mean of 0 and a standard deviation of 1. Hence, the new scores correspond to the standard normal distribution by definition since the standard normal distribution has a mean of 0 and a standard deviation of 1.

It follows from this that any distribution of scores may be transformed to the standard normal distribution. This allows us to use a single generic frequency distribution (the standard normal distribution) to describe the frequency distribution of any set of scores once it has been transformed to the standard normal distribution. Table S.2 gives a short version of this distribution.

Thus, if we know what a score is on the standard normal distribution we can use the table of the standard normal distribution to assess where it is relative to others. So if the score transformed to the standard normal

Table S.2 *Standard normal distribution (z distribution)*

z	% lower	z	% lower	z	% lower	z	% lower	z	% lower	z	% lower	z	% lower
−4.0	0.00	−2.2	1.39	−1.3	9.68	−0.4	34.46	0.5	69.15	1.4	91.92	2.3	98.93
−3.0	0.13	−2.1	1.79	−1.2	11.51	−0.3	38.21	0.6	72.57	1.5	93.32	2.4	99.18
−2.9	0.19	−2.0	2.28	−1.1	13.57	−0.2	42.07	0.7	75.80	1.6	94.52	2.5	99.38
−2.8	0.26	−1.9	2.87	−1.0	15.87	−0.1	46.02	0.8	78.81	1.7	95.54	2.6	99.53
−2.7	0.35	−1.8	3.59	−0.9	18.41	0.0	50.00	0.9	81.59	1.8	96.41	2.7	99.65
−2.6	0.47	−1.7	4.46	−0.8	21.19	0.1	53.98	1.0	84.13	1.9	97.13	2.8	99.74
−2.5	0.62	−1.6	5.48	−0.7	24.20	0.2	57.93	1.1	86.43	2.0	97.50	2.9	99.81
−2.4	0.82	−1.5	6.68	−0.6	27.43	0.3	61.79	1.2	88.49	2.1	97.72	3.0	99.87
−2.3	1.07	−1.4	8.08	−0.5	30.85	0.4	65.54	1.3	90.32	2.2	98.21	4.0	100.00

Special values: a z of 1.64 has 95% lower; a z of −1.64 has 5% lower; a z of 1.96 has 97.5% lower; and a z of −1.96 has 2.5% lower.

distribution is 1.96, Table S.2 tells us that only 2.5% of scores in the distribution will be bigger than it.

The quicker way of doing all of this is simply to work out the following formula for the score which comes from a set of scores with a known standard deviation:

$$z \text{ score} = \frac{\text{score} - \text{mean}}{\text{standard deviation}} = \frac{X - \bar{X}}{SD}$$

The z score is a score transformed to its value in the standard normal distribution. So if the z score is calculated, Table S.2 will place that transformed score relative to other scores. It gives the percentage of scores lower than that particular z score.

Generally speaking, the requirement of the bell shape for the frequency distribution is ignored as it makes relatively little difference except in conditions of gross skewness. See also: **standard deviation; z score**

statistic: a characteristic such as a mean, standard deviation or any other measure which is applied to a sample of data. Applied to a population exactly the same characteristics are described as parameters of the population.

statistical inference: see **estimated standard deviation; inferential statistics; null hypothesis**

Table S.3 *Symbols for population and sample values*

Concept	Symbol for population value (parameter)	Symbol for sample value (statistic)
Mean	μ (mu)	$\bar{X}$
Standard deviation	σ (sigma)	s
Correlation coefficient	ρ (rho)	r

statistical notation: the symbols used in statistical theory are based largely on Greek alphabet letters and the conventional (Latin or Roman) alphabet. Greek alphabet letters are used to denote population characteristics (parameters) and the letters of the conventional alphabet used to symbolize sample characteristics. Hence, the value of the population mean (i.e. a parameter) is denoted as μ (mu) whereas the value of the sample mean (i.e. the statistic) is denoted as $\bar{X}$. Table S.3 gives the equivalent symbols for parameters and statistics.

Constants are usually represented by the alphabetical symbols (a, b, c and similar from the beginning of the alphabet).

Scores on the first variable are primarily represented by the symbol X. Scores on a second variable are usually represented by the symbol Y. Scores on a third variable are usually represented by the symbol Z.

However, as scores would usually be tabulated as rows and columns, it is conventional to designate the column in question. So X_1

would be the first score in the column, X_4 would be the fourth score in the column and X_n would be the final score in the column. The rows are designated by a second subscript if the data are in the form of a two-dimensional table or matrix. $X_{1,5}$ would be the score in the first column and fifth row. $X_{4,2}$ would be the score in the fourth column and second row.

statistical package: an integrated set of computer programs enabling a wide range of statistical analyses of data usually using a single spreadsheet for the data. Typical examples include SPSS, Minitab, etc. Most statistical analyses are now conducted using such a package. See also: **Minitab; SAS; SPSS; SYSTAT**

statistical power: see **power of a test**

statistical significance: see **hypothesis testing; significant; t distribution**

stem and leaf diagram: a form of statistical diagram which effectively enables both the illustration of the broad trends of the data and details of the individual observations. It can be used to represent small samples of scores. There are no foolproof ways of constructing such a diagram effectively apart from trial and error. Take a look at the following diagram:

STEM LEAF

7	5	7					
8	2	4	7	8			
9	2	3	4	4	5		
10	1	1	3	4	6	7	8
11	2	5	6	7			
12	3	6	7				
13	1	4					
14	2	3					

Imagine that the diagram represents the IQ of a class of schoolchildren. The first column is the stem labelled 07, 08,…, 14. These are IQ ranges such that 07 represents IQs in the 70s, 13 represents IQs in the 130s. The leaf indicates the precise IQs of all of the children in the sample. So the row represents a child with an IQ of 75 and a child with an IQ of 77. The last row indicates a child with an IQ of 142 and another with an IQ of 143. Also notice how in general the pattern seems to indicate a roughly normal distribution.

Choosing an appropriate stem is crucial. That is, too many or too few stems make the diagram unhelpful. Furthermore, too many scores and the diagram also becomes unwieldy.

stepwise entry: a method in which predictors are entered according to some statistical criteria in statistical methods such as logistic regression, multiple regression, discriminant function analysis and log–linear analysis. The results of such an analysis may depend on very small differences in predictors meeting those criteria. One predictor may be entered into an analysis rather than another predictor when the differences between the two predictors are very small. Consequently, the results of this method always need to be interpreted with care.

stratified random sample: straightforward random sampling may leave out a particular class of cases. Thus, it is conceivable that a random sample drawn, say, from a list of electors will consist overwhelmingly of women with few men selected despite the fact that the sexes are equally common on the electoral list. Random sampling, theoretically, may lead to a whole range of different outcomes some of which are not representative of the population. One way of dealing with this is to stratify the population in terms of characteristics which can be assessed from the sampling frame. For example, the sampling could be done in such a way that 50% of the sample is male and the other 50% is female. For example, males may be selected from the list and then randomly sampled, then the process repeated for females. In this way, variations in sample sex distribution are circumvented. See also: **cluster sample; probability sampling**

structural equation modelling: a sophisticated and complex set of statistical procedures which can be used to carry out confirmatory factor analysis and path analysis on quantitative variables. It enables the statistical fit of models depicting the relationship between variables to be determined. Various statistical packages have been developed to carry it out including AMOS, EQS and LISREL. See also: **AMOS; attenuation, correcting correlations for; confirmatory factor analysis; discriminant function analysis; EQS; identification; just-identified model; LISREL; manifest variable; maximum likelihood estimation; over-identified model**
    Cramer (2003)

Student's t test: see **t test**

Student Newman–Keuls multiple comparison test: see **Newman–Keuls method, procedure** or **test**

studentized range statistic q: used in some multiple comparison tests such as the Tukey$_a$ or HSD (Honestly Significant Difference) test which determine which of three or more means differ significantly from one another. It is the difference or range between the smallest and the largest mean divided by the standard error of the range of means which is the square root of the division of the error mean square by the number of cases in a group:

$$q = \frac{\text{largest mean} - \text{smallest mean}}{\sqrt{\text{error mean square/number of cases in a group}}}$$

Table S.4 *The 0.05 critical values of the studentized range*

df for error mean square	df for number of means					
	2	3	4	5	6	7
8	3.26	4.04	4.53	4.89	5.17	5.40
12	3.08	3.77	4.20	4.51	4.75	4.95
20	2.95	3.58	3.96	4.23	4.45	4.62
30	2.89	3.49	3.84	4.10	4.30	4.46
40	2.86	3.44	3.79	4.04	4.23	4.39
60	2.83	3.40	3.74	3.98	4.16	4.31
120	2.80	3.36	3.69	3.92	4.10	4.24
∞	2.77	3.31	3.63	3.86	4.03	4.17

It is called 'studentized' after the pseudonym 'Student' – the pen name of William Sealey Gossett who also developed the *t* test.
    The distribution of this statistic depends on two sets of degrees of freedom, one for the number of means being compared and the other for the error mean square. With four groups of three cases each, the degrees of freedom for the number of groups being compared are 4 and for the error mean square is the number of cases minus the number of groups, which is 8 (12 − 4 = 8). The table for this distribution can be found in some statistics texts such as the one listed below. Values that this statistic has to be or exceed to be significant at the 0.05 level are given in Table S.4 for a selection of degrees of freedom. See also: **Duncan's new multiple range test; Newman–Keuls method; Tukey$_a$ and Tukey$_b$ tests**
    Kirk (1995)

subject: a traditional and increasingly archaic word for participant which denotes a person taking part in a study. Participant is a more acceptable term because it denotes the active participation of individuals in the research process as opposed to subject which tends to denote someone who obeys the will of the researcher. Case is commonly used in statistical packages as they need to be able to deal with other units of interest such as organizations. The term subject cannot totally be discarded because statistics include terms like related subjects design. Proband is another term sometimes used to describe a subject or person. This term is more commonly found in studies examining the influence of heredity. The term is derived from the Latin meaning tested or examined.

The term subject should be avoided except where traditional use makes it inevitable (or at least its avoidance almost impossible).

subject variable: a term which is sometimes used to describe the characteristics of subjects or participants which are not manipulated such as their gender, age, socioeconomic status, abilities and personality characteristics. A distinction may be made between subject variables, which have not been manipulated, and independent variables, which have been manipulated.

subtract: deduct one number from another. Take one number away from the other. See also: **negative values**

sum of squares (SS) or **squared deviations:** a statistic in analysis of variance which is used to form the mean square (MS). The mean square is the sum of squares divided by its degrees of freedom. Square is short for squared deviations or differences. What these differences are depends on what term or source of variation is being calculated. For the between-groups source of variation it is the squared difference between the group mean and the overall mean which is then multiplied by the number of cases in that group. The squared differences for each group are then added together or summed. See also: **between-groups variance; error sum of squares**

suppressed relationship: the apparent absence of a relationship between two variables which is brought about by one or more other variables. The relationship between the two variables becomes apparent when these other variables are statistically controlled. For example, there may be no relationship between how aggressive one is and how much violence one watches on TV. The lack of a relationship may be due to a third factor such as how much TV is watched. People who watch more TV may also as a result see more violence on TV even though they are less aggressive. If we statistically control for the amount of TV watched we may find a positive relationship between being aggressive and watching violence on TV.

suppressor variable: a variable which suppresses or hides the relationship between two other variables. See also: **multiple regression; suppressed relationship**

survey: a method which generally refers to a sample of people being asked questions on one occasion. Usually the purpose is to obtain descriptive statistics which reflect the population's views. The collection of information at one point in time does not provide a strong test of the temporal or causal relationship between the variables measured.

symmetry: usually refers to the shape of a frequency distribution. A symmetrical frequency distribution is one in which the halves above and below the mean, median or mode, are mirror images of one another. They would align perfectly if folded around the centre of the distribution. In other words, symmetry means exactly what it means in standard English. Asymmetry refers to a distribution which is not symmetric or symmetrical.

SYSTAT: one of several widely used statistical packages for manipulating and analysing data. Information about SYSTAT can be found at the following website:
http://www.systat.com/

systematic sample: a sample in which the cases in a population are consecutively numbered and cases are selected in terms of their order in the list, such as every 10th number.

Suppose, for example, we need to select 100 cases from a population of 1000 cases which have been numbered from 1 to 1000. Rather than selecting cases using some random procedure as in simple random sampling, we could simply select every 10th case (1000/100 = 10) which would give us a sample of 100 (1000/10 = 100). The initial number we chose could vary anywhere between 1 and 10. If that number was, say, 7, then we would select individuals numbered 7, 17, 27 and so on up to number 997.

T

t distribution: a distribution of *t* values which varies according to the number of cases in a sample. It becomes increasingly similar to a *z* or normal distribution the bigger the sample. The smaller the sample, the flatter the distribution becomes. The *t* distribution is used to determine the critical value that *t* has to be, or to exceed, in order for it to achieve statistical significance. The larger this value, the more likely it is to be statistically significant. The sign of this value is ignored. For large samples, *t* has to be about 1.96 or more to be statistically significant at the 95% or 0.05 two-tailed level. The smaller the sample, the larger *t* has to be to be statistically significant at this level.

The critical value that *t* has to be, or to be bigger than, to be significant at the 0.05 two-tailed level is shown in Table T.1 for selected samples increasing in size. Sample size is expressed in terms of (*df*) rather than number of cases because the way in which the degrees of freedom are calculated varies slightly according to the *t* test used for determining statistical significance. For samples of 20 or more this critical value is close to 2.00.

t test: generally determines whether two means are significantly different from each other or the mean of a sample is significantly different from that of the population from which it may have been drawn. It is also used to ascertain the statistical significance of correlations and partial correlations, and regression and partial regression coefficients.

Table T.1   *The 0.05 two-tailed critical value of t*

df	Critical value
1	12.706
5	2.571
10	2.228
20	2.086
50	2.009
100	1.984
1000	1.962
∞	1.960

The exact nature of the test depends on the use to which it is being put. The sign of the *t* test is ignored since it is arbitrary and depends on what mean is subtracted from the other. The larger the *t* value of the test, the more likely the test is statistically significant. The test can be two tailed or one tailed. A one-tailed test is used when there are good grounds for predicting the direction or sign of the difference or the association. When there are no such grounds a two-tailed test is applied. The *t* value has to be higher for a two- than a one-tailed test. So, the two-tailed test is less likely to be statistically significant than the one-tailed test. See also: **t test for one sample; t test for related samples; t test for related variances; t test for unrelated samples**

t test for one sample: determines whether the mean of a sample differs significantly from that of the population. It is the difference between the population mean and the sample mean divided by the standard error of the mean:

$$\frac{\text{population mean} - \text{sample mean}}{\text{standard error of the mean}}$$

The larger the t value, disregarding its sign, the more likely the two means will be significantly different. The degrees of freedom for this test are the number of cases minus one.

t test for related samples: also known as the paired-samples t test. It determines whether the means of two samples that come from the same or similar cases are significantly different from each other. It is the difference between the two means divided by the standard error of the difference in means:

$$\frac{\text{mean of one sample} - \text{mean of other sample}}{\text{standard error of the difference in means}}$$

The larger the t value, ignoring its sign, the more likely the two means differ significantly from each other. The degrees of freedom for this test are the number of pairs of cases minus one.

t test for related variances: determines whether the variances of two samples that come from the same or similar cases are significantly different from each other. The following formula can be used to calculate it, where r is the correlation between the pairs of scores:

$$\frac{(\text{large variance} - \text{smaller variance}) \times \sqrt{\text{number of cases} - 2}}{\sqrt{(1 - r^2) \times (4 \times \text{larger variance} \times \text{smaller variance})}}$$

The larger the t value, the more likely it is that the variances will differ significantly from each other. The degrees of freedom are the number of cases minus one.

McNemar (1969)

t test for unrelated samples: also known as the independent-samples t test. It is used to determine whether the means of two samples that consist of different or unrelated cases differ significantly from each other. It is the difference between the two means divided by the standard error of the difference in means:

$$\frac{\text{mean of one sample} - \text{mean of other sample}}{\text{standard error of the difference in means}}$$

The larger the t value, ignoring its sign, the more likely the two means differ significantly from each other.

The way in which the standard error is calculated depends on whether the variances are dissimilar and whether the group size is unequal. The standard error is the same when the group sizes are equal. It may be different when the group sizes are unequal. The way in which the degrees of freedom are calculated depends on whether the variances are similar. When they are similar the degrees of freedom for this test is the number of cases minus one. When they are dissimilar, they are calculated according to the following formula, where n refers to the number of cases in a sample and where subscripts 1 and 2 refer to the two samples:

$$\frac{[(\text{variance}_1/n_1)^2 + (\text{variance}_2/n_2)]^2}{\dfrac{(\text{variance}_1/n_1)^2}{(n_1 - 1)} + \dfrac{(\text{variance}_2/n_2)^2}{(n_2 - 1)}}$$

This formula in many cases will lead to degrees of freedom which are not a whole number but which involve decimal places. When looking up the statistical significance of the t values for these degrees of freedom, it may be preferable to round up the degrees of freedom to the nearest whole number making the test slightly more conservative. See also: **pooled variances**

Pedhazur and Schmelkin (1991)

T_2 test: determines whether Pearson's correlation between one variable and two others differs significantly when all three variables are measured in the same sample. For example, the correlation between relationship satisfaction and relationship conflict may be compared with the correlation between relationship satisfaction and relationship support. The statistical significance of the T_2 test is the same as the t test except that the degrees of freedom are the number of cases minus three.

Cramer (1998); Steiger (1980)

Tamhane's *T2* multiple comparison test: a *post hoc* or multiple comparison test which is used to determine which of three or more means differ from one another when the *F* ratio in an analysis of variance is significant. It was developed to deal with groups with unequal variances. It can be used with groups of equal or unequal size. It is based on the unrelated *t* test as modified in the Dunn–Sidak multiple comparison test and degrees of freedom as calculated in the Games–Howell multiple comparison procedure.

Kirk (1995)

test–retest reliability: the correlation coefficient between the scores on a test given to a sample of participants at time *A* and their scores at a later time *B*. It is then essentially a measure of the consistency of the scores from one time to the next. It allows one to assess whether the scores remain stable over time. Test–retest reliability indicates how likely it is that a person's score on the test will be similar relative to the scores of other participants from one administration to the next. In other words, it does not measure whether the actual scores are similar. For variables which ought to be stable over time (such as, say, intelligence) high test–retest reliability is a good thing. However, there are variables which may be fairly unstable over time (e.g. how happy a person feels) and may be expected to vary from day to day. In that case, a good and valid measure might be expected to be fairly unstable over time and hence have low test–retest reliability. See also: **reliability**

ties or **tied scores:** two or more scores which have the same value on a variable. When we rank these scores we need to give all of the tied scores the same rank. This is calculated as being the average rank which would have been allocated had we arbitrarily ranked the tied scores. For example, if we had the five scores of 5, 7, 7, 7 and 9, 5 would be given a rank of 1, 7 a rank of 3 [(2 + 3 + 4)/3 = 3] and 9 a rank of 5.

total: the amount obtained when a series of numbers or frequencies are added together. It is also known as the sum.

transformations: these are mathematical procedures or adjustments applied to scores in an attempt to make the distribution of the scores fit requirements. Statistical procedures are often affected by the presence of skewness or outliers. A transformation will often reduce the impact of these. The nature of the transformation will depend on the nature of the problem and they range from trimming to logarithmic transformations. Table T.2 illustrates some transformations though none may be ideal for a particular purpose. The transformations for values of 0 can be problematic and it is best to adjust the scores to give a minimum value of 1 before transforming them. Adding a constant to every score does not affect the outcome of the statistical calculations but one needs to readjust means, for example by subtracting the constant when reporting the findings. Variance is unaffected by adding a constant to every score.

There is nothing intrinsically good about carrying out a data transformation particularly as transformed scores cease to have any of the obvious meaning that they may have had in their original form. They are there to deal with difficult data. As such, they have a place but their use is relatively uncommon in modern practice. See also: **logarithm**

treatment group or **condition:** also known as the experimental group/condition. The

Table T.2 *Some examples of transformations*

Score	Log 10 transformation	Natural log transformation	Reciprocal transformation	Square root transformation
1	0.000	0.000	1.000	1.000
5	0.699	1.609	0.200	2.236
10	1.000	2.303	0.100	3.162
50	1.699	3.912	0.020	7.071
100	2.000	4.605	0.010	10.000
500	2.699	6.215	0.002	22.361
1000	3.000	6.908	0.001	31.623
5000	3.699	8.517	0.0002	70.711
10,000	4.000	9.210	0.0001	100.000

condition to which higher levels of the independent variable are applied as opposed to the control condition which receives no increased level of the independent variable. The treatment condition is the direct focus of the investigation and the impact of a particular experimental treatment. There may be several treatment groups each receiving a different amount or type of the treatment variable.

trend analysis in analysis of variance: may be used in analysis of variance to determine the shape of the relationship between the dependent variable and an independent variable which is quantitative in that it represents increasing or decreasing levels of that variable. Examples of such a quantitative independent variable include increasing quantities of a drug such as nicotine or alcohol, increasing levels of a state such as sleep deprivation or increasing intensity of a variable such as noise. If the F ratio of the analysis of variance is statistically significant, we may use trend analysis to find out if the relationship between the dependent and the independent variable is a linear or non-linear one and, if it is non-linear, what kind of non-linear relationship it is.

The shape of the relationship between two variables can be described in terms of a polynomial equation. A first-degree or linear polynomial represents a linear or straight line relationship between two variables where the values of one variable either increase or

decrease as the values of the other variable increase. For example, performance may decrease as sleep deprivation increases. A linear trend can be defined by the following equation, where y represents the dependent variable, b the slope of the line, x the independent variable and a a constant.

$$y = (b_1 \times x) + a_1$$

A minimum of two groups or levels is necessary to define a linear trend.

A second-order or quadratic relationship represents a curvilinear relationship in which the values of one variable increase (or decrease) and then decrease (or increase) as the values of the other variable increase. For instance, performance may increase as background noise increases and then decrease as it becomes too loud. A quadratic trend can be defined by the following equation:

$$y = (b_2 \times x)^2 + (b_1 \times x) + a_2$$

A minimum of three groups or levels is necessary to define a quadratic trend.

A third-order or cubic relationship represents a curvilinear relationship in which the values of one variable first increase (or decrease), then decrease (or increase) and then increase again (or decrease). A cubic trend can be defined by the following equation:

$$y = (b_3 \times x)^3 + (b_2 \times x)^2 + (b_1 \times x) + a_3$$

A minimum of four groups or levels is necessary to define a cubic trend.

A fourth-order or quartic relationship represents a curvilinear relationship in which the values of one variable first increase (or decrease), then decrease (or increase), then increase again (or decrease) and then finally decrease again (or increase). A quartic trend can be defined by the following equation:

$$y = (b_4 \times x)^4 + (b_3 \times x)^3 + (b_2 \times x)^2 + (b_1 \times x) + a_4$$

A minimum of five groups or levels are necessary to define a quartic trend.

These equations can be represented by orthogonal polynomial coefficients which are a special case of contrasts. Where the number of cases in each group is the same and where the values of the independent variable are equally spaced (such as 4, 8, 12 and 16 hours of sleep deprivation), the value of these coefficients can be obtained from a table which is available in some statistics textbooks such as the one listed below. The coefficients for three to five groups are presented in Table T.3. The procedure for calculating orthogonal coefficients for unequal intervals and unequal group sizes is described in the reference listed below. The number of orthogonal polynomial contrasts is always one less the number of groups. So, if there are three groups, there are two orthogonal polynomial contrasts which represent a linear and a quadratic trend.

The formula for calculating the F ratio for a trend is as follows:

$$F = \frac{[(\text{group 1 weight} \times \text{group 1 mean}) + (\text{group 2 weight} \times \text{group 2 mean}) + \cdots]^2}{\text{Error mean square} \times \left(\dfrac{\text{group 1 weight}^2}{\text{group 1 } n} + \dfrac{\text{group 2 weight}^2}{\text{group 2 } n} + \cdots\right)}$$

For the example given in the entry for the Newman–Keuls method there are four groups of three cases each. We will assume that the four groups represent an equally spaced variable. The four means are 6, 14, 12 and 2 respectively. The error mean square is 9.25. As there are four groups, there are three orthogonal polynomial contrasts which represent a linear, a quadratic and a cubic trend. The F ratio for the linear trend is 3.18:

Table T.3 Coefficients for orthogonal polynomials

Trends					
Three groups:					
Linear	−1	0	1		
Quadratic	1	−2	1		
Four groups:					
Linear	−3	−1	1	3	
Quadratic	1	−1	−1	1	
Cubic	−1	3	−3	1	
Five groups:					
Linear	−2	−1	0	1	2
Quadratic	2	−1	−2	−1	2
Cubic	−1	2	0	−2	1
Quartic	1	−4	6	−4	1

$$\frac{[(-3 \times 6) + (-1 \times 14) + (1 \times 12) + (3 \times 2)]^2}{9.25 \times \left(\dfrac{-3^2}{3} + \dfrac{-1^2}{3} + \dfrac{1^2}{3} + \dfrac{3^2}{3}\right)}$$

$$= \frac{(-18 + -14 + 12 + 6)^2}{9.25 \times \left(\dfrac{9}{3} + \dfrac{1}{3} + \dfrac{1}{3} + \dfrac{9}{3}\right)}$$

$$= \frac{-14^2}{9.25 \times \left(\dfrac{9 + 1 + 1 + 9}{3}\right)}$$

$$= \frac{196}{9.25 \times \dfrac{20}{3}} = \frac{196}{9.25 \times 6.67} = \frac{196}{61.70} = 3.18$$

This F ratio has two sets of degrees of freedom, one for the contrast or numerator of the formula and one for the error mean square or denominator of the formula. The degree of freedom is 1 for the contrast and the number of cases minus the number of groups for the error mean square, which is 8 (12 − 4 = 8). The critical value of F that the F ratio has to be or to exceed to be statistically significant at the 0.05 level with these two degrees of freedom is about 5.32. This value can be found in a table in many statistics texts and is usually given in statistical packages which compute this contrast. As the F ratio of 3.18 is less than the critical value of 5.32, the four means do not represent a linear trend.

The F ratio for the quadratic trend is 26.28:

$$\frac{[(1 \times 6) + (-1 \times 14) + (-1 \times 12) + (1 \times 2)]^2}{9.25 \times \left(\frac{1^2}{3} + \frac{-1^2}{3} + \frac{-1^2}{3} + \frac{1^2}{3}\right)}$$

$$= \frac{(6 + -14 + -12 + 2)^2}{9.25 \times \left(\frac{1}{3} + \frac{1}{3} + \frac{1}{3} + \frac{1}{3}\right)}$$

$$= \frac{-18^2}{9.25 \times \left(\frac{1 + 1 + 1 + 1}{3}\right)}$$

$$= \frac{324}{9.25 \times \frac{4}{3}} = \frac{324}{9.25 \times 1.333} = \frac{324}{12.33} = 26.28$$

As the F ratio of 26.28 is greater than the critical value of 5.32, the four means represent a quadratic trend in which the means increase and then decrease.

The F ratio for the cubic trend is 0.06:

$$\frac{[(-1 \times 6) + (3 \times 14) + (-3 \times 12) + (1 \times 2)]^2}{9.25 \times \left(\frac{-1^2}{3} + \frac{3^2}{3} + \frac{-3^2}{3} + \frac{1^2}{3}\right)}$$

$$= \frac{(-6 + 42 + -36 + 2)^2}{9.25 \times \left(\frac{1}{3} + \frac{9}{3} + \frac{9}{3} + \frac{1}{3}\right)}$$

$$= \frac{2^2}{9.25 \times \left(\frac{1 + 9 + 9 + 1}{3}\right)}$$

$$= \frac{4}{9.25 \times \frac{20}{3}} = \frac{4}{9.25 \times 6.67} = \frac{4}{61.70} = 0.06$$

As the F ratio of 0.06 is less than the critical value of 5.32, the four means do not represent a cubic trend.

Kirk (1995)

trimmed samples: sometimes applied to data distributions which have difficulties associated with the tails, such as small numbers of extreme scores. A trimmed sample is a sample in which a fixed percentage of cases in each tail of the distribution is deleted. So a 10% trimmed sample has 10% of each tail removed. See also: **transformations**

true experiment: an experiment in which one or more variables have been manipulated, all other variables have been held constant and participants have been randomly assigned either to the different conditions in a between-subjects design or to the different orders of the conditions in a within-subjects design. The manipulated variables are often referred to as independent variables because they are assumed not to be related to any other variables that might affect the measured variables. The measured variables are usually known as dependent variables because they are assumed to depend on the independent ones. One advantage of this design is that if the dependent variable differs significantly between the conditions, then these differences should only be brought about by the manipulation of the variables. This design is seen as being the most appropriate one for determining the causal relationship between two variables. The relationship between the independent and the dependent variable may be reciprocal. To determine this, the previous dependent variable needs to be manipulated and its effect on the previous independent variable needs to be examined. See also: **analysis of covariance; quasi-experiments**
    Cook and Campbell (1979)

true score: the observed score on a measure is thought to consist of a true score and random error. If the true score is assumed not to vary across occasions or people and the error is random, then the random error should cancel out leaving the true score. In other words, the true score is the mean of the scores. If it is assumed that the true score may vary between individuals, the reliability of a measure can be defined as the ratio of true score variance to observed score variance. See also: **reliability**

Tukey$_a$ or HSD (Honestly Significant Difference) test: a *post hoc* or multiple comparison test which is used to determine whether three or more means differ significantly in an analysis of variance. It assumes equal variance in the three or more groups and is only approximate for unequal group sizes. This test is like the Newman–Keuls method except that the critical difference that any two means have to be bigger than, to be statistically significant, is set by the total number of means and is not smaller the closer the means are in size. So, if four means are being compared, the difference that any two means have to exceed to be statistically significant is the same for all the means.

The formula for calculating this critical difference is the value of the studentized range multiplied by the square root of the error mean square divided by the number of cases in each group:

$$W = \text{studentized range} \times \sqrt{\text{error mean square}/\text{group } n}$$

The value of the studentized range varies according to the number of means being compared and the degrees of freedom for the error mean square. This value can be obtained from a table which is available in some statistics texts such as the source below.

For the example given in the entry for the Newman–Keuls method there are four groups of three cases each. This means that the degrees of freedom for the error mean square are the number of cases minus the number of groups, which is 8 ($12 - 4 = 8$). The 0.05 critical value of the studentized range with these two sets of degrees of freedom is 4.53. The error mean square for this example is 9.25.

Consequently, the critical difference that any two means need to exceed to be significantly different is about 7.97:

$$4.53 \times \sqrt{9.25/3} = 4.53 \times \sqrt{3.083}$$
$$= 4.53 \times 1.76 = 7.97$$

The means of the four groups are 6, 14, 12 and 2 respectively. If we look at Table N.1 which shows the difference between the four means, we can see that the absolute differences between groups 2 and 4 ($14 - 2 = 12$), groups 3 and 4 ($12 - 2 = 10$) and groups 2 and 1 ($14 - 6 = 8$) exceed this critical difference of 7.97 and so differ significantly.

Because the Tukey$_a$ test does not make the critical difference between two means smaller the closer they are, this test is less likely to find that two means differ significantly than the Newman–Keuls method. For this example, in addition to these three differences being significant, the Newman–Keuls method also finds the absolute difference between groups 3 and 1 ($12 - 6 = 6$) to be statistically significant as the critical difference for this test is 5.74 and not 7.97.

We could arrange these means into three homogeneous subsets where the means in a subset would not differ significantly from each other but where some of the means in one subset would differ significantly from those in another subset. We could indicate these three subsets by underlining the means which did not differ as follows.

<u>2 6</u>   <u>12 14</u>

Kirk (1995)

Tukey$_b$ or WSD (Wholly Significant Difference) test: a *post hoc* or multiple comparison test which is used to determine whether three or more means differ significantly in an analysis of variance. It assumes equal variances in each of the three or more means and is approximate for unequal group sizes. It is a compromise between the Tukey$_a$ or HSD (Honestly Significant Difference) test and the Newman–Keuls method. Both the Tukey$_a$ and the Newman–Keuls test use the studentized range to determine the critical difference two means have to exceed to be significantly different. The value of this range differs for the two tests. For the Tukey$_a$ test it depends on the total number of means being compared whereas for the Newman–Keuls test it is smaller the closer the two means are in size in a set of means. In the Tukey$_b$ test, the mean of these two values is taken.

The formula for calculating the critical difference is the value of the studentized range multiplied by the square root of the error mean square divided by the number of cases in each group:

W = studentized range
× √error mean square/group n

The value of the studentized range varies according to the number of means being compared and the degrees of freedom for the error mean square. This value can be obtained from a table which is available in some statistics texts such as the source below.

For the example given in the entry for the Newman–Keuls test there are four groups of three cases each. This means that the degrees of freedom for the error mean square are the number of cases minus the number of groups, which is 8 ($12 - 4 = 8$). The 0.05 critical value of the studentized range with these two sets of degrees of freedom is 4.53. For the Tukey$_a$ test, this value is used for all the comparisons. For the Newman–Keuls test, this value is only used for the two means that are furthest apart, which in this case is two means apart. The closer the two means are in size, the smaller this value becomes. So, for two means which are only one mean apart, this value is 4.04 whereas for two adjacent means it is 3.26.

The Tukey$_b$ test uses the mean of these two values which is 4.53 [($4.53 + 4.53)/2 = 9.06/2 = 4.53$] for the two means furthest apart, 4.29 [($4.53 + 4.04)/2 = 8.57/2 = 4.29$] for the two means one mean apart and 3.90 [($4.53 + 3.26)/2 = 7.79/2 = 3.90$] for the two adjacent means.

To calculate the critical difference we need the error mean square which is 9.25. The value by which the value of the studentized range needs to be multiplied is the same for all comparisons and is 1.76 ($\sqrt{9.25/3} = \sqrt{3.083} = 1.76$).

The critical difference for the two means furthest apart is about 7.97 ($4.53 \times 1.76 = 7.97$). For the two means one mean apart it is about 7.55 ($4.29 \times 1.76 = 7.55$), whereas for the two adjacent means it is about 6.86 ($3.90 \times 1.76 = 6.86$).

The means of the four groups, ordered in increasing size, are 2, 6, 12 and 14. If we take the two means furthest apart (2 and 14), we can see that their absolute difference of 12 ($2 - 14 = -12$) exceeds the critical value of 7.97 and so these two means differ significantly. If we take the two pairs of means one mean apart (2 and 12, and 6 and 14), we can see that both their absolute differences of 10 ($2 - 12 = -10$) and 8 ($6 - 14 = -8$) are greater than the critical value of 7.55 and so are significant differently. Finally, if we take the three pairs of adjacent means (2 and 6, 6 and 12, and 12 and 14), we can see that none of their absolute differences of 4 ($2 - 6 = -4$), 6 ($6 - 12 = -6$) and 2 ($12 - 14 = -2$) is greater than the critical value of 6.86 and so they do not differ significantly.

We could arrange these means into three homogeneous subsets where the means in a subset do not differ significantly from each other but where some of the means in one subset differ significantly from those in another subset. We could indicate these three subsets by underlining the means which did not differ as follows:

$$\underline{2\ 6}\quad \underline{12\ 14}$$

Howell (2002)

Tukey–Kramer test: a *post hoc* or multiple comparison test which is used to determine whether three or more means differ significantly in an analysis of variance. It assumes equal variance for the three or more means and is exact for unequal group sizes. It uses the studentized range to determine the critical difference two means have to exceed to be significantly different. It is a modification of the Tukey$_a$ or HSD (Honestly Significant Difference) test.

The formula for calculating this critical difference is the value of the studentized range multiplied by the square root of the error mean square which takes into account the number of cases in the two groups (n_1 and n_2) being compared:

W = studentized range
$$\times \sqrt{\left[\text{error mean square} \times \left(\frac{1}{n_1} + \frac{1}{n_2}\right)\right]/2}$$

The value of the studentized range varies according to the number of means being compared and the degrees of freedom for the error mean square. This value can be obtained from a table which is available in some statistics texts such as the source below.

For the example given in the entry for the Newman–Keuls method there are four groups of three cases each. This means that the degrees of freedom for the error mean square are the number of cases minus the number of groups, which is 8 ($12 - 4 = 8$). The 0.05 critical value of the studentized range with these two sets of degrees of freedom is 4.53. The error mean square for this example is 9.25.

Consequently, the critical difference that any two means need to exceed to be significantly different is about 7.97:

$$4.53 \times \sqrt{[9.25 \times (1/3 + 1/3)]/2}$$
$$= 4.53 \times \sqrt{[9.25 \times 0.667]/2}$$
$$= 4.53 \times \sqrt{6.17/2} = 4.53 \times \sqrt{3.09}$$
$$= 4.53 \times 1.76 = 7.97$$

This value is the same as that for the Tukey$_a$ or HSD (Honestly Significant Difference) test when the number of cases in each group is equal.

The means of the four groups are 6, 14, 12 and 2 respectively. If we look at Table N.1 which shows the difference between the four means, we can see that the absolute differences between groups 2 and 4 ($14 - 2 = 12$), groups 3 and 4 ($12 - 2 = 10$) and groups 2 and 1 ($14 - 6 = 8$) exceed this critical difference of 7.97 and so differ significantly.

Kirk (1995)

two-tailed level or **test of statistical significance:** see **correlation; directionless tests; significant**

two-way relationship: see **bi-directional relationship**

Type I or **alpha error:** the probability of assuming that there is a difference or association

between two or more variables when there is none. It is usually set at the 0.05 or 5% level. See also: **Bonferroni test; Dunn's test; Dunnett's T3 test; Waller–Duncan t test**

Type I, hierarchical or **sequential method in analysis of variance:** a method for determining the F ratio for an analysis of variance with two or more factors with unequal or disproportionate numbers of cases in the cells. In this situation the factors and interactions are likely to be related and so share variance. In this method the factors are entered in an order specified by the researcher.

Cramer (2003)

Type II or **beta error:** the probability of assuming that there is no difference or association between two or more variables when there is one. This probability is generally unknown. See also: **Bonferroni test; Waller–Duncan t test**

Type II, classic experimental or **least squares method in analysis of variance:** a method for determining the F ratio for an analysis of variance with two or more factors with unequal or disproportionate numbers of cases in the cells. In this situation the factors and interactions are likely to be related and so share variance. In this method main effects are adjusted for all other main effects (and covariates) while interactions are adjusted for all other effects apart from interactions of a higher order. For example, none of the variance of a main effect is shared with another main effect.

Cramer (2003)

Type III, regression, unweighted means or **unique method in analysis of variance:** a method for determining the F ratio for an analysis of variance with two or more factors with unequal or disproportionate numbers of cases in the cells. In this situation the factors and interactions are likely to be related and so share variance. In this method each effect is adjusted for all other effects (including covariates). In other words, the variance explained by that effect is unique to it and is not shared with any other effect.

Cramer (2003)

Type IV method in analysis of variance: a method for determining the F ratio for an analysis of variance with two or more factors with unequal or disproportionate numbers of cases in the cells. In this situation the factors and interactions are likely to be related and so share variance. This method is similar to Type III except that it takes account of cells with no data.

U

under-identified model: a term used in structural equation modelling to describe a model in which there are not sufficient variables to identify or to estimate all the parameters or pathways in the model. See also: **identification**

unequal sample size: generally speaking, there is little difficulty created by using unequal sample sizes in research although equal sample sizes should be regarded as an ideal. Some statistical techniques have their optimum effectiveness (power) when sample sizes are equal. Statistically unequal samples may lead to less precise estimates of population values but this is not a matter of great concern as the effect is usually small. However, some statistical calculations are much more difficult with unequal sample sizes. This is particularly the case for the analysis of variance. Of course, computer analyses of data are not affected by the issue of computational labour or difficulty. Nevertheless, researchers may come across publications in which calculations were done by hand. These probably will have ensured equal sample sizes for no reason other than to ease the difficulty of the computation. There is little reason to use equal sample sizes when carrying out analyses with computers. It is essential to have equal sample sizes when counterbalancing order, though equal sample sizes are an ideal to aim for when collecting data for maximum precision in many statistical analyses. See also: **analysis of variance**

uni-directional relationship: a relationship between two variables in which the direction of the causal relationship between the two variables is thought to be one-way in that one variable, A, is thought to cause the other variable, B, but the other variable, B, is not thought to cause the first variable, A. A bi-directional relationship is one in which both variables are thought to influence each other.

uni-lateral relationship: see **uni-directional relationship**

unimodal distribution: a distribution of scores which has one mode as opposed to two (bimodal) or more than one mode (multimodal).

unique method in analysis of variance: see **Type III, regression, unweighted means** or **unique method in analysis of variance**

univariate: the analysis of single variables without reference to other variables. The commonest univariate statistics are descriptive statistics such as the mean, variance, etc. There are relatively few univariate inferential statistics other than those which compare a single sample against a known population distribution.

Examples would be the one-sample chi-square, the runs test, one sample *t* test, etc.

unplanned or *post hoc* **comparisons:** see **Bonferroni test; multiple comparison tests; omnibus test;** *post hoc, a posteriori* or **unplanned tests**

unrelated *t* test: see ***t* test for unrelated samples**

unrepresentative sample: see **biased sample**

unstandardized partial regression coefficient or **weight:** an index of the size and direction of the association between a predictor or independent variable and the criterion or dependent variable in a multiple regression in which its association with other predictors and the criterion has been controlled or partialled out. The direction of the association is indicated by the sign of the regression coefficient in the same way as it is with a correlation coefficient. No sign means that the association is a positive one with high scores on the predictor going with high scores on the criterion. A negative sign shows that the association is a negative one in which high scores on the predictor go with low scores on the criterion.

The size of the regression coefficient indicates how much change there is in the original scores of the criterion for each unit change of the scores in the predictor. For example, if the unstandardized partial regression coefficient was 2.00 between the predictor of years of education received and the criterion of annual income expressed in units of 1000 euros, then we would expect a person's income to increase by 2000 euros (2.00 × 1000 = 2000) for every year of education received.

The size of the unstandardized partial regression coefficient will depend on the units or the scale used to measure the predictor. If income was measured in the unit of a single euro rather 1000 euros, and if the same association held between education and income, then the unstandardized partial regression coefficient would be 2000.00 rather than 2.00.

Unstandardized partial regression coefficients are used to predict what the likely value of the criterion will be (e.g. annual income) when we know the values of the predictors for a particular case (e.g. their years in education, age, gender, and so on). If we are interested in the relative strength of the association between the criterion and two or more predictors, we standardize the scores so that the size of these standardized partial regression coefficients is restricted to vary from -1.00 to 1.00. A higher standardized partial regression coefficient, regardless of its sign, will indicate a stronger association.

An unstandardized partial regression coefficient can be converted into its standardized coefficient by multiplying the unstandardized partial regression coefficient by the standard deviation (SD) of the predictor and dividing it by the standard deviation of the criterion:

$$\begin{matrix} \text{standardized} \\ \text{partial} \\ \text{regression} \\ \text{coefficient} \end{matrix} = \begin{matrix} \text{unstandardized} \\ \text{partial} \\ \text{regression} \\ \text{coefficient} \end{matrix} \times \frac{\text{predictor SD}}{\text{criterion SD}}$$

The statistical significance of the standardized and the unstandardized partial coefficients is the same value and can be expressed in terms of either a *t* or an *F* value. The *t* test for the partial regression coefficient is the unstandardized partial regression coefficient divided by its standard error:

$$t = \frac{\text{unstandardized regression coefficient}}{\text{standard error of the unstandardized regression coefficient}}$$

See also: **regression equation**

unweighted means method in analysis of variance: see **Type III, regression, unweighted means** or **unique method in analysis of variance**

V

valid per cent: a term used primarily in computer output to denote percentages expressed as a proportion of the total number of cases minus missing cases due to missing values. It is the percentage based on the actual number of cases used by the computer in the calculation. See also: **missing values**

validity: the extent to which a measure can be shown to measure what it purports or intends to measure. Various kinds of validity have been distinguished. See also: **concurrent validity; construct validity; convergent validity; discriminant validity; ecological validity; external validity; face validity; factorial validity; internal validity; predictive validity**

variable: a characteristic that consists of two or more categories (such as occupation or nationality) or values (such as age or intelligence score). The opposite of a variable is a constant, which consists of a single value. See also: **categorical variable; confounding variable; criterion variable; dependent variable; dichotomous variable; dummy variable; independent variable; intervening variable; operationalization; population; predictor variable, subject variable; suppressor variable**

variance or **population variance:** a measure of the extent to which the values in a population of scores vary or differ from the mean value of that population. The larger the variance is, the more the scores differ on average from the mean. The variance is the sum of the squared difference or deviation between the mean score and each individual score which is divided by the number of scores:

$$\frac{\text{sum of (mean score} - \text{each score)}^2}{\text{number of scores}}$$

The variance estimate differs from the variance in that the sum is divided by the number of scores minus one. The variance estimate is usually provided by statistical packages such as SPSS and is used in many parametric statistical tests. The difference in size between these two measures of variance is small, which becomes even smaller the larger the sample.

variance estimate, estimated population variance or **sample variance:** a measure of the degree to which the values in a sample vary or differ from the mean value of the sample. It is used to estimate the variance of the population of scores from which the sample has been taken. The larger the variance is, the more the scores differ from the mean. The variance estimate is the sum of the squared difference or deviation between the mean score and each individual score which is divided by the number of scores minus one:

$$\frac{\text{sum of (mean score} - \text{each score)}^2}{\text{number of scores} - 1}$$

The variance estimate differs from the variance in that the sum is divided by one less than the number of scores rather than the number of scores. This is done because the variance of a sample is usually less than that of the population from which it is drawn. In other words, dividing the sum by one less than the number of scores provides a less biased estimate of the population variance.

The variance estimate rather than variance is used in many parametric statistics as these tests are designed to make inferences about the population of scores from which the samples have been drawn. Many statistical packages, such as SPSS, give the variance estimate rather than the variance. See also: **dispersion, measure of; Hartley's test; moment; standard error of the difference in means; variance** or **population variance**

variance of estimate: a measure of the variance of the scores around the regression line in a simple and multivariate regression. It can be calculated with the following formula:

$$\frac{\begin{array}{c}\text{sum of squared residuals or squared}\\ \text{differences between the criterion's predicted}\\ \text{and observed scores}\end{array}}{\text{number of cases} - \text{number of predictors} -1}$$

It is also called the mean square residual. The variance of estimate is used to work out the statistical significance of the unstandardized regression or partial regression coefficient. The square root of the variance of estimate is the standard error of the estimate.

Pedhazur (1982)

varimax rotation, in factor analysis: a widely used method of the orthogonal rotation of the initial factors in a factor analysis in which the variance of the loadings of the variables within a factor are maximized. High loadings on the initial factors are made higher on the rotated factor and low loadings on the initial factors are made lower on the rotated factor. Differentiating the variables that load on a factor in this way makes it easier to see which variables most clearly define that factor and to interpret the meaning of that factor. Orthogonal rotation is where the factors are at right angles or unrelated to one another.

Venn diagram: a system of representing the relationship between subsets of information. The totality is represented by a rectangle. Within that rectangle are to be found circles which enclose particular subsets. The circles may not overlap, in which case there is no overlap between the subsets. Alternatively, they may overlap totally or partially. The amount of overlap is the amount of overlap between subsets. So, Figure V.1 shows all Europeans. One circle represents English people and the other citizens of Britain. The larger circle envelops the smaller one because being British includes being English. However, not all British people are English. See also: **common variance**

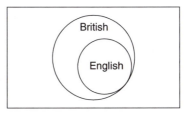

Figure V.1   *Illustrating Venn diagrams*

W

Waller–Duncan t test: a *post hoc* or multiple comparison test used for determining which of three or more means differ significantly in an analysis of variance. This test is based on the Bayesian *t* value, which depends on the *F* ratio for a one-way analysis of variance, its degrees of freedom and a measure of the relative seriousness of making a Type I versus a Type II error. It can be used for groups of equal or unequal size.

Table W.1   *Weighted and unweighted mean of three groups*

Groups	Means	Size	Sum
1	4	10	40
2	5	20	100
3	9	40	360
Sum	18		500
Number	3	60	60
Mean	6		8.33

weighted mean: the mean of two or more groups which takes account of or weights the size of the groups when the sizes of one or more of the groups differ. When the size of the groups is the same, there is no need to weight the group mean for size and the mean is simply the sum of the means divided by the number of groups. When the size of the groups differ, the mean of each group is multiplied by its size to give the total or sum for that group. The sum of each group is added together to give the overall or grand sum. This grand sum is then divided by the total number of cases to give the weighted mean.

Take the means of the three groups in Table W.1. The unweighted mean of the three groups is 6 [(4 + 5 + 9)/3 = 6]. If the three groups were of the same size (say, 10 each), there would be no need to weight them as size is a constant and the mean is 6 [(40 + 50 + 90)/30 = 6]. If the sizes of the groups differ, as they do here, the weighted mean is higher at 8.33 than the unweighted mean of 6 because the largest group has the highest mean.

Wilcoxon matched-pairs signed-ranks test: a non-parametric test used to determine whether the scores from two samples that come from the same or similar cases are significantly different from each other. The differences between pairs of scores are ranked in order of size, ignoring the sign or direction of those differences. The ranks of the differences with the same sign are added together. If there are no differences between the scores of the two samples, the sum of positive ranked differences should be similar to the sum of negative ranked difference. The bigger the differences between the positive and negative ranked differences, the more likely the two sets of scores differ significantly from each other.

Wilcoxon rank-sum or **Wilcoxon–Mann–Whitney W test:** see **Mann–Whitney U test**

Wilks's lambda or **λ:** a test used in multivariate statistical procedures such as canonical correlation, discriminant function analysis and multivariate analysis of variance to determine whether the means of the groups differ on a discriminant function or characteristic root. It varies from 0 to 1. A lambda of 1 indicates that the means of all the groups have the same value and so do not differ. Lambdas close to 0 signify that the means of the groups differ. It can be transformed as a chi-square or an F ratio. It is the most widely used of several such tests which include Hotelling's trace criterion, Pillai's criterion and Roy's *gcr* criterion.

When there are only two groups, the F ratios for Wilks's lambda, Hotelling's trace, Pillai's criterion and Roy's *gcr* criterion are the same. When there are more than two groups, the F ratios for Wilks's lambda, Hotelling's trace and Pillai's criterion may differ slightly. Pillai's criterion is said to be the most robust when the assumption of the homogeneity of the variance–covariance matrix is violated.

Tabachnick and Fidell (2001)

within-groups variance: a term used in statistical tests of significance for related/ correlated/repeated-measures designs. In such designs participants (or matched groups of participants) contribute a minimum of two separate measures for the dependent variable. This means that the variance on the dependent variable can be assessed in terms of three sources of variance:

1 That due to the influence of the independent variables (main effects).
2 That due to the idiosyncratic characteristics of the participants. Since they are measured twice, then similarities between scores for the same individuals can be assessed. The variation on the dependent variable attributable to these similarities over the two measures is known as the within-groups variance. So there is a sense in which within-groups variation ought to be considered as variation caused by within-individuals factors.

3 That due to unsystematic, unassessed factors remaining after the two above sources of variation, which is called the error variance or sometimes the residual variance.

Another way of conceptualizing it is that within-groups variance is the variation attributable to the personal characteristics of the individual involved – a sort of *mélange* of their personality, intellectual and social characteristics which might influence scores on the dependent variable. For example, if the dependent variable were verbal fluency then we would expect intelligence and education to affect these scores in the same way for any individual each time verbal fluency is assessed in the study over and above the effects of the stipulated independent variables. There is no need to know just what it is that affects verbal fluency in the same way each time just so long as we can estimate the extent to which verbal fluency is affected.

The within-groups variance in uncorrelated or unrelated designs simply cannot be assessed since there is just one measure of the dependent variable from each participant in such designs. So the influence of the within-groups factors cannot be separated from error variance in such designs.

within-subjects design: the simplest and purest example of a within-subjects design is where a single case (participant or subject) is studied on two or more occasions. Changes between two occasions would form the basis of the analysis. More generally, changes in several participants are studied over a period of time. Such designs are also known as related designs, related subjects designs or correlated subjects designs. They have the major advantage that since the same individual is measured on repeated occasions, many factors such as intelligence, class, personality, and so forth are held constant. Such designs contrast with between-subjects designs in which different groups of participants are compared with each other (unrelated designs or uncorrelated designs). See also: **between-subjects design; carryover** or **asymmetrical transfer effect; mixed design**

X

_x_ axis: the horizontal axis or abscissa of a graph. See also: **abscissa**

Y

y axis: the vertical axis or ordinate in a graph. See also: **ordinate**

Yates's correction: a continuity correction. Small contingency (cross-tabulation) tables do not fit the theoretical and continuous chi-square distribution particularly well. Yates's correction is sometimes applied to 2×2 contingency tables to make some allowance for this and some authorities recommend its universal application to such small tables. Others recommend its use when there are cells with an (observed) frequency of less than five. It is no longer a common practice to adopt it and it is possibly less misleading not to make any adjustment. If the correction has been applied, the researcher should make this clear. The correction is conservative in that the null hypothesis is favoured slightly over the hypothesis.

yea-saying: see **acquiescence**

Z

z score: another name for a standardized score. A z score is merely the difference between the score and the mean score of the sample of scores then divided by the standard deviation of the sample of scores:

$$z \text{ score} = \frac{\text{score} - \text{sample mean}}{\text{standard deviation}}$$

The computation is straightforward. z scores may have positive or negative values. A positive value indicates that the score is above the sample mean, a negative value indicates the score is below the sample mean. The importance of z scores lies in the fact that the distribution of z has been tabulated and is readily available in tables of the distribution of z. The z distribution is a statistical distribution which indicates the relative frequency of z scores. That is, the table indicates the numbers of z scores which are zero and above, one standard deviation above the mean and above, and so forth. The distribution is symmetrical around the mean. The only substantial assumption is the distribution is normal in shape. Technically speaking, the z distribution has a mean of 0 and a standard deviation of 1.

To calculate the z score of the score 11 in a sample of three scores consisting of 5, 9 and 11, we first need to calculate the mean of the sample = 25/3 = 8.333. The standard deviation of these scores is obtained by squaring each score's deviation, summing them and then finding their average, and then finally taking their square root to give a value for the standard deviation of 2.494:

$$\text{standard deviation} = \sqrt{\frac{\Sigma(X - \bar{X})^2}{N}}$$

$$= \sqrt{\frac{(5 - 8.333)^2 + (9 - 8.333)^2 + (11 - 8.333)^2}{3}}$$

$$= \sqrt{\frac{-3.333^2 + 0.667^2 + 2.667^2}{3}}$$

$$= \sqrt{\frac{11.109 + 0.445 + 7.113}{3}}$$

$$= \sqrt{\frac{18.667}{3}}$$

$$= \sqrt{6.222}$$

$$= 2.494$$

So the standard score (z score) of the score 11 is

$$\frac{11 - 8.333}{2.494} = \frac{2.667}{2.494}$$

$$= 1.07$$

Standardized or z scores have a number of functions in statistics and occur quite commonly. Among their advantages are that:

1   As variables can be expressed on a common unit of measurement, this greatly

facilitates the addition of different variables in order to achieve a composite of several variables.

2 As z or standardized scores refer to a distribution of known characteristics, the relative standing of a person's score expressed as a z score is easily calculated. For example, if a person's standardized score is 1.96 this means that the score is in the top 2.5% of scores. This is simply obtained from the table of the distribution of z scores.

See also: **correlation; standardized scores**

z test: determines whether Pearson's correlation from two unrelated samples differs significantly. When the correlation in the population is not 0, the sampling distribution of the correlation is not approximately normal. It becomes progressively skewed as the population correlation approaches ±1.00. As a consequence it is difficult to estimate its standard error.

To overcome this problem Pearson's correlation is transformed into a z correlation using the following formula, where $\log_e$ stands for the natural logarithm and r for Pearson's correlation:

$$z_r = 0.5 \times \log_e [(1 + r)/(1 - r)]$$

This transformation makes the sampling distribution approximately normal and allows the standard error to be calculated with the formula

$$1\sqrt{n - 3}$$

where n is the size of the sample.

The z test is simply a ratio of the difference between the two z correlations to the standard error of the two samples:

$$z = \frac{z_1 - z_2}{\sqrt{[1/(n_1 - 3)] + [1/(n_2 - 3)]}}$$

z has to be 1.65 or more to be statistically significant at the one-tailed 0.05 level and 1.96 or more at the two-tailed 0.05 level.

Table Z.1 z to r transformation

z	r	z	r
0.00	0.00	0.80	0.66
0.10	0.10	0.90	0.72
0.20	0.20	1.00	0.76
0.30	0.29	1.50	0.91
0.40	0.38	2.00	0.96
0.50	0.46	2.50	0.99
0.60	0.54	3.00	1.00
0.70	0.60		

Z_2^* test: determines whether Pearson's correlation between two variables differs significantly from that between two other variables from the same sample. For example, the one-year test-retest or autocorrelation for relationship satisfaction may be compared with that for relationship conflict. The statistical significance of this test is the same as that for the z test.

Cramer (1998); Steiger (1980)

z to r transformation: the change of a z correlation into Pearson's product moment correlation. This can be done by looking up the value in the appropriate table or using the following formula:

$$r = (2.718^{2 \times z_r} - 1)/(2.718^{2 \times z_r} + 1)$$

The values of the z correlation vary from 0 to about ±3 (though, effectively, infinity), as shown in Table Z.1, and the values of Pearson's correlation from 0 to ±1.

z transformation: see **Fisher's z transformation**

zero-order correlation: a correlation between two variables in which one or more variables are not partialled out. A first-order partial correlation is one in which one other variable has been partialled out, a second-order partial correlation one in which two variables have been partialled out, and so on.

zero point: the score of 0 on the measurement scale. This may not be the lowest possible score on the variable. Absolute zero is the lowest point on a scale and the lowest possible measurement. So absolute zero temperature is the lowest temperature that can be reached. This concept is not in general of much practical significance in most social sciences.

Some Useful Sources

Baltes, Paul B. and Nesselroade, John R. (1979) 'History and rationale of longitudinal research', in John R. Nesselroade and Paul B. Baltes (eds), *Longitudinal Research in the Study of Behavior and Development*. New York: Academic Press. pp. 1–39.

Cattell, Raymond B. (1966) 'The scree test for the number of factors', *Multivariate Behavioral Research*, 1: 245–276.

Cohen, Jacob and Cohen, Patricia (1983) *Applied Multiple Regression/Correlation Analysis for the Behavioral Sciences*, 2nd edn. Hillsdale, NJ: Lawrence Erlbaum.

Cook, Thomas D. and Campbell, Donald T. (1979) *Quasi-Experimentation*. Chicago: Rand McNally.

Cramer, Duncan (1998) *Fundamental Statistics for Social Research*. London: Routledge.

Cramer, Duncan (2003) *Advanced Quantitative Data Analysis*. Buckingham: Open University Press.

Glenn, Norval D. (1977) *Cohort Analysis*. Beverly Hills, CA: Sage.

Hays, William L. (1994) *Statistics*, 5th edn. New York: Harcourt Brace.

Howell, David C. (2002) *Statistical Methods for Psychology*, 5th edn. Belmont, CA: Duxbury Press.

Howitt, Dennis and Cramer, Duncan (2000) *First Steps in Research and Statistics*. London: Routledge.

Howitt, Dennis and Cramer, Duncan (2004) *An Introduction to Statistics in Psychology: A Complete Guide for Students*, Revised 3rd edn. Harlow: Prentice Hall.

Howson, Colin and Urbach, Peter (1989) *Scientific Reasoning: The Bayesian Approach*. La Salle, IL: Open Court.

Huitema, Bradley E. (1980) *The Analysis of Covariance and Alternatives*. New York: Wiley.

Hunter, John E. and Schmidt, Frank L. (2004) *Methods of Meta-Analysis*, 2nd edn. Newbury Park, CA: Sage.

Kenny, David A. (1975) 'Cross-lagged panel correlation: A test for spuriousness', *Psychological Bulletin*, 82: 887–903.

Kirk, Roger C. (1995) *Experimental Design*, 3rd edn. Pacific Grove, CA: Brooks/Cole.

McNemar, Quinn (1969) *Psychological Statistics*, 4th edn. New York: Wiley.

Menard, Scott (1991) *Longitudinal Research*. Newbury Park, CA: Sage.

Novick, Melvin R. and Jackson, Paul H. (1974) *Statistical Methods for Educational and Psychological Research*. New York: McGraw-Hill.

Nunnally, Jum C. and Bernstein, Ira H. (1994) *Psychometric Theory*, 3rd edn. New York: McGraw-Hill.

Owusu-Bempah, Kwame and Howitt, Dennis (2000) *Psychology beyond Western Perspectives*. Leicester: British Psychological Society.

Pampel, Fred C. (2000) *Logistic Regression: A Primer*. Newbury Park, CA: Sage.

Pedhazur, Elazar J. (1982) *Multiple Regression in Behavioral Research*, 2nd edn. Fort Worth, TX: Harcourt Brace Jovanovich.

Pedhazur, Elazar J. and Schmelkin, Liora P. (1991) *Measurement, Design and Analysis*. Hillsdale, NJ: Lawrence Erlbaum.

Rogosa, David (1980) 'A critique of cross-lagged correlation', *Psychological Bulletin*, 88: 245–258.

Siegal, Sidney and Castellan N. John, Jr (1988) *Nonparametric Statistics for the Behavioral Sciences*, 2nd edn. New York: McGraw-Hill.

Steiger, James H. (1980) 'Tests for comparing elements of a correlation matrix', *Psychological Bulletin*, 87: 245–251.

Stevens, James (1996) *Applied Multivariate Statistics for the Social Sciences*, 3rd edn. Hillsdale, NJ: Lawrence Erlbaum.

Tabachnick, Barbara G. and Fidell, Linda S. (2001) *Using Multivariate Statistics*, 4th edn. Boston: Allyn and Bacon.

Tinsley, Howard E. A. and Weiss, David J. (1975) 'Interrater reliability and agreement of subjective judgments', *Journal of Counselling Psychology*, 22: 358–376.

Toothaker, Larry E. (1991) *Multiple Comparisons for Researchers*. Newbury Park, CA: Sage.